POWER, DISCOURSE AND VICTIMAGE RITUAL IN THE WAR ON TERROR

To Angie

Power, Discourse and Victimage Ritual in the War on Terror

MICHAEL BLAIN
Boise State University, USA

Routledge
Taylor & Francis Group

LONDON AND NEW YORK

First published 2012 by Ashgate Publishing

Published 2016 by Routledge
2 Park Square, Milton Park, Abingdon, Oxon OX14 4RN
711 Third Avenue, New York, NY 10017, USA

First issued in paperback 2017

Routledge is an imprint of the Taylor & Francis Group, an informa business

British Library Cataloguing in Publication Data
Blain, Michael, 1943–
    Power, discourse and victimage ritual in the war on terror.
    1. Power (Social sciences) 2. Abuse of administrative power. 3. Social control.
    4. Terrorism – Prevention – Political aspects. 5. Terrorism – Prevention – Social aspects.
    I. Title
    303.3–dc23

Library of Congress Cataloging-in-Publication Data
Blain, Michael, 1943–
    Power, discourse, and victimage ritual in the war on terror / by Michael Blain.
        p. cm.
    Includes bibliographical references and index.
    ISBN 978–1–4094–3605–8 (marketing : alk. paper)
    1. Terrorism – Social aspects. 2. Political violence – Social aspects. 3. Power (Social sciences) I. Title.
    HV6431.B569 2012
    303.6'25–dc23   2012005212

ISBN 13: 978-1-138-11578-1 (pbk)
ISBN 13: 978-1-4094-3605-8 (hbk)

Contents

List of Diagrams and Charts

List of Tables

Acknowledgements

I am deeply indebted to my wife, Angeline Kearns Blain, for the continuing emotional support and encouragement needed to finish this project. I have benefited greatly from her distinctively Irish perspective on political violence, terrorism, and issues of colonial domination. Her research on the role of women in the peace movement has permanently altered my perspective on violence.

I would like to express special gratitude to my colleague, Edward McLuskie. His graduate seminar on "Communication, Power, and Critical Theory" was a crucial testing ground for many of the sharper theoretical and empirical points advanced in this work.

I would also like to acknowledge the continuing support of my colleagues in the Department of Sociology, Boise State University. I am particularly indebted to the Chairs of the Sociology Department while I worked on this project, Professors Martin Orr and Steven Patrick. In the face of tight budgets and severe time constraints, they provided much needed financial support and release time to facilitate the production of this book.

I am grateful to the following research assistants who have helped me collect and analyze the data reported in this book: Macy Boggs, Amity Harrison, Jennifer Simpson, Nikki Weihe, Eiko Strader, and Loraine Hand.

Many thanks to professional colleagues who read or discussed earlier publications or paper presentations relevant to the theme of this book: Mabel Berezin, Laura Edles, Jorge Capetillo-Ponce, Sam Binkley, Elaine Campbell, Don Winieki, William Bogard, Deborah Staines, Joan Kirkby, A. Dirk Moses, G. William Domhoff, John Walton, Paul Rabinow, and Hubert Dreyfus.

I would like to acknowledge the highly competent and compassionate editorial support of Neil Jordan (Commissioning Editor) and Mrs Celia Barlow (Senior Editor) at Ashgate Publishing Group. Thanks to the anonymous reviewers of the original proposal who were encouraging and thought-provoking in their recommendations. Tom Norton did a superlative job indexing the text. I am very gratified and grateful to Professor Vian Bekel for her kind and courageous endorsement of my controversial thesis concerning American political violence.

And, finally, thanks to our close personal friends who have supported Angeline and I in many ways: Ariel McLuskie, Lynn Lubamersky, Nick Miller, and Chad and Vashti Summerville.

Chapter 1
Cycles of Violence

They knew it, the fervent pupils of Pythagoras:
that stars and humans revolve in a cycle...
"The Cyclical Night" by Jorge Luis Borges (1967)

This book elaborates a new interpretation of the U.S. led global war on terrorism. The analysis merges concepts derived from Kenneth Burke's dramatism and theory of victimage rituals, with Michel Foucault's account of power relations and biopolitics in modern liberal societies. Blending these ideas with current thinking in the sociology of politics and violence, it fashions a critical perspective on the causes and effects of the war on terrorism. The global campaign against terrorism, it proposes, is a liberal mode of power and subjection by means of victimage ritual.

The war against terrorism provides the U.S. power elite with a new *pretext* for extending its hegemony over new territories and populations, and legitimating an intensification of "homeland security," domestic surveillance and social control (for discussion of power elite theory, see Domhoff 1990, 2006, 2010). The global war against terrorists is a *victimage ritual* employed by the power elite to mobilize masses as a calculated means to exercise power to achieve their objectives. This use of victimage ritual involves a perverse use of a religious system of thought to accomplish political purposes. The war on terror is just the most recent case. The juridical significance of this "political theology" as a justification for declarations of states of emergency and dictatorship (e.g., the 1933 Reichstag terror attack), was explicitly recognized in a 1922 essay by Karl Schmitt ("Political Theology," 1985: 36–52), the Nazi legal theorist:

> All significant concepts of the modern theory of the state are secularized theological concepts not only because of their historical development—in which they were transferred from theology to the theory of the state, whereby, for example, the omnipotent God became the omnipotent lawgiver—but also because of their systematic structure, the recognition of which is necessary for a sociological consideration of these concepts. The exception in jurisprudence is analogous to the miracle in theology (1985: 37).

Schmitt's statement is a strong gloss on his definition of Sovereignty: "Sovereign is he who decides on the exception" (1985: 5). By this Schmitt means an exception to the rule of law. More recent examples of this kind of "miracle" include President Bush's November 13, 2001 "military order" authorizing the "indefinite detention" and trial by "military commissions" of noncitizens suspected of involvement in terrorist activities (i.e., "illegal combatants"), and President Obama's May 1, 2011 executive order authorizing the Navy Seals to violate Pakistan's sovereignty and kill Osama bin Laden.[1]

If, as Schmitt argued, the friend/enemy criterion delineates the concept of the political and the political is theological in form, then the struggle against the enemy is a Manichean struggle of good against evil. Any actor who threatens the survival of the state—foreign or domestic enemies—is the incarnation of evil or the devil. The war on terror, in this sense, enacts a theological system of thought. The Islamic terrorist has been perfected in the role of international devil and "liberal" scapegoat. Osama bin Laden personifies the evil one who must be sacrificed.

As Kenneth Burke (1967) put it in his analysis of Adolf Hitler's *Mein Kampf* (1971), Nazi rhetorical practices involved a "bastardization of a fundamentally religious patterns of thought." Political scapegoats are materializations of a religious pattern of thought. In Nazi rhetoric the Jews were the terrorists threatening Germany's survival and standing in the way of the political program to build a Thousand Year Reich. The rhetorical function of the scapegoat, according to Burke, involves a displacement of responsibility and guilt for some problem—a projection of unacceptable desires, distracting attention away from existing modes of social domination in a society. The Nazi use of the anti-Semitic unifier projected all the political and economic ills of German society on to *das Juden* (see Longerrich 2010, particularly his discussion of the tactical polyvalence of the word, *judenpolitik*). Similarly, the global wars against communists and terrorists have functioned as unifiers as well as powerful mass distractions from underlying modes of class, race, and gender domination in U.S. society.

There is one aspect of the political in "political theology" not explicitly elaborated by Schmitt or Burke. This missing aspect is revealed in a remark made by President George W. Bush on the use of torture in the war. "Yeah, we waterboarded Kalid Sheikh Mohammed. **I'd do it again to save lives** [emphasis added: bold = glorifier / bold + italic = vilifier] (quoted in Froomkin 2010). The terrorist threatens individual "lives," not "good" understood in the Christian sense of moral virtue. This is why precious human life must be sacrificed in a heroic struggle against the "enemies of freedom." Michel Foucault captures this dimension of modern "liberal" politics more clearly and directly (see Foucault 1978: 135–159). The Nazi concept of race is biopolitical; it is specifically dependent on a knowledge

---

1   I try to avoid the implication that presidents are the individual authors of the documents and speech practices described. There is ample evidence that they are socially produced, vetted and modified by speech writers and numerous relevant players in the regime. For a good example see Powers' (2010) account of the power struggles and political pressures exerted on the CIA by the Bush regime regarding Iraq's WMD programs and the "outing" of CIA agent, Valerie Plame (see also Wilson 2004). At least since World War II and the emergence of "psychological warfare" programs, presidential speeches and official reports are best understood as tactical elements in a specific regime's political strategy or "psychological warfare" program (Simpson 1994).

of nineteenth-century racist biology. Formulated in these terms, the traditional theological system of good struggling against evil as personified by the Devil is translated into biopolitics. The Nazi war against the Jews is an ultimate struggle of the Aryan race *against* the Jews understood as *racial monsters* (see Blain 1995, 1988). The modern liberal state, on the other hand, governs society in the name of the health and welfare of each and every "individual" life. Each individual is understood to be a living being. The "soul" is not the object and target of political power; it is the life of the body and its health and welfare that matters.

The Sociology of Violence

One consequence of the war on terrorism has been to refocus attention on the problematic of mass violence in human social life. On the one hand, sociologists have had problems dealing with the phenomena of violence with any degree of clarity (for exceptions, see Giddens 1985, Jackman 2002, Collins 2008, 2012). Part of this has to do with the evasion of the problem by the Enlightenment philosophers and many social scientists (Saint-Amand 1996; Joas 1999). Advancing an optimistic view of human nature to augment their progressive political agendas, they fashioned a discourse of "modernity" that assumed that violence and terrorism were things of the past. When violence does happen, they argued, it was almost always represented as a regression to an earlier, uncivilized age of barbarism. People who resist liberal modernity are categorized as uncivilized savages and terrorists. Civilized people, allegedly, only use "force" reluctantly in response to savages who refuse to submit to Empire. The idea that social domination in the name of liberal modernity might generate "violence" is anathema. All "reasonable" people should agree.

On the other hand, an *objective* sociology of violence that seeks to avoid the pitfalls of ethnocentricity and partisan politics, must apply the concept of terrorism with some degree of equanimity to all parties involved in power struggles.[2] By "objective" I mean that the violent acts perpetrated by the dominant powers in a struggle can still count as *terrorism*, particularly the violent acts of those who have the authority to define the legitimacy and illegitimacy of violent acts. This should be the case for two reasons. First of all, the use of euphemisms to make light of violence perpetrated by legal authority figures is a widely recognized phenomenon (Allen and Burridge 1991, Jackman 2002, Bromwich 2008). According to Presidents Bush's and Obama's public statements, the U.S. government does not engage in "torture" or "terrorism" (e.g., see Bush's omissions and denials in his 2010 biography). Moreover, there is a realistic sense in which all *political* violence involves a Hobbesian element of terrorism, including the violence and terrorism

---

2   Chomsky (1969) raised similar issues regarding "objectivity" and "Liberal Scholarship" in the context of the Vietnam War. The one-sided focus on Vietcong "terrorism" was central to the debate about the war.

perpetrated by the legitimate authorities of the world. It is a serious analytic and empirical mistake to deliberately write "state terrorism" off-the-table in the field of the sociology of violence or "terrorism" studies by operationally defining terrorism as violence perpetrated by non-state actors (as, for example, Turk [2004], Lafree and Ackerman [2009], and Spilerman and Stecklov [2009] do). There should be no "hidden side" to "domestic terrorism" (Garland 2010, Sanchez-Cuenca and de la Callez 2009). This means there should always be a frank acknowledgement of the empirically observable, power struggles implicated in any specific situation of terrorism.

Secondly, so-called "state actors" frequently attempt to legitimate the use of "counter-*terrorism*" to fight "terrorists." Giddens (1985: 303–10) lists state terror as one of the four central elements of modern totalitarianism (along with intensified information coding and police surveillance, patriotic and moral totalism, and the presence of dictators). As a result, the discourse of terrorism is part and parcel of the phenomenon of contemporary political violence. Pape (2005), for example, argues with a good deal of empirical support that "suicide terrorism" is a strategic response to liberal Empire. Therefore, an objective sociology of violence cannot ignore the violent actions of the police and military against enemies of society, the nation, and the international community—actions aimed at deterring violations of the law and upholding the sovereign authority of the state (Nygengast 1994, Gareau 2005, Garland 2010).

In a June 22, 2011 speech by President Obama on the withdrawal of American troops from Afghanistan, he explicitly denies that America's use of military power is aimed at Empire. Rather, America seeks to extend "self-determination" to the Afghan people.

> In all that we do, we must remember that what sets America apart is not solely our power— it is the principles upon which our union was founded. We're a nation that brings our enemies to justice while adhering to the rule of law, and respecting the rights of all our citizens. We protect our own freedom and prosperity by extending it to others. We stand not for empire, but for self-determination.

The U.S. engages in "enhanced interrogations" for rational reasons to collect intelligence only under "ticking bomb" circumstances. Wars are fought as heroic struggles against villainous powers, military action in the name of national defense and as a defense of democracy. But terrorism is a very slippery concept. One group's political hero is another group's terrorist, and vice versa. From the standpoint of the sociology of violence, there is absolutely no way to escape this definitional conundrum (contra Jackman 2002). Terrorism is a contested concept in part because it is impossible to avoid some degree of methodological "relativity" in the study of the phenomena of political violence. The structural position of those who engage in the use of this categorization cannot be ignored (see Richard English 2009: 18–24, Laqueur 2002). The powerful describe things in a way that privileges their actions as legal, right and moral. The task of the social scientist is to describe how that "cover up" functions in power struggles.

In spite of this confusion social scientists do agree on one generalization regarding the patterning of social and political violence. As Borges' (1967) great poem[3] suggests, violence is "cyclical" and deeply embedded in the "dark" origins of Western culture. Scheper-Hughes and Phillipe Bourgois (2004: 1) assert, "It is mimetic, like imitative magic or homeopathy…So we can rightly speak of chains, spirals, and mirrors of violence…" Violence begets violence. An "eye-for-an-eye" makes everyone blind. "Whoever fights monsters should see to it that in the process he does not become a monster (one of Nietzsche's aphorisms discussed in Blain 1988). As we shall see, victimage ritual is the "cyclical night" of political violence. When "the good guys" perpetrate violence it is justified in euphemistic terms that "legitimate" it as "self-defense" and as a "heroic struggle against evil." U.S. support for oppressive regimes in the Middle East begets Al Qaeda's terrorism. In turn, Al Qaeda's terrorism begets the violence of so-called counter-terrorism and global war.

There is a certain degree of hypocrisy involved in the selective and one-sided use of the terrorist category to vilify adversaries and to describe their violence. Understanding this hypocrisy is central to the analysis presented in this book. It focuses directly on the functions of this categorization in the context of power struggles and Empire. The concept of Empire implies that an asymmetry of power exists between the various contending parties (i.e., NATO, or U.S. versus terrorists). The analysis that follows shows how the practice of categorizing opponents as "terrorists" or their acts as "terrorism," is part and parcel of the history of the practices of liberal democratic Empire.[4] A good example of the calculated character of this hypocritical practice is captured by two past events reported in the New York Times: "Nazis give French only two choices: all must be 'collaborationist' or 'terrorist'—no middle ground lies open" (Archambault 1942) and "British in Palestine ban use of word 'terrorist'" (British in Palestine, 1947). The vilification of opponents as terrorists is part and parcel of Empire—a mode of power or subjection by means of victimage ritual. Clearly, the British imperial administrators understood this hypocrisy as well as the Nazis. If people are moved to acts of political violence through the strategic use of victimage ritual, then vilifying opponents as "terrorists" is a tactic employed by political leaders to legitimate and motivate violence against their adversaries.

In reality, states and governments employ the threat and use of political violence to enforce the authority of the law and to terrorize (if necessary) opponents and populations into accepting domination. As Max Weber (1946: 43–76) put it in "Politics as a Vocation," the state is "a human community that (successfully)

---

3   Quoted at the opening of this chapter.

4   The link between Empire and colonization, and terrorism and torture, has been the subject of a spate of post 9/11 studies (Mann 2003, Ali 2004, Chomsky 2004, Mamdani 2004, Lazreg 2007).

claims the monopoly on the legitimate use of physical force within a territory." As Weber added, this is so because "The decisive means of politics is violence." Political domination depends on two conditions: moral authority and command of the material means of violence. By violence, Weber clearly meant the capacity to terrorize potential opponents. The demagogic "war of words" to generate moral authority is part and parcel of the process of political violence and victimage ritual; it is the discursive correlate to the "war of bullets and bombs." Political leaders must engage in a continuous rhetorical campaign to rally their loyal troops and sustain public support to achieve their political goals. Political actors in power struggles engage in the tactical use of ritual symbolism and rhetorical discourse, the vilification of opponents and glorification of heroes, to motivate people to engage in violence against their adversaries. One way to do this is to categorize your opponent's violence as "terrorism" and cast them in the role of "terrorists."

Politics and Culture

Culture and language play a central role in the social genesis and dynamics of politics (Hunt 1984, Ozouf 1988, Edles 1998, Smith and Riley 2009). The sociological study of politics has gone through a fundamental change or "cultural turn" in the last decade. This change in thinking was recognized by Mabel Berezin's (1997) *Annual Review of Sociology* article, "Politics and Culture: A Less Fissured Terrain." In this important review Berezin diagnosed the limits of "structuralism" and "frame analysis" as approaches to the study of how culture and discourse function in politics. As she asserts, "frame analysis" had led to an overly rigid approach to the study of political discourse, particularly for those analysts who were seeking a more nuanced sense of cultural and historical understanding (citing Blain 1994 as an example of the new approach). At the time, she argued, "An interest in rhetorical strategies or language and political mobilization is beginning to emerge and will be a major competitive paradigm to frame analysis" (Berezin: 375–376).

Implicit in this cultural turn was a new appreciation of the ethnological and cultural background of human social practices. The analyst's job is to describe these practical systems. Swidler (1986, 1995) also argued this point in regard to the cultural study of political phenomena like social movements. The analyst needs to focus on the practices that constitute movements. Political practices, vilifying opponents / glorifying heroes, are linked to interpretive understandings acquired by actors through socialization to a culture. These interpretations include understandings of Scene, Actor, and Audience. Symbolic interaction presupposes this kind of shared cultural background. Diagram 1.1 highlights the ethnological model of symbolic interaction. Culture is the total repertoire of practices available to actors in a society, including modes of power, truth, and subjection as well as (sometimes correlated) modes of political violence. Examples would be the tradition of revolutionary violence and terror inspired by the American and French revolutions.

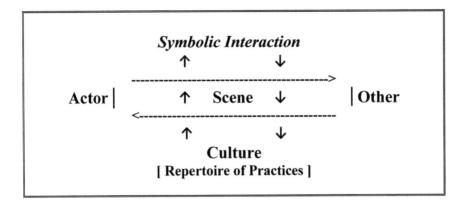

Diagram 1.1   Ethnological Model of Symbolic Interaction

Human beings are ethnocentric animals who acquire knowledge of the interactional strategies available to them through socialization. Culture is the total tool-kit of collective inventions of human beings and societies. Culture accumulates through the creation, storage and intergenerational transmission of symbol systems and artifacts. The Actor and the Audience must share a common cultural background to be able to engage in symbolic interaction. Knowledge of historical events and practices, including the background of revolutionary violence and warfare that constituted liberal democratic systems, is taught to each new generation. The agencies of socialization include mass public education systems and the celebration of national holidays (e.g., the Boston Tea Party, Fourth of July, Memorial Day).

Symbol systems like language, speech and writing, are material, meaningful, and magical. They are material in the sense that they are observable, recordable, and documentable practices. Interaction is symbolic because the Actor and the Auditor share a common sense understanding of the signs and symbols of social systems and structures, and their associated norms and values. Human action is ethnological because it depends on these background understandings. Everyone who learns about the history of Western Civilization studies the French "Revolution" (1789) and "the Great Terror." The material aspect of symbol-systems is captured by contemporary semiotic theory. Semiotics makes a basic distinction between signifier and signified. The Name is Not the Thing! It is in the play of associated signifiers that meanings, understandings, and interpretations are constituted (e.g., the strong association made between "revolution" and "terrorism," particularly by reactionary political elites). Symbol systems are magical because they have the power to produce social effects. Actors can use ritual and discursive symbolism rhetorically, to influence, incite, provoke others, to act on their actions. Some politicians can incite followers to engage in collective actions and power struggles against their adversaries. The constant linking of "Islam" and "terrorism"—"guilt by association" can provoke publics to applaud high-tech, homicide bombings of those who have been categorized as "Islamic terrorists" and their "Taliban" supporters.

Power and Subjection

The conceptualization of power and subjection employed in this book is derived from Michel Foucault's histories. Foucault (1978) defined power in terms of strategy: "One needs to be nominalistic," he stated, "power is not an institution, and not a structure; neither is it a certain strength we are endowed with; it is the name that one attributes to a complex strategic situation in a society" (1978: 93). A power relation is not simply a relationship between two parties, individual and collective, but a way of acting on the actions of others. Acting on the action of others involves practices of subjection and subjectification (see Foucault 1982, Rabinow 1984: 7–11, Barrett 1991, Butler 1997). Since the "others" are also actors with options, the exercise of power is agonistic, implicating relations of strategy and counter-strategy. A study or genealogy of a specific mode of power such as the global war on terror requires two things: a description of the theater of force relations in a situation and a description of how actors in that theater constitute themselves as subjects acting on self and others. One can constitute oneself as a war hero by joining the military, disciplining oneself as a warrior, and fighting in the war on terror, or by participating in Memorial Day or Veteran's Day celebrations one can constitute oneself as a patriotic American.

Foucault relates power relations to strategy in three ways. In its most general sense, a strategy refers to the totality of means put into operation to implement or maintain a power relation effectively. The second issue concerns the dynamic possibility of counter-action in a power struggle. Any move in a struggle can generate a new field of possible reactions. When actors engage in struggles, they calculate strategies and tactics on the basis of what they think their opponents might do or what they think their opponent's thinks the actor might do. A third way Foucault linked power to strategy concerns the free-play of antagonistic reactions in a confrontation. The moment of victory or stalemate arrives when this free-play is replaced by stable mechanisms. This conceptualization has important consequences for how we build resistance into an analysis of power struggles like the war on terror. Power relations are social relations. The "other" over whom power is exercised must be recognized as an agent who acts, and therefore, the agonism involving power and freedom's refusal to submit or resist cannot be separated. Any attempt to exercise domination over another agent generates a dynamic theater of possible counter-strategies. Low-tech suicide bombings can become a lethal counter to high-tech homicide bombings.

Strategy is a key term in this book, as it was for both Foucault and Kenneth Burke (Burke [1973] asserted, a symbolic act is a strategy for dealing with a situation). The war on terror is a strategy for dealing with a world that is resistant to Empire and U.S. domination. It is also a response to the need to constitute "existential" threats to justify the use of military power to police Empire. In the rhetorical vacuum created by 1989 and the collapse of the Soviet and "communist" threat, the power elite followed President Ronald Reagan's example and turned to Hollywood for an answer (Rogin 1987). Flora Lewis captured this shift in culture and discourse, a new name for the "new game" of power, in a 1999 *New York Review of Books* article:

> It is the Washington idiom but it sounds more like Hollywood-doom, disaster, Armageddon, absolute action. It is the guaranteed new threat to take the place of the run-down cold war, keep us all on our toes, out of pocket, in line, under surveillance. The name of the new game is "catastrophic terrorism" and it is very frightening, not just because it conceivably could happen but even more because of what people who choose to dwell on the possibility, however remote, want to do about it (Lewis 1999).

As evidence of this change Lewis summarized U.S. Secretary of Defense William Cohen's remarks at the time. The traditional "threat of reprisal," Cohen warned, will not work against "biological and chemical weapons and cyber-terrorism" because it is too hard to determine the perpetrators. "Deterrence is not going to be sufficient to prevent their use in future. We have to depend upon defense. We have to depend upon intervention, and we have to promote the safety of our citizens both here and abroad" (Cohen quoted in Lewis, 1999). Cohen spoke just before a new series of bombing attacks on Iraq to "degrade" Saddam Hussein's capacity to use exotic weapons. Lewis concluded that Cohen's remarks appeared "to launch an intense new campaign focused on weapons of mass destruction, or WMD, now the preferred initials in place of ABC, or atomic, biological, chemical weapons."

Foucault's (1978: 98–102) well-known history of sexuality is a paradigm example of subjection as a mode of power. It is also relevant because it is in this study that Foucault advanced his most original claim about modern society—the notion of biopower or biopolitics. The discourse of sexuality, he argued, was part and parcel of a distinctly modern politics of life. The knowledge that one has a sexual drive is itself a way of exercising power over bodies and populations. Discursive elements like "sexuality" are tactically polyvalent because they are tied to a multiplicity of power relations (e.g., parent / child relations; teacher / student relations, etc.). One can see a parallel to this tactical polyvalence in the notion of "terror" as a psychological state of extreme fright. The idea of normal and perverse "sexualities" can be the basis of a counter-strategy. Foucault described how the development of a *scientia sexualis* and its notions of perverse versus healthy forms of sexual desire, were historically correlated with the emergence of a bio-medical regime that took hold of the bourgeois family. Once constituted, elements of this discourse could be rearticulated in an opposing strategy. A movement for homosexual rights could emerge by the beginning of the twentieth century. Later, the sexual liberation and gay movements could critique modern bourgeois society as Victorian and sexually repressive (see Reich 1970). In the same way the eighteenth century Monarchs employed the Sovereign "terror" of public torture as a mode of punishment to constitute a sovereign / subject mode of power. French revolutionaries would turn the tables on the tyrant, adopting the "reign of terror" as a tactic of liberal-democratic and revolutionary politics. Once constituted, the liberal governments that emerged to manage modern society would differentiate between legitimate and illegitimate violence.

These ideas can be extended to the U.S. lead war on terrorism and the practices of torture. The modern concept of political terrorism emerged during the French revolutionary era (as described in detail in Chapter 2). Terror and torture are traditional tactics of political power and subjection. Garland's (2010) genealogy of the complex social functions of the American practice of the death penalty puts popular justice, mob violence, torture, and lynching at the center of his account. In contrast to Foucault's account of "sovereign torture," Garland argues "The spectacle lynching was not an official ceremony but a popular carnival—a 'lynching bee,' a 'negro barbecue'" (2010: 32). These activities were largely ignored by the federal government. Thus it should not be surprising that the U.S. government has provided military training and financial and logistical support to "friendly" regimes that have employed techniques of terror and torture as modes of power and subjection. Some of those regimes are in the Middle East. Resistance movements emerged in response to this violent subjection. These movements were duly indicted as "terrorist movements" by these regimes and the U.S. State Department, and members of the populations who are indicted as supporters of these movements are, in turn, tortured to elicit "intelligence" (McCoy 2006).

Victimage Ritual

The analysis presented in this book merges Foucault's concepts of power and subjection with Kenneth Burke's dramatism theory of victimage ritual. It argues that the war on terrorism is a mode of power and subjection by means of victimage ritual. In Burke's perspective social action is rhetorical precisely because it is always a strategy for acting on a situation (Gusfield 1989: 1–49, Swidler 1986). One tries, Burke asserted, "to develop a strategy whereby one 'can't lose'" and "one tries to fight on his own terms," but "one must also, to develop a full strategy, be *realistic*. One must *size things up* properly." Burke interprets political acts as "sincere" but "calculated" social actions designed to achieve political objectives.

This book views the war on terrorism from Kenneth Burke's perspective— dramatism and the related concept of victimage ritual—and the problematic of ruling liberal societies. Human beings are symbol using animals (Burke 1968, 1965). Victimage ritual is a consequence of this fact of human social life. It involves the polemical and melodramatic use of language to scapegoat an opponent in a power struggle to establish a common identification with an enemy (e.g., the Christian Church's vilification of the devil; the NAZI scapegoating of the Jews; the liberal crusade against Islamic terrorists). The language of victimage ritual is a symbolic fog that "screens," "directs" and / or "deflects" attention. It can be used by politicians to deflect attention from alternative ways of seeing power relations and modes of domination (the devil rather than the priests; the Jews rather than capitalists; terrorists rather than imperialists, etc.).

Victimage ritual is rooted in a deeply ingrained cultural practice derived from the history of Christianity. The crucifixion of Jesus by a Roman imperial administrator and his spiritual resurrection—redemption through vicarious victimage, Burke argued in the *Rhetoric of Religion* (1961), is the incunabula of Western culture (Ivie 2004, 2005). The sacrificial principle is a deeply resonant cultural rhetoric of motives. The *Oxford English Dictionary* (2010) defines victimage as "the practice of seeking out a victim, esp. a symbolic one, in order to expiate the guilt of some social group." The dictionary also quotes Burke's writings as the primary source of the word: "A principle of absolute 'guilt', matched by a principle that is designed for the corresponding absolute cancellation of such guilt. And this cancellation is contrived by victimage, by the choice of a sacrificial offering that is correspondingly absolute in the perfection of its fitness" (Burke, *Permanence and Change* 1954: 284). There are two dramatic moments in Christian victimage ritual: guilt and redemption. These two moments correspond to the scapegoating of Islamic terrorists, particularly Osama bin Laden, after the 9/11 attacks on U.S. soil. The second moment, as we shall see in detail, corresponds most completely to the May 1, 2011 killing of the perfect ritual scapegoat, the charismatic Osama bin Laden.

This book also deals with two problems in understanding contemporary forms of victimage ritual: 1) the first concerns the unique problems of ruling liberal societies founded on the right to engage in revolutionary violence against tyranny, and 2) the role of scientific practices in the perfection of modern scapegoats. The U.S. was founded on the principles elaborated in the *Declaration of Independence* which includes the right of the people to engage in revolutionary violence against tyranny. The *Preamble* to the Constitution of the United States asserts that the role of government is to "secure the blessings of Liberty." Threats to "government / security" are vilified as "terrorists" who threaten Liberty—the right to life, liberty, and the pursuit of happiness.

Burke acknowledged the unique problem of recognizing the forms that victimage ritual assumes in a scientific culture. Enlightened people are secular and scientific in their orientation to the world. Ritual scapegoating is barbaric; hence, pre-modern. "Dramatism", Burke admonished, "...asks not how the sacrificial motives revealed in the institutions of magic and religions might be eliminated in a scientific culture, but what new forms they take" (Burke 1968: 451). Burke's critique of the Nazi fusion of traditional religious thinking and "scientific racism" and the techniques of "psychological warfare" is a good example of this approach. As we shall see, Burke's approach to modern forms of scapegoating in a scientific culture provides an opening to Foucault's account of modern power / knowledge regimes, humanism, and the politics of the human and social sciences. These examples also provide useful clues to how to approach the war on terror and "humanitarian interventions" as liberal modes of power and subjection by means of victimage ritual.

Burke's perspective can be merged with Foucault's power / subjection analytic because both thinkers view rhetorical discourses and rituals as material practices that can exercise power effects. This merging is another way to link the issue of power and domination to Burke's critique of modern forms of victimage ritual (Burke 1965, Duncan 1962: 253–311). The exercise of power to maintain social domination can be easily lost in a symbolic fog of liberal rhetoric. Empire can be justified and extended in the name of "liberation." Political domination, seen in this light, can be mystified by being represented as a dramatic struggle of heroes against villainous powers. The heroes and villains are perfected in such a way that they personify the ultimate principles of social order. By casting our opponents in the role of a villain—terrorists who threaten life and liberty, we justify and motivate their ritual destruction. Political leaders perfect victims through a process of vilification. When effective this vilification generates a social need to witness the ritual destruction of the villain. Only through the violent destruction of a scapegoat can the world be purged of evil. The vicarious participation of publics in these spectacles generates a social need to punish the guilty and destroy evil. This need explains the controversy surrounding the killing of Osama bin Laden and his burial at sea. The demand for justice cloaked a perverse social need. The strong and insistent desire to witness the killing of Osama bin Laden by the Navy Seals by vicarious participation in the killing or seeing photographs of his corpse. The mystique of political authority is affirmed by such spectacles.

The moment of the kill was elaborated in great detail on the front page of the *New York Times* in an article titled, "Behind the Hunt for Bin Laden" (Mazzetti, Cooper, and Baker, May 3, 2011):

> On Sunday afternoon, as the helicopters raced over Pakistani territory, the president and his advisers gathered in the Situation Room of the White House to monitor the operation as it unfolded. Much of the time was spent in silence. Mr. Obama looked "stone faced," one aide said. Vice President Joseph R. Biden Jr. fingered his rosary beads. "The minutes passed like days," recalled John O. Brennan, the White House counterterrorism chief.

The code name for Bin Laden was "Geronimo." The president and his advisers watched Leon E. Panetta, the C.I.A. director, on a video screen, narrating from his agency's headquarters across the Potomac River what was happening in faraway Pakistan.

> "They've reached the target," he said.
> Minutes passed.
> "We have a visual on Geronimo," he said.
> A few minutes later: "Geronimo EKIA."
> Enemy Killed In Action. There was silence in the Situation Room.

Finally, the president spoke up.

"We got him."

Interpreting the War on Terror

It is the enemies of Empire who are most likely to be labeled with the terrorist category. Hardt and Negri (2000) argue that the "terrorist" category is "a rude conceptual and terminological reduction that is rooted in a police mentality" (2000: 37). The global war on terror is best understood as a strategic response to organized and violent resistance to a liberal regime of globalizing Empire. "Today military intervention is progressively less a product of decisions that arise out of the old international order or even U.N. structures" they argue, "More often it is dictated unilaterally by the U.S. which charges itself with the primary task and then subsequently asks its allies to set in motion a process of armed containment and/or repression of the current enemy of Empire" (2000: 370). The global war is a strategic response to the post-Cold-War (post-1989) world and perceived threats to liberalism and the defense and expansion of Empire (Berman 2004).

Diagram 1.2 (below) presents the overarching analysis of the war on terrorism advanced in this book; the diagram depicts the principal concepts and structural relations that organize this book's interpretation of the war. The war on terror is a mode of power and subjection by means of victimage ritual. This power system operates by means of two interrelated subjectifying practices working in tandem: victimage ritual and biopower. In this sense it is clear that the discourse of terrorism is tactically polyvalent. In the context of Sovereignty, power struggles that implicate the political authority of the state, the "terrorist" functions as a villainous scapegoat in a victimage ritual. In this regard the terrorist represents an ultimate threat to the survival of "liberal" forms of governance— the security system that protects and defends human life and individual liberty. These two discourses are part and parcel of two interrelated clusters of practices.

The following excerpts illustrate the two types of "terrorist" discourses. The first are derived from the Bush regimes' Weekly Whitehouse speeches and exemplify the "terrorist" as villainous scapegoat:

> Good morning. This weekend I am engaged in extensive sessions with members of my National Security Council, as we plan a comprehensive assault on terrorism. This will be a different kind of conflict against a different kind of enemy....

> This is a conflict without battlefields or beachheads, a conflict with opponents who believe they are invisible. Yet, they are mistaken. They will be exposed, and they will discover what others in the past have learned: *Those who make war against the United States have chosen their own destruction.* [emphasis added: bold = glorifier / bold + italic = vilifier] Victory against terrorism will not

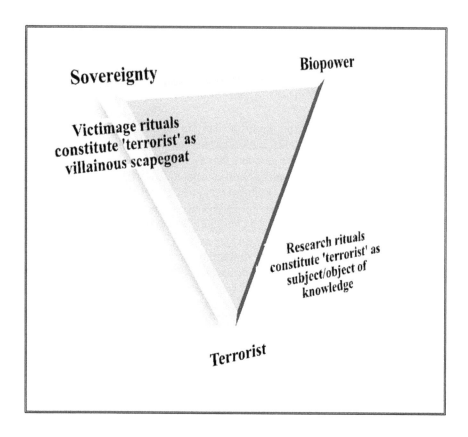

Diagram 1.2   Triangle of Power and Subjection by Means of Victimage Ritual

take place in a single battle, but in a series of decisive actions against terrorist organizations and those who harbor and support them....

We are planning a broad and sustained campaign to secure our country and *eradicate the evil* of terrorism. ("Attack Response," September 15, 2001)

Two months after the September 11, 2001 attacks, President Bush elaborated the global implications of these ideas in a speech to an international meeting of Pacific Rim nations convened in Shanghai, China. The "terrorists," he argued, must be destroyed to insure the survival of a global regime of "free trade":

The nations meeting here in Shanghai understand what is at stake. If we do not stand against terrorism now, every civilized nation will at some point be its target. We will defeat the terrorists by destroying their network...[and]...by building an enduring prosperity...

The terrorists attacked the World Trade Center. They fear trade because they understood that trade brings freedom and hope [emphasis added]. We're in Shanghai to advance world trade because we know that trade can conquer poverty and despair. *In this struggle of freedom against fear, the outcome is not in doubt—freedom will win* [emphasis added]... (Bush Radio Speech, October 20, 2001)

After the invasion of Afghanistan and the Shanghai conference, President Bush presented the 2002 State of the Union address to the Congress and nation, articulating the doctrine driving the war on terror:

What we have found in Afghanistan confirms that, far from ending there, our war against terror is only beginning. Most of the 19 men who hijacked planes on September the 11th were trained in Afghanistan's camps, and so were tens of thousands of others. *Thousands of dangerous killers, schooled in the methods of murder, often supported by outlaw regimes, are now spread throughout the world like ticking time bombs, set to go off without warning* [emphasis added].

Thanks to the work of our law enforcement officials and coalition partners, hundreds of terrorists have been arrested. Yet, tens of thousands of trained terrorists are still at large. *These enemies view the entire world as a battlefield, and we must pursue them wherever they are* (Applause) [emphasis added]. So long as training camps operate, so long as nations harbor terrorists, *freedom is at risk* [emphasis added]. And America and our allies must not, and will not, allow it (Applause).

Our nation will continue to be steadfast and patient and persistent in the pursuit of two great objectives. First, we will shut down terrorist camps, disrupt terrorist plans, and bring terrorists to justice. And, second, we must prevent the terrorists and regimes who seek chemical, biological or nuclear weapons from threatening the United States and the world (Applause). (2002 State of the Union Address)

The second type of "terrorist" discourse is constituted by practitioners of the human and social sciences. This discourse is biopolitical and a product of complex power / knowledge relations, government and privately sponsored research inside and outside institutions of higher education. In this discourse the "terrorist" and the social conditions of "terrorism" are objects of "rational" psychological and social scientific analysis (i.e., as reified social facts or realities with a discernible nature of their own). The subjectivity and psychological motivation of the "terrorist" as a social or psychological type has become a serious object of scientific study. Here is a representative extract from an article published by Jerrold Post (2005b), a psychiatrist who has consulted extensively with the CIA, and titled "The New Face of Terrorism":

...In contrast to social revolutionary and nationalist-separatist terrorists, for religious fundamentalist extremist groups, the decision-making role of the preeminent leader is of central importance. For these true believers, the radical cleric is seen as the authentic interpreter of God's word, not only eliminating any ambivalence about killing, but endowing the destruction of the defined enemy with sacred significance. These groups are particularly dangerous, for they are not seeking to influence the West but to expel the West with its secular modernizing values and hence are not constrained by Western reactions. They have shown a willingness to perpetrate acts of mass causality terrorism, as exemplified by the bombings of Khobar Towers in Saudi Arabia, the World Trade Center [extended list of examples followed by an elaboration on Osama bin Laden's *fatwa* about the moral duty of all Muslims to kill Americans] (Post 2005b: 451–452).

The article goes on to elaborate a scientific methodology. "To bring the reader into their minds we will draw upon the words of terrorists themselves, drawing on material from a research project...funded by the Smith Richardson Foundation involving semi-structured interviews with 35 incarcerated radical Middle Eastern terrorists, both radical Islamist terrorists from HAMAS, Islamic Jihad, and Hezbollah, and secular terrorists from Fatah and the Palestinian Front for the Liberation of Palestine, as well as interviews conducted by the author with an Abu Nidal terrorist and Al Qaeda terrorists in connection with federal trials" (Post 2005b: 453). The research leads to the following generalization: "...there is a clear fusion of individual identity and group identity." The more fusing of the individual and group identity, the more "personal" the struggle becomes for group members:

...Most interestingly and illustrative of this concept of individual and group fusion is the perception or characterization of the "the enemy"...The Islamist groups are fighting for a pure Islamic state...There is no concern about alienating any "earthly" population because the only "audience" they are seeking to satisfy is Allah. With their direction coming in the form of religious *fatwas* (religious edicts) and sanctioned by religious clerics and other figures, the identification of the enemy is clear and simple for those Islamist groups—whether Israel or the United States—it is anyone who is opposed to their world view (Post 2005b: 460–461).

The author goes on to draw out the policy implications of his research for "Counter-terrorist strategy." It should be based on an understanding of "what makes terrorists tick" and it is important to emphasize that "terrorists are psychologically normal." There activities should be theorized in terms of unique cultural, organizational, and social psychological processes. However, Post concludes, "Political terrorism is...a particularly vicious species of psychological warfare...violence as communication...[and]...until now the terrorists have had a virtual monopoly on the weapon of the television camera as they manipulate their target audience through the media…" This is, of course, a patently false historical assertion. There is solid historical evidence that states, including the U.S. have employed this kind of political terrorism in wars (see Simpson 1994; McCoy 2006, 2009; Dower 2010, particularly on "terror bombing" during World War II and the nuclear bombings of Hiroshima and Nagasaki). Post draws one major implication from his analysis: "One counters psychological warfare with psychological warfare" (2005b: 461–462).

From the standpoint of the perspective advanced here, relating these two different but correlated discourses and contexts, one explicitly political (part of a dramatic victimage ritual that vilifies the "terrorist" as international devil) and the other explicitly scientific and implicitly political (part of a rational psychological analysis, warranted by the meticulous rituals of scientific knowledge that objectifies the "terrorist" and the social conditions of "terrorism" with policy implications), the terrorist has become a tactically polyvalent discursive element in a strategy of global domination. The function of victimage ritual and ritual denunciation of the terrorist is to incite moral outrage and the desire for revenge to motivate the war against terrorism; the function of the biopolitical discourses is to provide a realistic policy for managing conflicts in the face of violent resistance to Empire.

Security, Surveillance, and Domination

Foucault invented the concept of biopower to name "a mode of power organized around the management of life rather than the menace of death" (Foucault 1978: 147). He contrasted this mode of power over life to the repressive practices of traditional Sovereignty and the Law (dividing practices, the legal / illegal; repression, public torture as mode of punishment, power / truth). Foucault associated this modern mode of power with the rise of liberalism, a cluster of governmental practices aimed at regulating the activity of "living beings" and "free" subjects (contra Marxist ideology critique). Biopower is a strategy that individualizes and totalizes, involving disciplinary techniques and subjectifying practices (dividing practices such as internment and incarceration, scientific classification, subjectification).

The contemporary relevance of biopolitics to the war on terrorism has been established by Agamben (2005, see Blain 2009b). He cites as his chief example, President Bush's (2002) executive order authorizing the use of indefinite detention in camps, torture, black-sites, etc. He also sees a striking parallel between the Nazi subjection of Jews and the current subjection of terrorists. They were placed beyond the pale and outside of any established legal framework (enemy combatants, absent ordinary liberties, rights). The "state of exception" occasioned by the war on terrorism is a paradigm of government in which the law encompasses living beings by means of its [the law's] own suspension (2002: 3). The objectification of the "terrorist" in social and psychological research coincides with the state of exception. Psychologists have played a front-line role in the revival of torture (e.g., euphemistically called "Enhanced Interrogation" programs). Anthropologists have played front-line roles in the cultural aspects of the counter-insurgency campaigns in Iraq and Afghanistan.

The passage of the Homeland Security Act (2002) has had major reverberations in the field of knowledge. U.S. Institutes of "Terrorism" have been constituted to produce "knowledge" tailored to the interests of Empire. The National Counterterrorism Center (NCTC), the official U.S. agency charged with tracking the incidence of terrorism, created in response to a critique of prior State Dept. reports (Data: 2005 →). The Memorial Institute for the Prevention of Terrorism (MIPT) was created in memory of the Oklahoma bombing in 1995 (Data: 1998 → 2006; now funded by U.S. Department of Homeland Security). MIPT has data on international terrorism only. Researchers associated with these institutions operationally define terrorism and count cases in ways that are consistent with the asymmetric logic of Empire. They define terrorism as intentional, politically motivated violence perpetrated by non-state groups against civilians and/or noncombatants. On the other hand, if government forces kill civilians they will not be counted as terrorism. Apparently, the political violence practiced by allied states does not count as "terrorism." In the early years these researchers only counted incidents of "international" rather than "domestic" terrorism. The dramatic increase in the number of deaths attributable to global terrorism after 2003 was caused by the dubious practice of counting all civilian deaths during the Iraq War as acts of international terrorism (*Human Security* 2007: 12).

Chapter Overview

Chapters 2 and 3 of the book elaborate a more detailed theoretical perspective on the functions of victimage ritual in violent political power struggles. Later chapters describe the contemporary functioning of the discourse of "terrorism" in the global war on terrorism. The book goes on to describe the link between the politics of victimage ritual and the intensification of political surveillance and domination produced by the global war, especially (and ironically) the dangers to civil liberty and freedom that result from the intensified surveillance and social control.

Chapter 2 presents the results of a historical genealogy of the concept of "political terrorism," particularly as it converges on the war on terrorism. If terror is tactically polyvalent, then it can be made to function in a meaningful way in a variety of strategic situations. Four types of Terror are discerned: Divine, Sovereign, Revolutionary; and Biopolitical. The pivotal historical event transforming its meaning in terms of modern democratic politics was the French Revolution (1789–1815).

Chapter 3 applies Burke's dramatism theory of victimage ritual to the war on terrorism. A dramatism model of the war is highlighted. A social-psychological theory of identification is advanced to explain why victimage ritual works, one that goes beyond the glib "dehumanization" thesis that dominates thinking in the sociology of violence. Charismatic leaders play a decisive role in socially organized warfare. Political leaders must play an active role in motivating warriors to fight wars. The emotions and desires involved must be stirred up and sustained through intensive and frequent participation in victimage rituals. These rituals create a stage on which authorities can vilify enemies as threatening powers who must be destroyed so that we might live. These ideas are elaborated in detail by means of a review of past research on America's wars, particularly its wars against communism and drugs. The chapter concludes with a theoretical discussion that relates victimage ritual to power struggles like the war on terrorism and to the rhetorical analysis of discourse.

Chapter 4 applies the concept of victimage ritual to a detailed analysis of the war on terror. Employing the results of a discourse analysis of U.S. presidential rhetoric (the Bush and Obama regime's Weekly Whitehouse speeches) two subjectifying practices are highlighted: two systems for differentiating the field of power relations, friends versus enemies and patriots versus traitors, and the amplification of these differences employing the tactics of vilification and glorification. The cast of characters includes villains (terrorists, tyrants), heroes (troops; armed forces; veterans, martyrs), leader (President Bush or Obama, Commander in Chief), spectators (public, patriots "supporting the troops"). While much attention has been paid to "dehumanization" in the original incitement to political violence, one of the key aims of this part of the analysis is to demonstrate the tragic symbolic force of the glorification of the hero, the flip-side of the vilification of the enemy in victimage ritual, in sustaining political violence. Collins (2011) concludes without detailed explanation, that "ideological polarization between opponents" sustains violent conflicts. He diagrams how "external polarization" gives way to emergent internal factions and conflict identities, pitting victory vs. peace factions, and concludes that idealization promoted at the outset of conflict becomes an obstacle to resolving the conflict in the end (2011: 18).

Chapter 5 highlights the dangers of security by describing two major social consequences of the "emergency" or "state of exception" caused by the global war on terrorism and the victimage ritual against "international" terrorists. The first effect of the emergency has been an intensification of the surveillance and policing of populations (i.e., domestic and foreign). This, in turn, provoked a major reorganization and consolidation of existing "security" programs in a new federal "Department of Homeland Security." It also spawned a global network of "Black Sites" and "Detention Centers for the interrogation and incarceration of "enemy combatants." At the practical level, the "state of exception" also caused a recrudescence of the practices of torture in the guise of "enhanced interrogation" and the production of "intelligence." A second major effect of the "emergency" has been in the order of knowledge. The use of "torture" to produce "actionable intelligence" corresponds to the use of "social science" to produce "knowledge." The global victimage ritual against "terrorists" has produced a new subject / object of knowledge. The correlates of terrorism and the characteristics of terrorists have become established fields of investigation. New "Institutes" and "Centers of Counterterrorism" have been established at universities funded by the Department of Homeland Security. Their practical aim is to provide knowledge to inform the policies of the U.S. power elite and the management of Empire.

Chapter 2
Genealogy of Terrorism

The category and concept of terrorism can be traced to the problematic of ruling liberal-democratic societies prone to civil war, destructive class conflicts, and revolutionary violence (Foucault 2003b: 59–62; Blain 2007). The emergence of this concept was a tactical response to the complicated circumstance that the first liberal nation-states were constituted through acts of political violence and terror—the American War of Independence and the French revolution. These struggles had consecrated a powerful cultural tradition, a cluster of national rituals and myths that continues to inspire resistance to tyranny and oppression right into the 21st century (Hunt 1984, 2003). Governing a "free people" who can claim a legitimate right to engage in revolutionary violence in reaction to tyranny creates special problems, including the constant threat of terrorism (e.g., by abolitionists, Ku Klux Klan, Indians, anarchists, Communists, right-wing militias, Tea Party, etc.). As a consequence there was a practical need to differentiate legitimate and illegitimate political violence. The concepts of terrorism and of terrorists seem to resolve that conceptual and political problem. Political violence directed against liberal-democratic regimes can be denounced as terrorist.

Genealogy traces the history of power struggles and the emergence of new practices and discourses. Michel Foucault's histories reveal how our concepts of "criminality" and "terrorism" emerged in response to the rise of the liberal-democratic state. The force driving these developments was the constant "emergency" provoked by the persistent threat and reality of civil and revolutionary warfare. Liberalism, Foucault concluded, was the great intervening event between the pre-modern state and modern democratic states (Gordon 1991). Liberalism was not just a "bourgeois ideology," but involved new approaches to political rule. This new "governmental rationality" involved a "sovereignty of all and each"—a tricky fusion of the ancient "Greek-city" game and the Christian Church's pastoral "Shepherd / Flock" games, i.e., *Omnes et Singulatim* or "all is each"). This powerful new form of sovereignty has proliferated ever since, intensifying government surveillance of every aspect of life.

The exercise of power and authority in the pre-modern European state had been based almost exclusively on a sovereignty founded on the Prince's divine "right of death." The Prince's laws were backed-up by the menace of death by means of terrifying torture. Wars were conceived as "duels" fought by monarchs in defense of their personal sovereignty. The modern "liberal-democratic" state is a "biopolitical" regime. The practices that constitute this regime involve a govern*mentality* oriented toward the security, health and welfare of each citizen. "There had been a parallel shift in the right of death," Foucault asserts, "or at least a tendency to align itself with the exigencies of a life-administering power…" or, "… the ancient right to take life or let live was replaced by a power to foster life or disallow it to the point of death" (1978: 136–138). These changes were also reflected in changes in the discourses and practices of warfare:

> Wars are no longer waged in the name of a sovereign who must be defended, they are waged on behalf of the existence of everyone; entire populations are mobilized for the purpose of wholesale slaughter in the name of life necessity: massacres have become vital. It is as managers of life and survival, of bodies and the race, that so many regimes have been able to wage so many wars, causing so many men to be killed…informed by the naked question of survival (Foucault 1978: 137).

The idea that governments must be capable of mass slaughter to secure the life and liberty of each individual member of society has become the biopolitical principle that defines the strategy of states. As recent events in the war on terrorism confirm, "torture" and "terror' did not disappear with the pre-modern state. Instead these practices have been reinterpreted in biopolitical terms as "enhanced interrogation" and "homeland security."

According to Foucault's (1978: 100) rule of the tactical polyvalence of discourses, it is the multiple uses of categories like "terrorism" that determine their historical appearance and functioning in the field of modern power relations. The discourse of sexuality linked a biomedical knowledge of the individual's body to the need for government regulations to insure the health of populations. Research shows how the "drug" problem was immediately linked to the war on terrorism (Blain 2002). If drug abusers snort cocaine or smoke crack, then they aid and abet terrorists in Columbia. The fact that these discursive elements can be put into play in multiple strategies creates a coincidence of interests among multiple constituencies. The problem of terrorism can be adopted by government agencies at the federal, state and local levels. Private contractors and security firms can get into the act as well. Within months of the 9/11 terrorist attacks, the U.S. Office of National Drug Control, had reinterpreted the war on drugs as a fight against terrorists. It is mentioned in the President's letters that preface the Annual Reports as well as at many points in the texts (see ONDC 2002–2008).

In February 2002, the Bush White House issued its first annual *National Drug Control Strategy* (NDCS 2002). Seizing the political opportunities of the moment, this new strategy statement articulates a direct link between the war on drugs and the war on terrorism. The letter signed by President George Bush that prefaces the document vilifies illegal drugs and glorifies the war on drugs by linking each to terrorism:

> ***Illegal drug use threatens everything that is good about our country. It can break the bonds between parents and children. It can turn productive citizens into addicts, and it can transform schools into places of violence and chaos.***

Internationally, it finances the work of terrorists who use drug profits to fund their murderous work. [emphasis added: bold = glorifier / bold + italic = vilifier] **Our fight against illegal drug use is a fight for our children's future, for struggling democracies, and against terrorism** (ONDC 2002).

This attack on "illegal drug use" reflects a two-pronged, domestic and global agenda. Part III of the strategy statement elaborates its "international" dimension: "Disrupting the Market: Attacking the Economic Basis of the Drug Trade." U.S. global strategy emphasizes "Going to the Source":

The illegal drug proceeds of the Taliban represent just part of a global problem in which drug revenue helps fuel terrorist violence; 12 of the 28 international terrorist groups listed by the U.S. Department of State are alleged to be involved to some degree in drug trafficking. In Columbia, all three of the major terrorist groups are involved in the drug trade as a source of operational funding. [emphasis added: bold = glorifier / bold + italic = vilifier] **This underscores the need to ensure that cooperative international law enforcement operations target those trafficking organizations that directly or indirectly help bankroll international terrorism** (White House, NDCS 2002: 26).

If one were to accept these statements at face value, one would have to conclude that drug users support terrorism and the illegal drug trade finances terrorist movements that "threaten democracy." It should be enough to note at this point that the biopolitics of the "drug problem" has frequently been employed by the U.S. power elite to legitimate its wars and policies as a means to achieve its domestic and global objectives (Scott 2003, Nadelmann 1993, Andreas and Nadelmann 2006).

The pre-revolutionary concept of terror was associated with a sovereign "right of death" or the Monarch's right to take or give life in defense of sovereignty. This right was made manifest in the spectacular victimage rituals of public torture described by Foucault in his study of the birth of the prison. In the liberal critique of tyranny that informed revolutionary thought, the tyrant is "the King of terror." Following the French revolution, a shift in perspective with regard to the locus of the terrorist threat took place. The tyrant's terror was understood to be top-down. The right to use terror descended from the top of the power hierarchy. After the revolution, terror was associated with the democratic threat of revolutionary violence, variously referred to in positive terms as the "people" or negative terms as the "mob" or "rabble," that is, as a threat from below or the bottom of the power hierarchy. Terrorism was redefined as a tactic of the "the dangerous classes," enemies of society such as revolutionaries, criminals, and terrorists (Hunt 2003). From its eighteenth century inception, the "social movement" has been associated with violence (Tarrow 1998). Hence, there was a practical need in governing liberal societies to differentiate illegitimate from legitimate forms of political violence. Violence by the police and military would have to be differentiated from illegitimate forms of criminal or terrorist violence.

Two consequences flowed from this. First, terror in defense of the sovereign was confined to enclosed spaces and kept secret to mask the scandalous face of naked violence—the prison and interrogation center (Foucault 1977). And second, there was a need for new interpretations of violence and modes of knowledge such as the social sciences that would focus on the regulation of populations and individuals. As a result of shifts in the configuration of power/knowledge, new interpretations of war, diplomacy, morality, criminality, poverty, sexuality, terrorism and peace emerged (Foucault 1978: 137; Der Derian 1987, Dean 1991, Mahon 1992). The evidence for these changes is derived from detailed archaeologies of texts and artifacts to establish the events that have led us to constitute ourselves and to recognize ourselves as subjects of what we are doing, thinking, saying. Foucault's concept of subjection refers therefore to the practices that constitute us as subjects. The invention of a discourse of terrorism was a response to the ever present possibility of dangerous insurrections. Once invented it could be deployed through basic regulatory practices of subjection.

At the same time similar problems were posed by the need of liberal states to justify occupying and administering their colonial empires. Wallerstein (1983: 105) has argued that liberalism as ideology and practical policy has been associated with all three major instances of hegemony in the history of the capitalist world economy (17th C. Dutch; 19th C. British; 20th C. U.S.). At any rate, by the end of the 19th Century the concept of terrorism had been abstracted from its specific reference to the French Revolution, allowing governments to "kill many birds with one stone" (e.g., the Irish, the Russians, Communists, etc). After World War II, with the emergence of movements of national liberation and decolonization, the practice of categorizing resistance to imperial domination as terrorism began to be radically contested.

Edward Said has described how the "Orient" emerged as an object of a power / knowledge complex in tandem with European imperial domination of the Middle and Far East. Said defined "orientalism" as "the vocabulary employed whenever the Orient is spoken or written about" (Said 1978: 71). It is, he elaborated, a set of ethnocentric figures in which the Orient functioned as the Other to Europe and western civilization. The most extreme example was the terrifying image of conquering Islamic movements. The crusades were described as holy wars of Christian crusaders against Islamic devils, and a mode of dramatic deliverance from civilization's enemy. Islam was turned into a synonym for ignorance, despotism, slavery, and base servitude. Hence, Muslims had to be conquered and controlled (Said 1978: 172). Orientalist knowledge was a tactical component of an imperial containment strategy developed in response to the resistance by the Muslim, Ottoman, or Arab to European dominance. The images of Osama bin Laden, Palestinian and Islamic terrorists and suicide bombers, are the most recent reincarnations of that terrifying Other.

It is the enemies of Empire, according to Hardt and Negri (2000), who are most often labeled with the terrorist category. By Empire, they mean something different than imperialisms of the past. It is spatially and temporally limitless, covering the entire space of the civilized world. As a regime, it is "outside history" or "at the end of history," a new "eternal" global order:

> Empire not only manages a territory and population but also creates the very world it inhabits. It not only regulates human interactions but also seeks directly to rule over human nature. The object of its rule is social life in its entirety, and thus Empire presents the paradigmatic form of biopower. Finally, although the practice of Empire is continually bathed in blood, the concept of Empire is always dedicated to peace—a perpetual and universal peace outside of history (Hardt and Negri 2000, xv).

Organized resistance and political violence threatens world peace. The global war on terror is best understood as a strategic response to the problem of policing Empire:

> Today military intervention is...dictated unilaterally by the U.S., which charges itself with the primary task and then subsequently asks its allies to set in motion a process of armed containment and / or repression of the current enemy of Empire. These enemies are most often called Terrorist, a rude conceptual and terminological reduction that is rooted in a police mentality (Hardt and Negri 2000: 37).

The "policing" function of the war is signified by the selection of the "terrorist" as the chief enemy. As they go on to elaborate, the strategies and practices developed in the nineteenth century movement to constitute the U.S. as a North American Empire—establishing territories and gradually admitting these territories to the U.S. and delegating powers to govern those individual states—were later extrapolated and redeployed globally in the 20th Century. The so-called global war on terrorism is a strategic response to the post-cold-war, post-1989 global situation and perceived threats to the defense and expansion of Empire.

Etymology of Terrorism

If the interpretation advanced above is correct, then changes in the discourses and practices of political power should be registered in the etymological record of the English language. The use of etymologies in genealogical investigations of this type was introduced in 1887 by Friedrich Nietzsche in *On the Genealogy of Morals* (1967). Nietzsche posed the question, "What light does linguistics, especially the study of etymology, throw on the history of the evolution of moral concepts?" Concepts of good/bad and good / evil have changed. He interpreted these changes in the perspective of power relations by posing the question, "Who speaks?" The Christian priests had reinterpreted good/bad as good/evil to advance their struggle with Rome and later the domination of Pagan populations. The question posed here is "What light does the study of etymology throw on the history of the evolution of terror concepts?" As we shall also see, the first explicitly political concept of terror appeared in the English language during the power struggles of the French Revolutionary era.

Edward Rose (1960, 1994) has employed this method to explore how new English words have emerged to satisfy the practical need to name specific types of persons and social situations. Following Rose's method the precisely dated and detailed etymologies in the *Oxford English Dictionary* are used to trace the genealogy of terror concepts in the English language. Changes in word meanings happen in two principle ways: old words acquire new meanings or new words are invented (Allan and Burridge 1991). Old words acquire new meanings by being rearticulated with different terms. Take the English word "revolution." Its earliest meaning (*c.* 1390) is related to "the movement of celestial objects" in astronomy. In 1600, revolution acquires a new meaning: "the complete overthrow of an established government." As we shall see, evidence for at least four meanings or concepts of terror can be differentiated: Divine, Sovereign, Revolutionary, and Biopolitical.

According to the *Oxford English Dictionary* (2010) "terrorism" and "terrorist" first entered the English lexicon in 1795 during the French Revolution. By adding suffixes to terror-, two new words were created, terrorism and terrorist, and two new objects of knowledge were constituted. The pre-revolutionary concepts of terror were associated with a Divine and Sovereign "right of death"—the right to take or give life, dramatized in the spectacular victimage rituals of public torture and pre-modern forms of warfare. The liberal critique of tyranny had associated the tyrant with illegitimate and arbitrary terror. Terror was understood in its religious sense as the personification of death (see terror *n*. #3, "King of Terror," *Bible*, 1611). After the French Revolution, the discourse of terrorism would prove to be tactically polyvalent. Terrorism would be a category employed to interpret political violence by society, the demos or people, savages, the dangerous classes, and social movements.

This new concept provided a practical solution to the problem of differentiating legitimate political violence by the state from illegitimate political violence. But it also created a gaping hole in the political understanding of violence and terrorism. If an act or practice is NOT illegal, then it is NOT categorized or understood as violence. Jackman (2002) is highly critical of this obfuscating practice in sociological discourse. This use of the "violence" category screens out many forms of violence that have not been criminalized—drone attacks that kill civilians or noncombatants. This problem has been particularly acute in liberal-democratic societies with Empires such as the British, the U.S. and the French. Consecrated through revolutionary violence, Empire does not categorize its use of "force" as political violence. Henceforth, the legal use of force in domestic and colonial contexts could be differentiated from illegal forms of political violence, particularly political resistance and the violence of the "dangerous classes." Actors who engaged in acts of collective violence against liberal, democratic states could be vilified and criminalized as terrorists.

Pre-Revolutionary Terror

The evidence from the etymology of terror corroborates this account of the emergence of a discourse of political terrorism. The word "terror" derives from Middle English *terrour*, from Old French *terreur*. The Old French *terreur* was derived from the Latin noun, *terror*, and the verb, *terrere*, glossed as "to frighten" in English. There are four major senses of terror, including one political concept. Terrorist, terrorism, and terrorize, according to the *Oxford English Dictionary*, are invented during and after the French revolution. Nine of the thirteen total senses (terror + terrorist + terrorism + terrorize) appeared during or after the French Revolution, establishing a strong association between revolutions and terror.

Table 2.1   Number of English Concepts of Political Violence in Relation to the French Revolutionary Era, 1789–1815

Category	<1789	1789–1815	>1815
tyranny	24	0	0
regicide	3	1	0
revolution	6	7	5
terrorism	0	2	0
terrorist	0	2	2
terrorize	0	0	2

Note: Plus suffixed forms

Source: Data derived from *On-line Oxford English Dictionary* 2010

Table 2.1 enumerates various *Oxford English Dictionary* concepts of political violence, tyranny, regicide, revolution, and terror in relation to the French revolutionary era, 1789–1815. The earliest concept refers to an individual's state of being (1375). It means "greatly frightened" or "intense fear or dread." The first three examples are religious, e.g., "The terrors of death are fallen upon me"

(1560). The second sense appears in the 1500s. A terror is an action or quality of something that causes dread or intense fear: a person (1375), "the Messiah cloathed with so much Terrour and Majesty" (1667), "the ferocious Bedoweens" (1788), the night (1834), etc. Fiction is specifically mentioned, as in Gothic "tales of terror" (1834). In 1598, terror was used in combination with war, "Curses… through the sterne throte of terror-breathing warre", which anticipates its later political associations

A third religious sense associated with the actions of divine powers appears in the 1611 edition of the Bible, the Book of Job. The "king of terrours" is "Death personified." The early association between king, death, and terror reflect the needs of a regime of absolute sovereignty and right of death, the Law, the Divine Right of Kings to take life and impose the ultimate sanction of death—the king of terror. Terror is imposed by God and the sovereign. The English revolution dates from 1600, when the issue of Absolutism was resolved in favor of an uneasy balance of power between the monarchs and the Parliament. Henceforth, monarchs would devote themselves to extending their sovereignty over colonial empire. The emergence of the French Revolution signals further discursive shifts.

Revolutionary Terror

The association between democratic government by and for "the people," and revolutionary terror was clearly articulated by Maximilien Robespierre:

> …In times of peace, virtue is the source from which government of the people takes its power. During the Revolution, the sources of this power are virtue and terror: virtue, without which terror will be a disaster; and terror, without which virtue is powerless" (Speech delivered to the Convention, Feb. 5, 1794, "Report on the Principles of Public Morality," Hachey and Weber 1972: 17).

The modern democratic state did not arrive peacefully. The tyranny of state terror, public executions and spectacular tortures, and warfare played a decisive role in the pacification of the people. At the same time, the development of a capitalist economy produced new actors and class networks, a print industry and literary culture, and the material means to challenge tyranny (Tarrow 1998). All the *Oxford English Dictionary* senses of tyranny, regicide, and assassination were elaborated prior to the French Revolutionary era (<1789). The social movement as a political practice emerged as a democratic counter to the strategy of absolute sovereignty. Monarchs were vilified as tyrants and their governmental policies as tyranny. The concept of political revolution emerges during the English civil war (1600). The American War of Independence (1776) and French Revolution (1789–1795), fought in the name of the individual liberty and rights, were potent signs of the power of this new democratic movement.

While the term terror was available to describe the violence associated with the English and American revolutions, it was not specially designated for that purpose. It is the French Revolution that permanently forges an indelible association between revolutionary violence and terrorism. The first explicitly political concepts of terror in the English language refer directly to the French Revolution (1789–1794). Henceforth, the modern concept of political terrorism, including its prior association with intense fear and death, are inextricably bound up with "illegitimate" revolution against the governing power structure. One of the three new concepts that appear during the revolutionary era is that of a "Reign of Terror" (1801). The *Oxford English Dictionary* provides a brief note to contextualize the concept:

> 4. reign of terror, a state of things in which the general community live in dread of death or outrage; esp. (with capital initials) French Hist. the period of the First Revolution from about March 1793 to July 1794, called also the Terror, the Red Terror, when the ruling faction remorselessly shed the blood of persons of both sexes and of all ages and conditions whom they regarded as obnoxious.

Several points about this change in meaning should be noted. First, this concept refers to a state of the general community, not the individual. Second, this general community lives in dread of repression by a "ruling faction" that engages in "organized intimidation." The *Oxford English Dictionary* states that this concept is applied to other episodes of "remorseless repression in various countries," or simply to "a similar period of repression." Finally, the earlier associations to the word do not disappear; they accumulate. The new political use includes the earlier association to "intense fear" and "death." Moreover, the use of "reign" ties terror to the violence of absolutist monarchy. This association is reinforced by the religious concept of Death personified as "The King of Terror."

The new revolutionary concepts of terror are marked by morphological changes: terrorist (1795) and terrorism (1795). The suffix -ist is used to mark some special feature of an agent, a specialist like a sociologist for example, or an adherent of specific doctrine, a Marxist. The first use of terrorist was a specific reference to Jacobins and their agents in the French Revolution, especially those involved with the Revolutionary tribunals during the "Reign of Terror." The quotes illustrating this concept emphasize that terrorists are "cruel" and act with "merciless severity." They are described as "Hell-hounds…let loose on the people" (1795). The fact that terrorists engage in attacks on civilians is a key to its status as an illegitimate form of political violence.

Post-Revolutionary Terrorism

The French Revolution was a watershed event in human history, spawning a new culture of practices that would exert an enormous international influence as a dangerous example of democratic rule (Hunt 1984: 203). The Napoleonic wars involved much of Europe until the British defeat the French at Waterloo in 1815. The British then turned their attention increasingly to extending and maintaining the Empire, fighting fifty colonial wars between 1803 and 1901 (Giddens 1985: 223). In an attempt to contain anti-colonial resistance, one of the British political elite's preferred tactics was to caricature it as akin to the illegitimate example set by French revolutionary terrorism (Dupuy 1996). Henceforth, the British and Americans would vilify any anti-colonial movement that threatened their national interests as terrorist (e.g., Irish Republicans; Anarchists, Labor movements, the Vietnamese).

By the late nineteenth century the concept of the political terrorist had been abstracted from its specific French revolutionary reference. A terrorist was "anyone who attempts to further his views by a system of coercive intimidations." The first *Oxford English Dictionary* reference is to a Wexford (Ireland) terrorist (1866). In the 1880s it was specifically applied to members of one of the "extreme revolutionary societies in Russia." By the twentieth century, casting one's political opponents in the role of terrorist had become a standard polemical tactic. Both Adolf Hitler and Winston Churchill used it to vilify their opponents. Hitler made the following accusation in *Mein Kampf* "...they [workers, social democrats, Jews] made use of the weapon which most readily conquers reason: terror and violence" (1971: 40). In World War II the "terror-bombing" of "enemy" populations was official Allied war-fighting policy. The terror bombing of German and Japanese cities, John Dower (2010: 187–192) concludes was a form of "psychological warfare" intended to "shock and awe" populations. The strategic goal was to lower enemy morale and boost American morale.

After World War II. British administrators would smear the Kenyan Mau Mau movement by categorizing it as a terrorist campaign organized by World War II veterans against British imperial rule (Anderson 2005; Elkins 2005). The pattern is again observable in the Algerian struggle against French colonial rule, as famously described in Franz Fanon's (1963) *The Wretched of the Earth* and Gillo Pontecorvo's (1966) great docudrama, *The Battle of Algiers*. In the 1960s it was used to vilify "ultra-left" groups like the American Weather Underground and the German Baader-Meinhoff gang.

The use of terrorism to vilify anti-colonial opponents was first contested in the 1950s. The *Oxford English Dictionary* cites a 1956 diary entry remarking on the crisis in Cyprus: "When people rise against foreign oppression, they are hailed as patriots and heroes; but the Greeks whom we are shooting and hanging in Cyprus are dismissed as terrorists. What cant!" A second example appears in a 1973 South African newspaper, *Cape Times*: "The Minister cannot expect journalists to do violence to the English language by describing guerilla warfare as terrorism at all times and in all circumstances." More examples appear in the *New York Times*: "Nazis give French only two choices: all must be 'collaborationist' or 'terrorist'— no middle ground lies open" (Archambault, 1942), and "British in Palestine Ban Use of Word 'Terrorist'"(1947).

The Birth of Social Science

The birth of the "social" sciences, especially sociology in France, and the growing discursive authority of the social sciences in the nineteenth century was driven by the "emergency" generated by the threat of French revolutionary terrorism (Nisbet 1943; Rabinow 1989; Donzelot 1979, 1991, 1993). The association between the urgent practical need to manage the threat of civil war and revolutionary terror, and the rise of social science is explicitly noted by the recent Gulbenkian Commission, *Open the Social Sciences*:

> In many countries, certainly in Great Britain and France, it was the cultural upheaval brought about by the French Revolution that forced a certain clarification of the debate. The pressure for political and social transformation had gained urgency and a legitimacy that could not easily be contained any longer simply by proclaiming theories about a supposedly natural order of social life. Instead many argued that the solution lay rather in organizing and rationalizing the social change that now seemed to be inevitable in a world in which the sovereignty of the 'people' was fast becoming the norm (Wallerstein 1996: 8).

The emergency of World War II and the triumphal movement of the U.S. into a position of world dominance following the war also influenced the social sciences. George's (1994) study of the dominant political discourse that emerged at the time describes its narrative form as rigidly state-centric and focused on the opposition between a realm of (domestic) sovereign identity, rationality, and social coherence and a realm of (international) anarchy, fragmentation, and threat contextualized as "out there." Of course this would necessitate that this threat be disciplined, ordered, and controlled in the name of the common good. Under this discursive regime the U.S. is constituted as a unitary identity in contrast to an easily identified Them—a homogeneous "Self" confronting a threatening (terrorist) Other. By this means, a free, open, pluralistic social system can be distinguished from its closed, totalitarian counterparts; and a particular (Western scientific-rationality) way of knowing the world can be intellectually and institutionally legitimated in its struggle against the forces of ideology, irrationality, distortion, and untruth (George 1994: 223; also Campbell 1993). Luke (1989, also Simpson 1994) shows how the movement of the U.S. into a position of global dominance after World War II coincided with the "the data gathering revolution in the social sciences."

The "political-culture" concept, used in an invidious way to differentiate traditional from modern cultures as part of various development schemes, was elaborated in response to problems associated with managing and policing Empire in the teeth of democratic resistance and "terrorism" in developing countries. These new data gathering programs fostered by U.S. government caused a major controversy surrounding the role social scientists played in Project Camelot (Horowitz 1965). This was a research program financed by the Department of

Defense (1963–1965) to study the nature and causes of revolutionary insurgencies in Third World countries. The intent was to inform the Central Intelligence Agency's covert operations and military interventions around the world in order to contain revolutionary or "national liberation movements" that threatened U.S. interests specifically and "liberal" Empire in general. At the time, this program provoked political controversy with Latin American governments and an ethical controversy among American social scientists about the propriety of participating in sponsored research of this kind.

In addition to solving the conceptual problem of how to differentiate legitimate from illegitimate forms of political violence, the threat of terrorism added dramatic urgency to the movement to constitute the social sciences as adjuncts to government. There was a need for new modes of knowledge that would facilitate the social regulation of "free" individuals and populations. The threat of revolutionary terrorism and civil war added impetus to the development of these programs. So-called Third World populations needed to be politically socialized to modern norms and values by means of disciplinary technologies such as schools. By these means individuals could be fashioned into productive members of society and good citizens. There was a need to study social problems to prevent civil strife and explosive class conflicts, or delinquency and criminality that had the potential of destabilizing domestic and colonial societies.

Western "colonization" plays an important role in Foucault's (1970: 377) history of the human sciences. This is particularly evident in his discussion of the unique critical function of psychoanalysis and ethnology in the modern episteme. "There is a certain position of the Western ratio that was constituted in its history and provides a foundation for the relation it can have with all other societies..." Just as psychoanalysis can be deployed only in "the calm violence" of a particular relationship and the transference it produces, "so ethnology can assume its proper dimensions only within the historical sovereignty—always restrained, but always present—of European thought and the relation that can bring it face to face with all other cultures as well as with itself." Foucault assigned particular significance to Freud's (1950 [1913]) *Totem and Taboo*:

> ...Since *Totem and Taboo*, the establishment of a common field for these two [ethnology and psychology], the possibility of a discourse that could move from one to the other without discontinuity, the double articulation of the history of individuals upon the unconscious of culture, and of the historicity of those cultures upon the unconscious of individuals, has opened up, without doubt, the most general problems that can be posed with regard to man (1970: 379).

Stoler (1995) shows how the colonizing situation was very much on Foucault's mind in the development of his account of biopolitics. The history of European "race war" has its counterpart in the modern history of European colonial subjection of North American, Asian, and African "savages." The "take-off" of social science is associated with the emergence of scientific racism and colonial projects to fashion the colonized as desiring subjects (e.g., North American reservations and Indian Schools).

Like the western discourse of "sexuality," the discourse of "terrorism" is tactically polyvalent. It can be put to use in multiple political games; its sheer political utility determined its selection. There are numerous ways it can be combined with other discourses. Just to name a few examples from the war on terror: global—legitimates U.S. imperial activities; war—constitutes Bush as Commander-in-Chief, a new mission for the U.S. Department of Defense, troops as heroes, the public as patriotic supporters of the troops; terrorism and terrorists—villainous powers, ambiguous enough to deploy against a variety of obstacles and targets. It was also used to reinvigorate the U.S. war on narcoterrorists in Columbia. Domestically, drug abusers could be attacked as supporters of terrorism; internationally, drug producers and distributors could be indicted as "narcoterrorists." Moreover, it could be used to re-elect President George W. Bush as Commander in Chief in 2004. Six years later, it was redeployed in attacks on immigrants and the politics of immigration. In 2008, it is employed to discredit Presidential nominees opposed to the Bush regime's approach to the war on terrorism (see the satirical cover art depicting Barack and Michelle Obama as terrorists, "The Politics of Fear," *The New Yorker*, July 21, 2008).

Terrorism in U.S. Political Discourse

Burke's theory of victimage ritual can be merged with Foucault's ideas about liberalism in a way that can illuminate the genealogy of terrorism in U.S. history. The logologic implicit to the American liberal-democratic order (understood in biopolitical terms) entails the following:

- If (liberal) order (security of life and liberty), then the possibility of (illiberal) disorder (insecurity) and guilt (criminals who violate the law, tyrants and terrorists who threaten security);
- If guilt, then need for redemption and vicarious victimage ritual.

In Bush regime rhetorical discourse, Osama bin Laden (the terrorist) and Saddam Hussein (the tyrant) personified ultimate threats to the American liberal order; therefore, as enemies of "freedom" they had to be "taken out."

The emotional meaning of "freedom" is drilled into Americans through the repetition of patriotic rituals that directly link it to human sacrifice. These rituals include songs and pledges of allegiance to the American flag which contain "liberty" and "freedom" many times. Its meaning is drilled into American children at schools and public events. The *Pledge of Allegiance* to the American Flag has gone through several reiterations since Francis Bellamy invented it in 1892. It has always included the following language: "I pledge allegiance to…one nation, with *liberty* [emphasis added] and justice for all." In 1954 President Eisenhower encouraged Congress to add the words "under God" to mark America's difference from the communist nations during the Cold-War. Another powerful example is the patriotic song, "My Country, "Tis of Thee'," based on a poem written by Samuel Smith (1831) and first performed in public that year on the Fourth of July. Many Americans know this song by heart. The first stanza is illustrative:

> My country, 'tis of thee',
> Sweet land of liberty,
> Of thee I sing;
> Land where my fathers died,
> Land of the pilgrims' pride,
> From ev'ry mountainside
> Let freedom ring!

The prayer that introduces Irving Berlin's (1918, 1938) song, "God Bless America" also references freedom.

> While the storm clouds gather far across the sea,
> Let us swear allegiance to a land that's free,
> Let us all be grateful for a land so fair,
> As we raise our voices in a solemn prayer.

It should also be noted that the 1918 and 1938 publication dates reference the end and the beginning of the two world wars that America had participated in.

In spite of this deep core of common understandings, the meanings of "freedom" and "liberty" are hotly contested in contemporary American politics. Quinby (1991) has conducted a detailed genealogy of the concept of "freedom" as the defining characteristic of the "subject of America." Through a detailed critical reading of a wide range of classic political and literary texts, she describes an "esthetics of liberty"—an American ethical tradition that involves the creation of self as an exercise of personal freedom and civic responsibility. This tradition, Quinby argues is the chief way Americans challenge domination. Lakoff (2006) shows how these terms mean very different things to liberals and conservatives. Ironically, he demonstrates through detailed linguistic analysis that liberals have a more "traditional" conception of freedom; that is, they have a more progressive understanding of these terms than do conservatives. Conservatives have fashioned an opposed understanding of liberty as simply the negative of tyranny and government control. He concludes that conservatives are winning the rhetorical battle to redefine these terms.

This kind of political culture is founded on biopolitical understandings of the right to individual life and liberty—"freedom and justice for all." Or to put it more succinctly, liberal government is biopolitics. According to the *Preamble* of the U.S. Constitution, Americans are guaranteed rights to "life, liberty, and the pursuit of happiness." The role of government is to "insure" life, liberty, to secure "the blessings of liberty," and promote "the general welfare." To be secure, one must be free of risks to life and limb, danger and violent attack. Over time we see that modern societies have accumulated a long list of types of security (national, social), and more recently, homeland security. The order, "life, liberty, and the pursuit of happiness," enshrined in the Declaration is significant. In liberal discourse, security (= freedom from risks to one's life) is logically prior to the possibility of freedom and the pursuit of happiness. Hence, there is a need for some kind of governmental regime to insure security. Freedom depends on "law and order" and the willingness of members of society to submit to the law. Conversely, there is a corresponding need to continuously refine and perfect the existing security systems as well as to identify new threats and forms of insecurity to legitimate new government expenditures and programs.

Political leaders frequently define new "security" threats to mobilize and move publics, legislatures, and militaries to engage in collection action. The articulation of a link between "social" and "security" by President Franklin Roosevelt was accomplished during the emergency caused by the Great Depression of the 1930s (Agamben 2005: 21–22). Modern politics is largely a struggle over definitions of what constitutes clear and present dangers to security (e.g., disease, old age, unemployment, crime, terrorism, global warming or climate change). Victimage rituals allow leaders to engage in rhetorical attacks, vilifying those actors who are the putative cause of the insecurity (e.g., savages, Indians, anarchists, Communists, terrorists) At the same time the acts of those who fight those villains can be glorified in struggles to destroy the threatening Other. There have been numerous witch-hunts and national crusades against security threats in U.S. history. Spectacular events like Pearl Harbor and the 9/11 terrorist attacks provide political actors with new opportunities to achieve their goals (e.g., election or reelection to office, global dominance and Empire, expansion by invasion and occupation of new territory in Afghanistan or Iraq and new domestic programs such as "The Patriot Act" and departments of government, "The Office of Homeland Security", etc.).

The genealogy of terrorism in U.S. political discourse confirms the power / subjection thesis advanced here. This thesis was tested by tracing the nexus of terrorism in two bodies of texts: Presidential "*State of the Union Messages to the Congress*" (1790–2011) and *New York Times* editorials (1860–2006). *Times* editorials were included in the data set if they contained terrorism or terrorist(s) in the title, resulting in 182 total editorials. The editorials were coded for "actor labeled terrorist," "geographic scene of action" (e.g., Texas, Japan, Europe), and "Victims."

Employing the results of past research on waves of U.S. imperial activity, the *State of the Union Messages* were chronologically ordered into three periods: North American Empire, 1790–1896; Rise to World Power, 1897–1945; Empire, 1946–2008 (Go 2007). These three historical periods constitute distinguishable geostrategic contexts. The decade of the 1890s was significant for a number of reasons: the end of the Indian Wars, the closing of the western frontier in 1790, the Spanish-American War (1898), and the creation of an open-door policy with China (Kinzer 2006; Johnson 2004; Reynolds 2009). President McKinley was assassinated in 1901 by an "anarchist" and "terrorist." The end of World War II in 1945 marks a watershed event in U.S. geostrategic history, bringing to fruition the movement of the U.S. power elite into a leadership position in Empire.[1]

Table 2.2   Mean Frequency (Standard Deviation) of References to "Territory" and "World" in *State of the Union Messages* in Geostrategic Context, 1790–2011

Context	Territory#	World##
North American Empire		
1790–1896	8.81	2.97
(n = 108)	(10.72)	(3.21)
Rise to World Power		
1897–1945	3.73	12.63
(n = 48)	(5.93)	(6.76)
Empire		
1946–2011	0.38	17.79
(n = 67)	(0.93)	(9.83)
Total		
1790-1896	5.16	9.54
(n = 223)	(8.76)	(9.34)

One-way ANOVA, F = 24.36; df = 2, p < .001

One-way ANOVA, F = 112.14; df = 2, p < .001

Source: Data derived from *American Presidency Project*, http://www.presidency.ucsb.edu/sou.php/

---

1   "By the power elite," Mills wrote, "we refer to those political, economic, and military circles which, as an intricate set of overlapping cliques share decisions having at least national consequences (1956: 18). Domhoff's definition is more precise: "I define the power elite as the leadership group of the upper class. It consists of active-working members of the upper class and high-level employees in profit and nonprofit institutions controlled by members of the upper class through stock ownership, financial support, or involvement on the board of directors. This does not mean that all members of the upper class are involved in governing. Some are only playboys and socialites; their social gatherings may provide a setting where members of the power elite mingle with celebrities, and sometimes they give money to political candidates, but that is about as close as they come to political power." (see Domhoff 2010: 116, also http://sociology.ucsc.edu/whorulesamerica/power/class_domination.html , accessed 13 July 2011).

The results of a text analysis of presidential *Messages* presented in Table 2.2 supports the validity of this periodization of the chronology of U.S. geostrategic history. *WordCruncher 6.0* (2004), a text-indexing and rapid retrieval program, was employed to analyze the texts. The average frequency of references to North American "territories" by president corresponds to struggles and disputes produced by the settlement and conquest of the American frontier and the constitution of the "North American Empire." The highest average frequency occurs in *Messages* between 1790 and 1896 (about 9 per *Message*, reaching as high as 49 references in a single speech), the period of North American conquest and annexation of "territory" by the United States. The *Messages* reference territorial struggles and disputes with foreign governments, Empires, and Indian tribes. The following excerpt from the1805 *Message* is an early but typical example:

> Inroads have been recently made into the **Territories of Orleans and the Mississippi** [emphasis added], our citizens have been seized and their property plundered in the very parts of the former which had been actually delivered up by Spain, and this by the regular officers and soldiers of that Government. I have therefore found it necessary at length to give orders to our troops on that frontier to be in readiness to protect our citizens, and to repel by arms any similar aggressions in future (Jefferson 1805).

By the end of the Mexican War of 1848, the "territory" in contention has moved to the southwestern frontier:

> I also beg leave to call your attention to the propriety of extending at an early *day* our system of land laws, with such modifications as may be necessary, over the State of California and the Territories of Utah and New Mexico. The mineral lands of California will, of course, form an exception to any general system which may be adopted.

> The annexation of Texas and the acquisition of California and New Mexico have given increased importance to our Indian relations. The various tribes brought under our jurisdiction by these enlargements of our boundaries are estimated to embrace a population of 124,000. *Texas and New Mexico are surrounded by powerful tribes of Indians, who are a source of constant terror [emphasis added] and annoyance to the inhabitants*...[emphasis added: bold = glorifier / bold + italic = vilifier] (Fillmore 1850)

References to "territory" go through a rapid decline in the 20th Century (rounded up, the average is less than one per Presidential *Message*).

If the power / subjection thesis is correct, there should have been a dramatic and statistically significant increase in average numbers of references to the "world" in presidential *Messages*—an indicator of a shift in the field of power struggles from the settlement of the territories of the American west to the phase of Empire,

1946–2008 (rounded up, from about 3 references per Message to 18, ranging as high as 48 references in one speech). The Truman regime (1946–1952) *Messages* contain more "world" references than any other president (range = 14–48). The following excerpt is a pivotal example of how the "world" forces the President into a new role:

> But our times are not easy; they are hard-as hard and complex, perhaps as any in our history. Now, the President not only has to carry on these tasks in such a way that our democracy may grow and flourish and our people prosper, but *he also has to lead the whole free world in overcoming the communist menace— and all this under the shadow of the atomic bomb.* ...[emphasis added: bold = glorifier / bold + italic = vilifier] (Truman 1953)

If the pattern of liberal and terrorism discourses are a function of power struggles provoked by shifting geostrategic aims (e.g., the need to contend with organized resistance to the constitution of the North American Empire), then we should expect to see positive and statistically significant coefficients of correlation between these terms. As these struggles intensify, the Messages should reflect this fact through an increase in "terrorist" threats to security and freedom. The correlation analysis of the frequencies of liberal terms in individual *Messages* in each geostrategic context are presented in Table 2.3. The pattern of correlations tends to confirm this expectation. The increase in the use of security and freedom (or liberty) in individual *Messages* is positively correlated in all three contexts (.429, .341, .215) as well as for the data set as a whole (.406). The exceptions are the *Messages* after 1980. The increasing references to terrorism in these *Messages* are positively correlated with increases in references to security (.459), replacing references to freedom. As should be expected, positive correlations also exist between terror / security in the two geostrategic situations of North American Empire (.161) and world Empire (.283). Both of these contexts involve power struggles associated with resistance to the assertion of Empire, the U.S. settlement of the North America continent and the management of global Empire.

North American Empire

Charts 2.1 and 2.2 (below) present the results of a text-analysis of the pattern of terrorism discourse appearing in presidential *Messages* and *New York Times* editorials in the three geostrategic contexts. The change in the percentage of terror speeches can be interpreted as a measure of the change in the level of concern for the terrorist threat. As we shall see, the distribution of these texts over time is a direct function of the intensity of power struggles involved. We do in fact see the texts are correlated to the various historic power struggles that have defined U.S. geostrategic history. A typical example is taken from a Presidential Message focusing on democratic "terrorism" by "White Leagues" targeting "colored laborers" after the Civil War:

Table 2.3   The Correlation of Key "Liberal" Terms Deployed in Presidential
***State of the Union Messages* in Geostrategic Context, 1790–2008**

Context	Security & Freedom+	Terror & Security	Terror & Freedom+
North American Empire 1790–1896 (n = 108)	.529**	.161*	.162*
Rise to World Power 1897–1920 (n = 48)	.341**	-.062	-.241
Empire 1946–2011 (n = 67)	.215*	.283*	.013
Empire Extended 1980–2011 (n = 31)	.018	.459**	.088
Total 1790–2011 (n = 223)	.406**	.190**	.233**

* *Tau_b* ≤ .05 (2-tailed) ** *Tau_b* ≤ .01 (2-tailed)

Note: + includes liberty

Source: Data derived from *American Presidency Project*, http://www.presidency.ucsb.edu/sou.php/

I regret to say that with preparations for the late election decided indications appeared in some localities in the Southern States of a determination, by acts of violence and intimidation, to deprive citizens of the freedom of the ballot because of their political opinions. Bands of men, masked and armed, made their appearance; *White Leagues and other societies were formed; large quantities of arms and ammunition were imported and distributed to these organizations; military drills, with menacing demonstrations, were held, and with all these murders enough were committed to spread terror among those whose political action was to be suppressed, if possible, by these intolerant and criminal proceedings.* [emphasis added: bold = glorifier / bold + italic = vilifier] In some places colored laborers were compelled to vote according to the wishes of their employers, under threats of discharge if they acted otherwise; and there are too many instances in which, when these threats were disregarded, they were remorselessly executed by those who made them (Grant 1874).

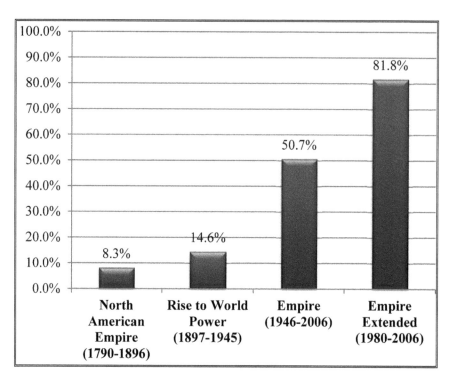

Chart 2.1   Percentage of President's *State of the Union Messages* Containing References to Terrorism in Geostrategic Context, 1790–2006

Source: Data derived from *The Presidential Project*, http://www.presidency.ucsb.edu/sou.php/

The majority of *New York Times* Editorials at the time focus on the democratic terrorism associated with the clash of Abolitionists and Pro-Slavery forces. Southerners, whites and blacks, are described as perpetrators and victims of terrorism. One editorial of the seven that are published during this period discusses the use of terrorism by British imperialists. Another discusses the "Mine Unions" involvement in terrorism.

The most frequent references to terrorism in Presidential *Messages* in this period concern Indians who attacked *white settlers* encroaching on traditional Indian lands. The following excerpt taken from the 1886 Message is illustrative:

> **In September and October last the hostile Apaches who, under the leadership** *of Geronimo, had for eighteen months been on the war path, and during that* *time had committed many murders and been the cause of constant terror to* *the settlers of Arizona*, surrendered to General Miles, the military commander who succeeded General Crook in the management and direction of their pursuit.
> [emphasis added: bold = glorifier / bold + italic = vilifier]

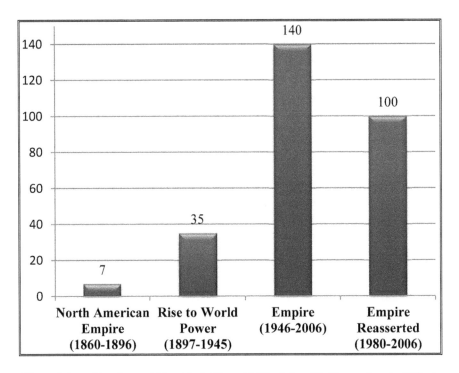

Chart 2.2 **Number of *New York Times* Editorials with Terrorism in Title in Geostrategic Context, 1860–2006**

Source: Data derived from the *New York Times* archive

> Under the terms of their surrender as then reported, and in view of the understanding which ***these murderous savages seemed to entertain of the assurances given them, it was considered best to imprison them in such manner as to prevent their ever engaging in such outrages again, instead of trying them for murder...*** (Cleveland 1886).

Rise to World Power

The percentage of Presidential *Messages* containing references to terrorism increases slightly to 14.6% in the geostrategic context of America's ascent to the status of world power (14.6%) and leader of Empire. As a result of this change in geostrategic situation and the shift to objectives located outside of the North American Empire, the actors cast in the role of terrorists also change.

Two types of discourses of terrorism, sovereign and democratic, are invoked with monotonous regularity in the Presidential texts. Consider the following two examples of the sovereign types, the kind that can justify a policy of expansion and Empire by means of military action and warfare. The first appears in the 1904 *Message*, delivered in the wake of the Spanish American War (1898) that resulted in the "liberation" of Cuba and the Philippines to a benevolent U.S. occupation and tutelage:

> The steady aim of this Nation, as of all enlightened nations, should be to strive to bring ever nearer the day when there shall prevail throughout **the world** [emphasis added] the peace of justice. There are kinds of peace which are highly undesirable, which are in the long run as destructive as any war. ***Tyrants and oppressors have many times made a wilderness and called it peace.*** [emphasis added: bold = glorifier / bold + italic = vilifier] Many times peoples who were slothful or timid or shortsighted, who had been enervated by ease or by luxury, or misled by false teachings, have shrunk in unmanly fashion from doing duty that was stern and that needed self-sacrifice, and have sought to hide from their own minds their shortcomings, their ignoble motives, by calling them love of peace. ***The peace of tyrannous terror, the peace of craven weakness, the peace of injustice, all these should be shunned as we shun unrighteous war.*** The goal to set before us as a nation, the goal which should be set before all mankind, is the attainment of the peace of justice, of the peace which comes when each nation is not merely safe-guarded in its own rights, but scrupulously recognizes and performs its duty toward others (Roosevelt 1904).

The shift in geostrategic orientation from a focus on the North American Empire to the "world" is clearly enunciated in this excerpt. "Tyrannous terror" is a threat to world peace. Only by "righteous war" can "world peace" be secured.

The second example of the use of the discourse of sovereign terrorism occurs in the 1945 *Message* toward the end of World War II:

> One of the most heartening events of the year in the international field has been the renaissance of the **French people** [victim] and the return of the French Nation to the ranks of the United Nations. Far from having been crushed by ***the terror of Nazi domination*** [emphasis added: bold = glorifier / bold + italic = vilifier] **the French people have emerged with stronger faith than ever in the destiny of their country and in the soundness of the democratic ideals to which the French Nation has traditionally contributed so greatly** (Roosevelt 1945).

After "ending the "Nazi-Fascist reign of terror in Europe" and defeating "the malignant power of imperialistic Japan" by means of the conspicuous use of "terror-bombing," the U.S. power elite assumed a dominant role in Empire as the leader of the "free-world."

A good example of democratic terrorism in a Presidential *Message* appears in the 1919 *Message*. The context is domestic politics and the infamous "Red

Scare." But the discourse appears after World War I (1914–1918) in the wake of the Russian Revolution (1917) and casts "labor" in the role of "terrorists" who threaten "liberty and justice":

> This is the hour of test and trial for **America. By her prowess and strength, and the indomitable courage of her soldiers, she demonstrated her power to vindicate on foreign battlefields her conceptions of *liberty and justice.*** [emphasis added: bold = glorifier / bold + italic = vilifier] Let not her influence as a mediator between capital and ***labor*** [emphasis added] be weakened and her own failure to settle matters of purely domestic concern be proclaimed to the world. ***There are those in this country who threaten direct action to force their will, upon a majority. Russia today, with its blood and terror is a painful object lesson of the power of minorities.*** It makes little difference what minority it is; ***whether capital or labor, or any other class no sort of privilege will ever be permitted to dominate this country*** (Wilson 1919).

The *New York Times* editorials include several references to terrorist acts in the U.S.: "criminals," "communists," "anarchists," "Strike leaders," "Unionists" and "Workers." There are fourteen editorials in 1934, the most frequent of any single year. They mainly focus on terrorism in Europe: "Spanish socialists," "Irish Republicans," "Austrian Nazis," "Macedonian revolutionaries," "Budapest Bakers," "Barcelona anarchists," "U.S. strike leaders," "Croats," "German Nazis," and "Palestinian Arabs." Once the war with Germany starts, the editorials make numerous references to "Hitler," "Germans," and the "Gestapo." There is *one* editorial that discusses the British Royal Air Force and the issues associated with the policy of "terror bombing."

Empire

Given the global scope of Empire, the number of potential opponents and terrorist threats multiply. As should be expected, the percentage of Presidential *Messages* containing "terrorism" triples to 50.7% of total after 1946. Again, there are two distinct types of terrorism: sovereign and democratic terrorism. A seamless shift takes place from Nazi-Fascist "terrorism" to a focus on Communist "terrorism." The following excerpt from a Message delivered in 1953 is typical of the kind of the Cold-War rhetoric that dominated "security" discourse until 1989:

> ***But it*** [the Soviet Union, the Stalinist World, Soviet satellites such as China*]* ***is also a world of great man-made uniformities, a world that bleeds its population white to build huge military forces; a world in which the police are everywhere and their authority unlimited; a world where terror and slavery are deliberately administered both as instruments of government and as means of production; a world where all effective social power is the state's monopoly –***

yet the state itself is the creature of the communist tyrants. [emphasis added: bold = glorifier / bold + italic = vilifier] (Truman 1953)

The second type of discourse occurs in response to anti-colonial struggles and National Liberation Movements:

> A satisfactory settlement in Laos would also help to achieve and safeguard the peace in Vietnam—*where the foe is increasing his tactics of terror* [emphasis added: bold = glorifier / bold + italic = vilifier]—where our own efforts have been stepped up – and where the local government has initiated new programs and reforms to broaden the base of resistance. *The systematic aggression now bleeding that country is not a "war of liberation"—for Viet Nam is already free. It is a war of attempted subjugation—and it will be resisted.* (Kennedy 1962)

A second example of the same type of revolutionary terrorism from the later stages of the Vietnam War reveals the managerial orientation of Empire in the clearest possible terms:

> **Our South Vietnamese allies are also being tested tonight. Because they must provide real** *security* **to the people living in the countryside.** [emphasis added: bold = glorifier / bold + italic = vilifier] *And this means reducing the terrorism and the armed attacks which kidnapped and killed 26,900 civilians in the last 32 months*, to levels where they can be successfully controlled by the regular South Vietnamese security forces. It means bringing to the villagers an effective civilian government that they can respect, and that they can rely upon and that they can participate in, and that they can have a personal stake in. We hope that government is now beginning to emerge. (Johnson 1967)

Empire Extended

The percentage of Presidential *Messages* stressing terrorism increases dramatically after 1979 to 82% of *Messages*. The following example is from the 1980 Presidential *Message*. Written in response to the Iranian revolution and the Soviet invasion of Afghanistan, it signals the increasing burdens involved in managing Empire:

> *At this time in Iran, 50 Americans are still held captive, innocent victims of terrorism and anarchy. Also at this moment, massive Soviet troops are attempting to subjugate the fiercely independent and deeply religious people of Afghanistan. These two acts—one of international terrorism and one of military aggression—present a serious challenge to the United States of America and indeed to all the nations of the world.* [emphasis added: bold =

glorifier / bold + italic = vilifier] Together, we will meet these threats to peace (Carter/1980/193).

Almost every subsequent Presidential *Message* contains at least one or more references to terrorism, and the number of times terrorism is mentioned in each *Message* escalates. This was also the first *Message* to use "international terrorism" to describe the problems confronted the "modern world" (reiterated in *Messages* delivered in 1984, 1998). About fifty percent of the *Times* editorials refer to "terrorism" associated with geopolitics in the Middle East. In response to the Al Qaeda 9/11 attacks on the "homeland," every *Message* mentions terrorism at least once. In fact, the *Messages* between 2002–2009 reference terrorism an average of 26 times per message—a literal reign of rhetorical terror!

The history of the discourse of "terrorism" correlates with the history of resistance to efforts by the U.S. government to extend its sovereignty over new territories, regions, and populations. There is a move, counter-move, and counter counter-move logic to this game. When "Southerners" resisted northern hegemony after the Civil War it was interpreted as "White Leagues" terrorize "negroes." When Indians respond to white encroachment on Indian lands with violence, it is "savages" terrorizing "settlers." This passive-aggressive pattern is replayed over and over again in U.S. history and the global dynamics of Empire. Israeli settlers move into Palestinian territory. Palestinians resist. The Palestine Liberation Organization is defined as a terrorist organization. Resistance to American moves to extend or defend Empire in the Middle East, Africa, and Central Asia is reinterpreted as terrorists threatening the American way of life. In response to resistance to projects to extend U.S. sovereignty to secure new territories and populations, U.S. presidents have staged victimage rituals. The rhetoric melodramatizes the scene of action. The discourse typically features American heroes and their allies struggling to defeat terrorist villains (e.g., Indians, Anarchists, criminals, unions, Nazis, Communists, and Al Qaeda). Victimage ritual is a source of political power employed to legitimate dominion over new territories and subjected populations— to render them secure and to liberate their populations.

Several patterns emerge from the analysis of terrorism discourse in the two sets of texts. The most obvious is the increasing frequency of *State of the Union Messages* and *New York Times* editorials devoted to policy questions that deal with terrorism. The second is the increasingly more "abstract" and protean character of the discourse of terrorism. By the end of the 19th century, as noted in the etymology of this discourse, terrorism had come to function as a generalized vilifier that could be applied to any opponent who engages in organized, premeditated political violence against an established authority, not matter the context. By the early 20th century, the *New York Times* editors are using it to label domestic anarchists, unionists, workers, revolutionaries, communists. This is most evident in editorials published between 1902 and World War II, a period of violent capital and labor conflicts. It is also used to vilify Nazis and Japanese militarists in the 1930s.

Terrorism and the terrorist have become sui-generis, social facts and problems to be known and managed.

A third geostrategic pattern also emerges. Once the U.S. power elite assumed a leadership role in the management of Empire after World War II the Presidential *Messages* and *Times* editorials begin to address the problem of terrorists at the "world" level much more frequently. Increasingly, these so-called terrorists are situated outside of European and American contexts. The titles of the *Times* editorials tell the story: "The Age of Terrorism" (1958), "Terrorism in the Americas" (1970), "Terrorism Act" (1972), "Arab Terrorism" (1975), "Combating Terrorism" (1976), "Talking about Terrorism" (1981), "Dealing with Arab Terrorism by the Rules" (1984), etc. By the 1970s and 1980s, *Times* editorials are more and more frequently responding to critical questions about terrorism policy: "Terrorism and Fit News" (1977). "Dealing with Terrorism by the Rules" (1984), "Snatching Terrorists Abroad" (1986), "Denied: A Shield for Terrorists" (1987).

The *Times* editorial advocating the denial of "A Shield for Terrorists" (1987) is illustrative of how the discourse of "terrorism" is tailored to the power perspective of Empire. This editorial supports President Reagan's decision to not ratify revisions to the 1949 Geneva Conventions. "If he said yes, that would improve protection for prisoners of war and civilians," they state, "but at the price of new legal protection for guerrillas and possible terrorists." Given the logic of power at work in the definition of who gets cast in the role of terrorist, it only appears to be hypocritical that President Reagan would take this position while secretly supporting the Contra "terrorist" campaign to overthrow the Sandinista government in Nicaragua. The concern about Israel also seems paramount. The problem with the revision of Article 1 of the protocol is that the provision that enhances the protection for prisoners of war and civilians, would also apply to "nations" or "peoples" who "are fighting against colonial domination and alien occupation and against racist regimes in the exercise of their right of self-determination." The editors comment that these are "nice words," but retort they are also "possible grounds for giving terrorists the legal status of P.O.W.'s." The protocol is doubly problematic, they argue, because they would also allow "regional groups like the Organization for African Unity and the League of Arab States" to decide which "peoples" constitute a legitimate party in an armed conflict. Presumably the only parties that can legitimately make these decisions are the leaders of Empire, typically the agents of U.S. power elite and its European allies.

Chapter 3
Victimage Ritual

Once constituted the political discourse of terrorism became part of the existing tool-kit of possible vilifiers that political actors could deploy to attack an opponent in a power struggle. The "guilt" of the perpetrators of the September 11, 2001 attacks on the American homeland created a political opportunity for the U.S. power elite to mobilize the American public to seek "redemption" through a global war against terrorism that has, in turn, destroyed nations, killed thousands, and victimized many more around the world. The war in Afghanistan or "Operation Enduring Freedom" (2001–present) has always been legitimated as part of the "The Hunt for Bin Laden" and as a war against his supporters, members of Al Qaeda and/or the Taliban. After the September 11 attacks Bin Laden became the most infamous personification of "international terrorism" in history, the perfect symbol of "evil" villainy. A video tape broadcast three months after the 9/11 attacks showing Osama bin Laden gloating about the success of the jetliner attacks on the World Trade Center was particularly provocative (Wilgoren 2001). In this sense he was the symbolic target of every military action. Every innocent victim of collateral damage was Bin Laden's surrogate victim.

This chapter begins with a detailed treatment of the social psychological basis of Kenneth Burke's dramatism and theory of victimage ritual.[1] These ideas are elaborated in terms of two problems: 1) the problem of ruling liberal societies founded on the right to engage in revolutionary violence, and 2) the role of scientific culture and biopolitics in victimage ritual. These issues are resolved through a merging of Burke's conceptions with those of Michel Foucault. These ideas are applied to the social-psychological basis for an *identification* with the victims and heroes of the 9/11 attacks. Why did the Bush regime decide to declare a global war against terrorism rather than a more limited response against the perpetrators of the 9/11 attacks? The decision to go with the declaration of a global war against terrorism is a major tactical component in the global functioning of Empire, justifying the world-wide projection of U.S. political authority and

---

1   Kenneth Burke's dramatism has had an important influence on American social thought. For examples, see Mills 1940, Duncan 1962, 1968, Edelman 1971,Jameson 1978, 1981, Swidler 1986, Gusfield 1989, and Wess 1996. Dramatism has been applied to a variety of social and political phenomena, including everyday life (Goffman 1974), the cold-war (Mills 1960, Ivie 1980, 1986, 1987), the drug war (Szasz 1974, Gusfield 1981), nuclear war (Cuzzort 1989), social movements (Klapp 1969, Zygmunt 1972, Blain 1994), the French Revolution (Hunt 1984), terrorism (Wagner-Pacifici 1986, Ivie 2004, 2005, Ivie and Giner 2007), and rituals (Cohen 1974; Kertzer 1988).

military power (see Mann 2003, Johnson 2004). The history and implications of the rhetoric of "World War" as a melodramatic device and component of victimage ritual is discussed.

Politicians know how to stage victimage rituals to move people to fight great, transcendent struggles to enhance their political power. Victimage ritual is a part of the stock of political knowledge available to political actors seeking to build their authority in the eyes of the masses. This is why the following two Nazi quotes are so widely available and familiar:

> If you tell a lie big enough and keep repeating it, people will eventually come to believe it. The lie can be maintained only for such time as the State can shield the people from the political, economic and/or military consequences of the lie. It thus becomes vitally important for the State to use all of its powers to repress dissent, for the truth is the mortal enemy of the lie, and thus by extension, the truth is the greatest enemy of the State (Joseph Goebbels, 2010).

And again,

> Naturally the common people don't want war; neither in Russia, nor in England, nor in America, nor in Germany. That is understood. But after all, it is the leaders of the country who determine policy, and it is always a simple matter to drag the people along, whether it is a democracy, or a fascist dictatorship, or a parliament, or a communist dictatorship. Voice or no voice, the people can always be brought to the bidding of the leaders. That is easy. All you have to do is to tell them they are being attacked, and denounce the pacifists for lack of patriotism and exposing the country to danger. It works the same in any country (Herman Goering, 2010).

These well-known quotes contain what Burke called "equipment for living" (Burke 1973). The practice of subjection by means of victimage ritual has become an established technique of political power, a necessary if not sufficient condition for provoking and prosecuting a war. Politicians aided by their technical support staff, hired from public relations and public polling firms, market war to the masses like corporate advertising campaigns market commercial products to consumers. The difference, of course, is that unlike most commercial products the *real* violence of dead and wounded bodies can be used to generate intense emotions and mobilize collective energies that can be directed along lines of retaliatory political violence. As we shall see, the so-called "unprovoked" 9/11 terror attacks on the American "homeland" can be dramatized as cosmic events to provoke victimage rituals with disastrous consequences. Politicians can tap into this energy by stirring up strong desires for revenge and retribution, which can be mobilized and deployed in global power struggles.

Politicians dramatize great wars as ultimate battles of good against evil, right against wrong, or freedom against terrorism. The U.S. government and global military establishment has contributed to some of the most horrible atrocities of the twentieth century. These wars have included great struggles against empires and savages, fascism, communism, narcotraffickers, and terrorists. In every case political leaders have resorted to the intensive and frequent use of victimage ritual and its corresponding melodramatic rhetorical discourse to accomplish their aims. In speech after speech, at memorial after memorial, this ritual rhetoric has been disseminated to the world by means of newspapers, radio, film and television. As Burke (1967) concluded in his 1941 study of Nazi ritual rhetoric, in politics as in advertising and marketing, the ritual repetition of the same carefully selected key terms can make a powerful political difference. There is in this theory an implied social psychological process of emotional amplification (Blain 1976, 1988).[2] As we shall see in Chapter 4, it is now possible to quantify with a much greater degree of precision, the frequency and intensity of this phenomenon by means of computerized text-indexing procedures.

The Nazi Paradigm

"Dramatism," Burke asserted, "is a method of analysis and a corresponding critique of terminology designed to show that the most direct route to the study of human relations and human motives is via a methodical inquiry into cycles or clusters of terms and their functions" (Burke 1968: 451). The discussion of Burke's dramatism theory that follows employs examples from his critique of Nazi victimage ritual (Burke 1967). It goes on to interpret a series of American lead global wars since World War II as gigantic victimage rituals that have functioned as crucial tactical components of Empire. They include the Cold War (1948–1989), war on drugs (1972–present), and the war on terrorism (2001–present). These global dramas have been enacted on a world-wide stage made possible by the modern revolution in mass media technology (i.e., newspapers, radio, movies, television, internet, broadcast by means of a global telecommunications systems). The ritual persecution and destruction of "communists" and "terrorists" have functioned as highly effective modes of power and subjection.

In Burke's perspective, the function of political discourse in victimage ritual is to move people to certain lines of action. In this sense it can be understood as "action" on "action." One of the primary functions of victimage discourse is to constitute the desire in those addressed to attack and destroy a villain whose actions have violated or threaten cherished values. Political speeches are part and parcel of staged ritual performances such as marches and memorials, demonstrations and rallies. The actual physical site of these community dramas is crucial. The

---

2   Lakoff (2006: 9–15) makes a similar point in succinct, neuro-linguistic terms *"We think with our brains." "Repetition of language has the power to change brains" "Most thought is unconscious.," "All thought uses conceptual frames." Language can be used to reframe a situation." "Frames trump facts,"* etc.

Nazis created physical centers to mount their campaigns, special places with deep historical and cultural significance, stages, shrines, and memorials. The function of these symbolic actions is to add rhetorical force to the constitution of political identities, friends and enemies, to move the masses to support and participate in power struggles.

The structure of victimage discourse is melodramatic. The specific melodramatic formula utilized in a struggle is often borrowed more or less consciously from popular culture. Using popular culture has the advantage that it is familiar to the masses. The Nazi party adopted Nordic myths involving Teutonic knights and Wagner's epic operas in its propaganda campaigns (Blain 1995). A classic example is Leni Riefenstahl's (2006) masterpiece, the 1935 documentary film, *Triumph des Willens*. Nazi film makers consciously borrowed from popular nineteenth century German middle class melodramas to fashion anti-Semitic movies. John Kennedy adopted the mythology of the western frontier, a powerful and deeply resonant story in American history (see Slotkin 1973, 1985, 1992). To justify his budget request for international development to aid emerging nations, Kennedy invoked the "frontiers of human freedom." (*State of the Union Message*, 1961). To gain public support for his space program to go to the moon, Kennedy invoked "the new frontier of science, commerce and cooperation, the position of the United States and the Free World" (*State of the Union Message*, 1962). President Ronald Reagan famously adopted the language and rhetoric of the evil empire to vilify "communists" directly from George Lucas' epic space opera the 1977 Hollywood movie, *Star Wars* (Rogin 1987).

The key to understanding how leaders are able to persuade their followers to participate in and personally identify with the violence of victimage ritual is in a theory of identification. Identification is a dramatic social psychological process that involves the use of ritual rhetoric to persuade people to take sides in a power struggle, support or oppose politicians and programs, participate in movements, or fight and die in wars to defeat enemies. The ultimate moment of identification is victimage—the personification and ritual destruction of those powers that threaten the survival of society. Burke summed up his theory this way:

> In the selection of terms for describing a scene one automatically prescribes the range of acts that will seem reason/able, implicit, or necessary in that situation…By tracing and analyzing such terms, a dramatistic analysis shows how the negativistic principle of guilt implicit in the nature of order combines with the principles of thoroughness (or "perfection") and substitution that are characteristic of symbol systems in such a way that the sacrificial principle of victimage (the 'scapegoat') is intrinsic to human congregation (1968, 450).

He obviously thought that some form of scapegoating ritual was intrinsic all forms of human congregation. One does not need to accept this ethnocentric proposition to see the value of his insight. It should be enough to argue that the political violence of scapegoating is a function of the so-called "higher" symbolic capacities of human beings, not a fall into some kind of "lower" or latent "animality" (Blain 1988). The enemy is transformed and perfected through symbolic practices of vilification. The "enemy" is perfected in his role by being transformed into a condensation of negativity. We "throw everything in the book" at the enemy by "digging up all the dirt" we can find. Burke's account can be better understood as an insightful diagnosis of a historically unique cultural practice, "a bastardization of a religious form of thought" that has acquired new political functions as a component of the world wars and political violence that have constituted Empire.

At the foundation of this cultural complex is a perversion of the Judeo-Christian practice of ritual human sacrifice. Jesus gave his life for the sins of mankind; the warrior and soldier give their lives for the survival of the nation. The social function of this form of symbolic interaction is to constitute by means of power and subjection a common "us" against a common "them," or, as Burke put it, "congregation through segregation" (e.g., Christians against the devil; NAZIs against the Jews; liberals against Islamic terrorists). We are all in one boat together as patriots in our identification with the struggle against one common enemy. The ultimate symbol of that commitment is the willingness to sacrifice one's life for the cause. The discourse of victimage ritual functions like a "screen" to "direct" the attention and / or "deflect" attention from other ways of seeing the world (e.g., Lucifer rather than the power of the Roman Catholic Church, Savages rather than colonizers, Jews rather than the Nazis, terrorists rather than Empire, etc.). It not only functions to unite us and distract us, it also incites us to torture, wound, and kill.

The symbol systems and principles deployed by political leaders in victimage rituals must already exist. One of the properties of symbol systems is their capacity for "extensive elaboration" (Cuzzort and King 1980: 331) Principles of social order are linguistically and symbolically elaborated and idealized, or perfected way beyond any possibility of realization. The Nazis employed the ideals of German nationalism and scientific racism to recruit, intensify commitment, mobilize and incite their followers to engage in political violence against their enemies. Ordinary citizens can be transformed into "patriots" and "war heroes" by gaining, sustaining, and intensifying their identification with victimage ritual. Enemies are perfected in their roles by means of vilification. Employing the established repertoire of vilifiers Hitler perfected the Jews as ultimate threats to the survival of the Aryan Race, culture, and German nation. Nazi discourse constituted his loyal followers as racially pure "Teutonic Knights" caught up in a modern crusade against an archaic racial enemy to build a thousand year Reich. The victors would be the "lords of this world."

Once values or principles are materialized in a symbol system (e.g., Bible, Ten Commandments, U.S. Constitution, Rights of Man, *Mein Kampf,* manifestos or the legal codes), then a dynamic of obedience and disobedience is set in motion. Burke called this dynamic *logologic.* If the language of the code specifies that "Thou shalt not kill," then murder is a willful choice to kill and the negative or logical contradiction of obedience to that commandment. The Bush regime's rhetoric perfected the "terrorist" as perfect enemy to justify declaring a global war to liberate the world of monsters. The dramatic 9/11 attack provided spectacular evidence of the villainy of the terrorists. They are ultimate "enemies of freedom" and therefore the threatening "killer of the ideal" who must be destroyed.

Identification Theory

There is a social psychological basis to the identification of human beings with victimage ritual. Burke developed his ideas in open dialogue with Freud's psychoanalytic theory. This connection can be more deeply appreciated by considering Foucault's observation toward the end of history of the human sciences regarding Freud's contribution to modern thought:

> ...Since Totem and Taboo, the establishment of a common field for these two [ethnology and psychology], the possibility of a discourse that could move from one to the other without discontinuity, the double articulation of the history of individuals upon the unconscious of culture, and of the historicity of those cultures upon the unconscious of individuals, has opened up, without doubt, the most general problems that can be posed with regard to man (1970: 379).

This is clearly evident in Freud's use of Sophocles' tragic drama, *Oedipus Rex*. This drama involves [attempted] infanticide and [successful] patricide. Oedipus' father, the King of Thebes, tries to kill him twice, as an infant and as a young man. Unknowingly, Oedipus kills his father and marries his mother. Burke, like Freud, also employed Greek tragic drama as a paradigm of victimage ritual (Burke 1965).

To fully appreciate Freud's use of Greek drama in the development of his social-psychological theory of identification, it is necessary to underscore the purely symbolic and psychological character of the dramatic process. While this process is provoked by the circumstances of family life, identification happens in the imagination, the theater of the human mind, not in reality. Freud differentiated two modes of thought. The primary processes of thought are hallucinatory. They are wish-fulfillments; intense imaginings of the experience of satisfaction or consummation of some pleasurable experience. These fantasies are experienced as intense and real in the way that we experience dreams, but they are thought realities. The secondary processes of thought are reality oriented and develop through symbolic interaction and socialization to a culture. According to the theory, we learn how to differentiate fantasy or internal "object-relations" from real or external "object relations," and this testing is an ongoing task.

With this qualification in mind, the Freudian theory of the Oedipus Complex involves imaginary violence in at least two major ways: 1) guilt—the murderous desires of the son toward the father provoked by the father's patriarchal dominance, and 2) redemption—the mourning and idealization of the father in the son's reaction to the imagined crime. The son engages in a shift from a passive to an active role in fantasy, or from the "nightmare" of oppression and helplessness to an "identification with the aggressor" and the satisfaction of the desire for revenge (Jones 1971: 22, A. Freud 1966: 113). This process is articulated in victimage ritual by symbolic means by a shift in the rhetoric from a focus on the villain's sadistic relationship to the victim, to a focus on the hero's triumph over the villain.

Mourning and the dynamics of guilt was Freud's model of identification (Freud 1961: 97–112, 1963, Blain 1976, Butler 2003: 167–97). In the son's remorse in response to the imagined patricide, the imagined loss of the father, he represses his erotic and violent desires and identifies himself with the aggressor. The Oedipus conflict is driven by emotional ambivalence, the simultaneous love and hate of the father as a symbol of patriarchal family authority. The son's frustrated desire for his mother causes him to form a desire to remove the father, the symbol of coercive authority and dominance. At the same time this thought conflicts with his equally strong desire to have the security of the father's protection (anxiety / defense mechanism). Redemption is accomplished through repression of these conflicting impulses. This repression is accomplished by means of the displacement and projection of these forbidden desires on to external objects, and by an identification with the father. Freud was the first to clearly describe how the superego can disguise murderous impulses in the cloak of moral righteousness and higher political purposes. This projection allowed the Nazis to persuade their followers that the Jews were the murderous ones who were out to destroy the Aryan Race and Germany. It was the Jews who were the persecutors and terrorists. They engaged in the "ritual murder" of Christian babies as part of their religious practices, leavening their ceremonial bread with Christian blood.

This model was further elaborated in Melanie Klein's "object relations" and "object-loss" theory of identification (Segal 1979). Klein's point of departure was Freud's 1917 paper on "Mourning and Melancholia" (1963). She and her disciples pushed Freud's analysis of these thought processes back to the pre-Oedipal infant's relation to the mother, and the anxiety and rage provoked by the experience of object-loss and social separation (Bowlby 1960, 1961). Klein (1940) described the thought process provoked by separation of the baby from its mother as "the infantile depressive position." "In short," she argued, "persecution (by "bad" objects) and the characteristic defense against it, on the one hand, and pining for the loved ("good") object, on the other, constitute the depressive position" (1940: 125–153). These paranoid thoughts of persecution by the bad objects, in turn, provoke a primary process of defensive thoughts of retaliation against the bad-objects and the idealization of the "good" objects. Anger replaces anxiety and fear. There are clear parallels found in the societal response to acts of political violence.

The mourning of the victims of political violence and the onset of victimage ritual are crucially related. The shock and awe of violence against innocent and helpless victims provokes the compulsive repetition of victimage (often purely symbolic) and ritual destruction of scapegoats. "Never forget!" The compulsive repetition of the crucifixion and resurrection of Jesus in the Eucharist is a paradigm of this process. Many historical episodes of political persecution parallel this unconscious process (Storr 1972; Cohn 1975). Germany's loss of World War I and all the martyred heroes who died in vain as a result was caused by "bad objects"— Jews or communists who had "crucified" Germany by stabbing the German people in the back. Many Germans died as a result of World War I. The ideals of the German nation were destroyed. Nazi discourse "split" society into good and bad groups, portraying the Jews and their dupes as persecutors. Pining for the loved good objects, the old Germany and those who had sacrificed for the cause, was an important part of Nazi victimage ritual. There is also a parallel in the Nazi idealization of the martyred war heroes and veterans of World War I in extensive memorial rites (also depicted in Riefenstahl's film).

The similarity between the psychoanalytic theory of infantile identifications and Burke's dramatism is not coincidental. Burke studied Freud's theories closely (see Duncan's discussion, 1962: 3–17, 1968: 30–32). The difference is that according to Burke's theory the emotions and motives involved are aroused in and through symbolic interaction. The emotional effects of political violence depend on how it is publically signified and, therefore, socially understood. Mass killings repeatedly and publically dramatized as "the cold-blooded slaughter of innocent people" will have a different emotional impact than the same violence formulated as "the heroic struggle of our troops to defeat the terrorists." Political victimage rituals are public dramas. They involve ritual practices and discourses that enunciate principles believed necessary to the survival of social orders. Political authority can be created or destroyed in these dramas. They are formulated as ultimate battles of good groups against bad groups, or groups representing life against groups inflicting death.

The double articulation of ethnology and psychology puts us in a better position to understand how political actors, deploying victimage ritual, can succeed in motivating people to kill and die in power struggles. This unconscious cultural-psychological complex can be invoked by political leaders using violence to beget violence. Political violence can be mystified by the discourses of victimage ritual. Diagram 3.1 depicts the stages in the social psychology of the identification process.

There are two moments of identification in a victimage ritual. Central to this model is the division of the social scene into two subject-objects (the good versus the bad) and an inversion of power perspective. Political leaders must rhetorically constitute their opponents and enemies as villainous subjects of power, terrorists and tyrants who must be fought and destroyed in ultimate struggles of good against evil. Nazi discourse was racist, involving a two-part system of equations and opposing terms signifying racial traits (That is, they were inborn or in the "blood"):

- Patriots = Germans, Aryan race (as victims and heroes) = honest, altruistic, creative
- Traitors = Jews and their duped allies (as villains, scapegoats, enemies) = cunning, egoistic, destructive

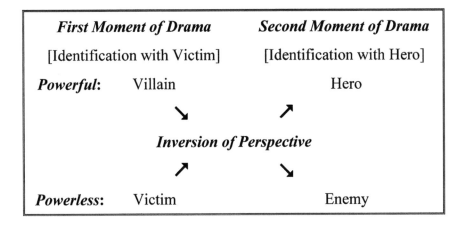

Diagram 3.1   Inversion of Power Relations and Identification in Victimage Ritual

The first moment of the drama involves an "Identification with the Victim." In this moment the powerful one is the villain persecuting the powerless victim, the subject who maliciously violates the victim. Identification with the victim provokes moral outrage at the villainy of the enemy. How could anyone act this way? In Nazi discourse, they were racially driven to be morally evil. The murderous is projected on to some convenient scapegoat. In the Nazi perversion of Christian ritual, the first moment is still guilt. Jesus, the personification of perfect good, was crucified by the Roman imperial authorities. But it was the Pharisees, a group of Jewish priests, who had conspired with Pilot to crucify Jesus. Nazi rhetoric picks up on this narrative by pinning the destruction of Germany on the Jews. Disguised as pacifists and social democrats, Marxists and international bankers, the cunning Jews had stabbed the country in the back. The Jews were responsible for the loss of World War I, personifying the humiliating "war guilt" and horrible loss of life symbolized by the "tomb of the unknown soldier." It is in the name of these "innocent victims" and "altruistic" martyrs that the victimage of the Jews and Germany's war with the world was justified.

The second dramatic moment in a victimage ritual is some kind of resolution of the conflict, redemption, or justice. In this moment leaders must constitute their followers (militias, troops, police or military forces) as heroic power subjects, agents who are ready, willing and able to kill and die in life and death struggles to destroy those villainous powers. This moment involves an inversion of perspective from the point of view of the powerless, the violation of the victim by the villain, to the standpoint of the hero and the triumph of the will. The Nazi goal was rebirth and the creation of a German empire in the form of a "Thousand year Reich." The *denouement* of any victimage ritual is sacrifice—the destruction of the villainous scapegoat who personifies the negation of social order. The final solution of the

Jewish question was extermination. The holocaust was set in motion by a political act—the ritual persecution of the Jews and their allies in the form of a great war to build a Thousand Year Reich. This provoked a counter victimage ritual to destroy the Nazi and fascist villains in Germany and Japan called World War II. The "terror bombings" that killed millions of civilians in World War II are horrific examples of the satisfaction of this symbolically generated desire to destroy the destroyers.

Biopolitics

Burke discussed the problem of recognizing modern forms of victimage ritual in a scientific culture that rejects traditional religious practices like scapegoating as irrational. Enlightened people are supposed to be "rational" and "scientific" in their orientation to the world. Ritual scapegoating is viewed as a regressive and barbaric practice; hence, not modern. Acutely aware of this cultural bias, "Dramatism," Burke asserted, "asks not how the sacrificial motives revealed in the institutions of magic and religions might be eliminated in a scientific culture, but what new forms they take" (Burke 1968: 451). Burke's critique of the Nazi use of "scientific racism" and "mass psychology" are good examples of modern forms of victimage ritual. Thomas Szasz (1974) has extended these ideas to the medical mistreatment of the "mentally ill" and the ritual persecution of "drug users" flowing from the war on drugs. These issues can also be addressed through a merging of Burke's ideas with Michel Foucault's account of modern liberalism and biopolitics. These examples can also provide a useful bridge to the discussion in Chapter 5 of the role of biopolitics, the current power / knowledge regime, the human and social sciences, and the consequent intensification of "homeland security" and surveillance that has resulted from the war on terrorism.

Actors who threaten "government / security" are vilified as "criminals" or "terrorists" who threaten individual rights to life, liberty, and the pursuit of happiness. This sets up the following logologic:

> If security, then life, liberty, happiness;

> But liberty also implies the logological possibility of revolutionary violence, "terrorism"

> Ergo: need for victimage ritual and the conspicuous sacrifice of "individual life" (e.g., use of deadly force against criminals, torture of terrorists, drone attacks to kill terrorists, etc.)

In Bush regime rhetorical discourse, Osama bin Laden and Saddam Hussein personified ultimate threats to life and liberty, specifically the American way of life, the lives and livelihood of the American people, and the so-called "free world". Therefore, they had to be "taken out" (Berman 2004).

Identification with 9/11 Victims

The form of ritual victimage is melodramatic. Actors in power struggles identify with actors who are cast into the roles of victims and villains, heroes and enemies, spectators and the public. In warfare the blood of innocent victims is used to establish the villainy of the opponent and to motivate the destruction of the enemy. The blood sacrifice of heroic martyrs is used to glorify the warriors. The villains and heroes as power subjects are defined in terms of historically specific antonyms and synonyms. These terms are ritually repeated again and again. The particular mix of terms deployed in power struggles depends on the actor's knowledge and background as well as variations in political context and audience addressed. The terrorist is constituted in the compulsive repetition of specific terms such as civilized/terrorist, freedom/tyranny, rational/extremist, peace loving/murderous and savage. The adversary's motives and actions are described in terms of the negative poles of the antonym, the heroes' in terms of the positive. The American victims of the 9/11 attacks were innocent, altruistic, and freedom-loving people. The terrorists were characterized as murderous and savage enemies of freedom. Later, Saddam Hussein would be [falsely] accused of secretly supporting the attackers. When that failed to convince, Saddam was repeatedly characterized as a murderous tyrant who had used chemical weapons to attack his own people.

As we shall see, the sacred sites created to memorialize the 9/11 attacks are symbols that can be mobilized to deepen the identification with victims and enhance the villainy of the "terrorists." Memorials to the victims of the 9/11 attacks have been built at the World Trade Center, New York City (http://www.911memorial.org/), the Pentagon in Washington, D.C. (http://www.whs.mil/memorial/), and at the "Flight 93 National Memorial" near Shanksville, Pennsylvania (http://www.nps.gov/flni/index.html). These sacred sites and monuments constitute the "scene of the crime"; as such, they are powerful condensations of political significance. Once they exist, political actors can use them to stage political events, ceremonies and hold press conferences to orchestrate their campaigns of ritual victimage against their political enemies, foreign and domestic.

President George Bush's September 20, 2001 televised address was politically decisive in setting the ritual victimage of global war into motion. The speech was delivered before a "Joint session of the Congress" (including an audience of members of the House of Representatives and Senate). It was televised to the whole world. Its theme was "U.S. Response to the Terrorist Attacks of September 11." Significantly, it was not an appeal to the Congress for a formal Declaration of War as specified in the Constitution. It was a strong appeal to the world to identify with the victims and martyrs of the 9/11 attacks. The speech positions the President as speaking to, for, and on behalf of the "American People," and to, for, and on behalf of the "civilized world." The first paragraphs focus almost exclusively on "the American people" and their heroic and self-sacrificing actions in response to the "terrorist" attack:

In the normal course of events, Presidents come to this Chamber to report on the state of the union. Tonight, no such report is needed. It has already been delivered by the American people.

We have seen it in the courage of [airline] passengers, who rushed terrorists to save others on the ground, passengers like an exceptional man named Todd Beamer. [emphasis added: bold = glorifier / bold + italic = vilifier] And would you please help me to welcome his wife, Lisa Beamer, here tonight. [*Applause*]

We have seen the state of our Union in the endurance of rescuers, working past exhaustion. We have seen the unfurling of flags, the lighting of candles, the giving of blood, the saying of prayers in English, Hebrew, and Arabic. We have seen the decency of a loving and giving people who have made the grief of strangers their own.

My fellow citizens, for the last 9 days, the entire world has seen for itself the state of our Union, and it is strong.

Tonight we are a country awakened to danger and called to defend freedom. Our grief has turned to anger and anger to resolution. Whether we bring our enemies to justice or bring justice to our enemies, justice will be done.

The emphasis on the "heroic" and "supportive" response is a plea for the audience's sympathy and personal identification with the plight of the American people. There is little emphasis placed on the helpless and innocent victims killed by the actual attacks and its horrific aftermath. The stress is on the positive, the essential courage and goodness of the American people as a whole. Not everyone would automatically associate these national virtues with the people who live and work in New York City (see Niebuhr 2001). It has often been associated with sin and evil, Jews and blacks, crime and violence, the American Civil Liberties Union, and liberals. This plea for the audience to identify with the essential goodness of the American people obviates this "divisive" negativity. There is a thinly veiled threat to kill in the observation that "our grief has turned to anger and anger to resolution" and the threat that directly follows it to "bring justice to our enemies." The plea continued with a series of brief statements of gratitude to the Congress, two political parties, and world for their support. Invoking the many nationalities of the victims who died in the Towers, Bush states, "Nor will we forget the citizens of 80 other nations who died with our own: dozens of Pakistanis; more than 130 Israelis; more than 250 citizens of India; men and women from El Salvador, Iran, Mexico, and Japan; and hundreds of British citizens." The speech is an attempt to get all "civilized" people to identify with all the victims of the terror attacks.

The transition to victimage rhetoric and the negative is introduced next. The 9/11 attack was synonymous with an attack on "freedom." It is the American commitment to the principle of "freedom" that is the crux of the attack and the terrorist's motivation:

On September 11th, *enemies of freedom committed an act of war against our country*. [emphasis added: bold = glorifier / bold + italic = vilifier] Americans have known wars, but for the past 136 years, they have been wars on foreign soil, except for one Sunday in 1941. Americans have known the casualties of war, but not at the center of a great city on a peaceful morning. Americans have known surprise attacks, but never before on *thousands of civilians*. All of this was brought upon us in a single day, and night fell on a different world, a world where freedom itself is under attack.

Later in the speech, the question of why the attacked us is broached again. Their motivation is answered again in terms of "freedom":

Americans are asking, why do they hate us? *They hate what we see right here in this Chamber, a democratically elected government. Their leaders are self-appointed. They hate our freedoms—our freedom of religion, our freedom of speech, our freedom to vote and assemble and disagree with each other.* [emphasis added: bold = glorifier / bold + italic = vilifier]

And who are these "enemies of freedom"? The perpetrators have to be precisely identified and vilified. The speech poses the question as one posed by the American people, "Americans are asking, who attacked our country?" The answer specifies "loosely affiliated terrorist organizations known as Al Qaeda," "murderers indicted for bombing American Embassies...[and]...bombing the U.S.S. Cole... who practice a fringe form of Islamic extremism," "kill Christians and Jews, kill all Americans, and make no distinctions among military and civilians, including women and children." Al Qaeda is led by Osama bin Laden. Its goal is to "remake the world" and impose "their radical beliefs on people everywhere." Lastly, they are linked to many other organizations and to "thousands of terrorists in more than 60 countries."

The specificity of the enemy is important. The speech goes to great lengths to differentiate Al Qaeda and Bin Laden from "Muslims throughout the world."

We respect your faith. It's practiced freely by many millions of Americans and by millions more in countries that America counts as friends. Its teachings are good and peaceful and those who commit evil in the name of Allah blaspheme the name of Allah. *The terrorists are traitors to their own faith, trying, in effect, to hijack Islam itself.* [emphasis added: bold = glorifier / bold + italic = vilifier] The enemy of America is not our many Muslim friends; it is not our many Arab friends. Our enemy is a radical network of terrorists and every government that supports them.

Muslims in general are not the enemy. Al Qaeda has to be clearly and precisely differentiated from the "millions" of Muslims, whose teachings are "good and peaceful." Al Qaeda wants to overthrow existing governments in many Muslim countries and "drive Israel out of the Middle East." To sharpen the point and drive it in deeper, the speech vilifies "the terrorists" by equating them to the other great "enemies of freedom."

> We are not deceived by their pretenses to piety. We have seen their kind before. ***They are the heirs of all the murderous ideologies of the 20th century. By sacrificing human life to serve their radical visions, by abandoning every value except the will to power, they follow in the path of fascism and nazism and totalitarianism.*** [emphasis added: bold = glorifier / bold + italic = vilifier] And they will follow that path all the way, to where it ends, in history's unmarked grave of discarded lies.

In addition to refining and clarifying the difference between "the good and peace-loving" Muslims of the world and the Islamic terrorists, this statement is a crucial move to set the stage for a cosmic global war against "evil."

These systems of terms, antonyms and synonyms, depending on political context, would continue to function with greater or lesser frequency and intensity and violence until the last years of the Bush Administration:

- Victims = Americans, American way of life, Jews and Christians, civilians, women and children, freedom, civilization
-
- Villains = terrorists = Al Qaeda = Bin Laden, Islamic extremists, Jihadists, hateful, murderers, killers

Bush refers to "terror" 34 times. The Al Qaeda terrorists are murderers, killers, full of hate, pretend to religious and moral piety, and ultimate "enemies of freedom." "Freedom and fear" are at war. Americans, by contrast, have many virtues. Americans are freedom-loving and peaceful, a decent and generous people, who are strong, courageous and resolved in the face of danger. The killing of Americans is hateful, murderous, and evil. This is especially so since it was on their own soil in the middle of a "peaceful" city filled with 'innocent" American civilians. The cosmic character of this conflict is clearly underscored by the many references to World War II and Pearl Harbor, the provocation that caused the U.S. to enter World War II. These threatening Others are malevolent killers of the American dream. They are distributed around the world in 60 countries. They must be destroyed in a global crusade against terrorism.

Identification with Heroic Struggle

The second dramatic moment of the war on terror as a victimage ritual was the decision to mount a global war in response to the September 11th terrorist attacks. Victimage ritual, particularly in the stock melodramatic form of a Great War against enemies personified as evil powers, has been a major source of political power and authority in the modern world. These terrifying and spectacular incidents of human sacrifice have been created and sustained through the intensive and frequent use of victimage ritual. The war of words is the first stage in the ritual. The second stage in the ritual is the heroic struggle to defeat the enemy. Victimage ritual has played a decisive role in some of the most horrendous social catastrophes involving the murder of millions of human beings in the twentieth century. The rhetorical discourse is melodramatic in form, featuring heroes struggling against villainous powers to secure the survival of nations, races, individual human lives, and the ultimate values of the free world. As we have seen this lethal, more or less unconscious, cultural complex is deeply rooted in the Judeo-Christian tradition.

The "holy" war is the most common form of political victimage ritual. The struggle of good against evil is tailor-made to the call for a heroic struggle against a common enemy (Duncan 1962: 131–132). Defining the appropriate response to the 9/11 attacks as a "global war against terrorism" raises the stakes. The problems and personal struggles of the day as topical identifications can be transformed into an identification with a cosmic crisis, "angels locked in ethereal battle before the ramparts of heaven." Ordinary problems can assume cosmic proportions. Hyperbole is the idiom of victimage ritual and political violence. Political leaders use language "to make mountains out of molehills" and transform a power struggle into a cosmic war of good against evil. The fight against the 9/11 crime becomes a global war against terrorism. This world scene is depicted in apocalyptic terms. The survival of our way of life is at stake. As a result, the war on terror can be fought by any means, including mass military violence that destabilizes whole populations, extrajudicial assassinations, high-tech homicide bombings with drones, torture at black sites, and indefinite detention in camps. All of this is necessary, because the terrorists represent an "existential threat."

The fight against the Nazis in World War II, who perfected the political art of propaganda to its highest possible level at the time, taught the glorious victors of that vicious fight that victimage ritual is a source of great political power and authority. The victors were transformed by the victory. There is no way to avoid the terrible truth that much of this horrific violence was organized and perpetrated by liberal-democratic regimes that claimed to be defending "humanistic" principles of reason and freedom. The "terror bombings" by the Allied powers during World War II, that destroyed whole cities, killed and maimed millions of people are exemplary in this regard. The interpretation of this phenomenon has been covered-up by a one-sided focus on the Nazi, communist, or terrorist devils. In the process of fighting "monsters," the U.S. power elite that assumed the leading role in Empire subsequently adopted many of their "monstrous" means.

Given this history, the references in Bush's war speech to World War II and the Cold-War signal a final shift toward the end of the speech to a more epochal and cosmic level:

> After all that has just passed, all the lives taken and all the possibilities and hopes that died with them, it is natural to wonder if America's future is one of fear. Some speak of an age of terror. I know there are struggles ahead and dangers to face. **But this country will define our times, not be defined by them. As long as the United States of America is determined and strong, this will not be an age of terror; this will be an age of liberty, here and across the world.** [emphasis added: bold = glorifier / bold + italic = vilifier]

> Great harm has been done to us. We have suffered great loss. And in our grief and anger, we have found our mission and our moment. Freedom and fear are at war. The advance of human freedom, the great achievement of our time and the great hope of every time, now depends on us. **Our Nation—this generation— will lift a dark threat of violence from our people and our future. We will rally the world to this cause by our efforts, by our courage. We will not tire; we will not falter; and we will not fail.**

This passage is followed up with a final invocation of the heroic courage of "a man who died at the World Trade Center trying to save others." The speech concludes with President Bush's personal pledge to "not forget" those who inflicted this "great harm" on the American people:

> ***...I will not forget this wound to our country and those who inflicted it.*** [emphasis added: bold = glorifier / bold + italic = vilifier] **I will not yield; I will not rest; I will not relent in waging this struggle for freedom and security for the American people.** ...The course of this conflict is not known, yet its outcome is certain. Freedom and fear, justice and cruelty have always been at war, and we know that God is not neutral between them.

As the speech suggests, there is a transcendent dimension to this conflict. Just as everyone knows what side God is on.

Power and Victimage Ritual

Why a global war? In a discussion recorded by Borradori (2003) in *Philosophy in a Time of Terror*, Jacques Derrida asked why "9–11" had been turned into a "major event" rather than some other horrific events involving equal amounts of terror? The frequent use of "9–11" as the name for the "event," Derrida argued, suggested a "repetition compulsion." Schmitt's work on "war" is discussed in the context of "the war on terrorism." Derrida thought that the use of the term "war" to define a "war on terrorism" was confusing. The official and media discourse of the "event" relied too heavily on "received concepts" like "war" and "terrorism." There is no "enemy" in the traditional sense of war, where two states and their armies engage in armed conflicts. The conflict with "Bin Laden and Al Qaeda" is not a traditional war between clearly defined groups (Purdum 2001). What "interests," Derrida asked, could such an abuse of rhetoric actually serve? What new situation, he asked, had made this new kind of conflict possible? It was, he thought, Al Qaeda's use of "technoscience" that blurred the distinction between traditional war and terrorism. This new "technoscience" [information systems and networks; hijacked airliners] allowed a small number of people possessing very few resources and minimal means to successfully attack the greatest power on earth.

The targets of these attacks were highly symbolic: the World Trade Center Towers, Washington D.C., and specifically the Pentagon. These sites and institutions are central to the functioning of the U.S. power elite and contemporary Empire. Members of the elite have been central players in the development of twentieth century Empire. Domhoff (2010) argues that the power elite is situated at the intersection of three social networks: the American social upper class, the corporate community, and a policy-planning network. The elite are that fraction of the social class that actively participates in the corporate community and policy planning network to rule America. Representatives of this class, for example the Roosevelt and Bush families, have played a dynastic role in the historical development of the U.S. power elite and Empire (see Phillips 2004 genealogy of the "House of Bush"). They use a variety of means to shape public opinion, party politics, and government policy. As far as foreign policy is concerned, according to his analysis:

> The opinion-shaping network achieves its clearest expression in the area of foreign policy, where most people have little information or interest and are predisposed to accept unilateral or bellicose actions by top leaders out of patriotism or fear of the foreign, even though polls show that the general public has more liberal and less militaristic views than those members of the power elite and the policy planning network who focus on foreign policy... Although the efforts of the foreign-policy groups are important [especially, the Foreign Policy Association, based in New York], the actions of the president and his top foreign-policy officials are the strongest influences on public opinion on specific foreign policy issues (Domhoff, 2010: 130–131).

As evidence he cites public opinion polls conducted before and after an escalation in the war in Vietnam. Before the bombing of Hanoi and Haiphong began in late spring 1966, the public was split fifty-fifty over the question of bombing. When asked in July, 1966, after the bombing began 85 percent were in favor. However, as Domhoff also notes there are limits to the power elite's influence on public support for wars. As casualties mounted during the Korean and Vietnam wars, public support declined. Public support for the Vietnam War in particular was negatively affected by the social disruption caused by anti-war protests. Even so, as he also observes, the same surveys show that the public disliked the anti-war "protesters" more than they disliked the war. The "protesters" were categorized as "traitors" by many who thought they were threatening U.S. troops by aiding and abetting the enemy. This fact is a testament to the rhetorical power of victimage ritual to shape public opinion.

A rhetorically effective victimage ritual must accomplish two things: 1) constitute a knowledge of the field of power struggle—argue the truth of some threat, injustice, or danger, and establish via vilification who the antagonists are (victims and villains, heroes and enemies); 2) constitute an ethical or moral incitement to political struggle—argue for solutions in an activating way. Edward Said has highlighted these two features of the Anglo-American discourse of Empire:

> Take as a case in point the emergence of 'terrorism' and 'fundamentalism' as two key terms of the 1980s. For one, you could hardly begin (in the public space provided by international discourse) to analyze political conflicts involving Sunnis and Shi'is and Iraqis, or Tamils and Sinhalese, or Sikhs and Hindus—the list is long—without eventually having to resort to the categories and images of 'terrorism' and 'fundamentalism,' which derived entirely from the concerns and intellectual factories in metropolitan centers like Washington and London. They are fearful images that lack discriminate contents or definition, but they signify moral power and approval for whoever uses them, moral defensiveness and criminalization for whomever they designate. These two gigantic reductions mobilized armies as well as dispersed communities... (1993: 309).

Narrating the field of power and the necessity of heroic struggle is a socially symbolic act. Indeed, as Frederic Jameson (1981) has argued, the study of these "reductions" is the royal road to the "political unconscious." From the standpoint of Empire, its official representatives and mandarins, terrorism is synonymous with abnormality, irrationality, and extremism, while the use of retaliatory military force has become a synonym for normality, rationality, and moderation. Victimage rhetoric functions to mobilize consent, eradicate dissent, and promote patriotism. By these means potentially disruptive demands for democracy by the multitudes can be more contained. In U.S. domestic context Homeland Security transforms citizens into patriotic subjects of the Commander in Chief.

Victimage Ritual and Discourse Analysis

Three principles guide the analysis of power struggles and discourse in the war on terror presented in the next chapter. Taken together, they constitute the basis for a genealogy of the dynamics of "the discourse of terrorism" in the war on terror. This kind of analysis is particularly useful in detecting novel tactical shifts in the discourses that emerge in the midst of power struggles (Blain 2005). The description of these "emergent" features of the discourse is one of the main benefits of an analysis of this type.

A power struggle perspective seems particularly well suited to an understanding of terrorism. As Richard English, a historian who has written an influential, some argue definitive, history of the Irish Republican Army struggle against the remnant of Empire in Ireland, seems to recognize, albeit rather obliquely, that terrorism cannot be understood except in the context of power relations of some kind. Terrorism, in one of its most important aspects, English asserts, "embodies the exerting and implementing of power, and the attempted redressing of power relations; it represents a subspecies of warfare, and as such it can form part of a wider campaign of violent and non-violent attempts at political leverage" (2009: 24). The idea advanced here is that the categorizing of an opponent as a "terrorist" is itself a way of exerting a power relation.

The first rule concerns the relations between power struggles and subjectifying practices. As we shall see, the mode of subjection by means of victimage ritual shifted during the Iraq war. After the "liberation" produced an organized counter-insurgency campaign, the opponents were characterized as "terrorists." As the "surge" was mounted in response to the terrorism, the opponents were categorized more frequently as "extremists." The way discourse functions in most power struggles is according to the model of war—an agonism of strategies. The exceptions to this rule are struggles guided by the Gandhi method of *satyagraha* or method of truth which explicitly opposes agonology (Fisher 1980, Blain 1989). One must avoid deliberately inflicting harm on an adversary by vilifying them. One must treat an opponent with honor and respect. Most politicians fight rhetorical battles against their opponents the way that generals engage in warfare, by mobilizing forces, calculating ritual strategies and discursive tactics to achieve their objectives, and seizing opportunities. The aim is to win the war by all necessary means including character assassination. Changes in strategic opportunities can alter actor's calculations of the probability of successful action and, therefore, their willingness to engage in political action. This proposition has been verified in much scholarly research on the dynamics of contentious politics (Tarrow 1998, McAdam, Tarrow, and Tilly 2001).

There is a predictable sequence of power relations set into motion by Empire. Empire is always on the move and as such a constant provocation. The global deployment of U.S. and NATO military forces, the existence of hundreds of foreign military bases, is a constant incitement to resistance or "terrorism." Agents of empire make moves into new geostrategic spaces, provoking organized resistance and political violence. The construction of a huge military base in Saudi Arabia following the Iranian revolution of 1979 is a clear case in point. Losing a base in Iran, American military planners exploit the occasion to move to Saudi Arabia. The groups that resist the move are categorized as "terrorists." A victimage ritual is orchestrated against them justifying and inciting campaigns to destroy the villains. As described in Chapter 2, this pattern was deeply embedded in American political culture by the end of the nineteenth century as a result of the settlement, occupation, and annexation of the North American territories. It is true that the American Revolution was an anti-colonial struggle. But Empire is at the very heart of the more (agents of U.S. power elite and Empire) or less (American public) conscious American political understanding of how the United States of America was constructed. Rhetorically speaking, America is the so-called anti-Empire, Empire. This cultural irony is behind the constant charge of hypocrisy leveled against the "Empire of Liberty" (Reynolds 2009). The settlement of the American west was aided and abetted by the U.S. Federal government. The constitution and expansion of the American Empire, of course, provoked organized resistance by "Indians" against "white settlers," who really were encroaching on Indian lands. This evoked vicious victimage rituals against the uncivilized "savages," inciting violent retaliation and campaigns of extermination against Indians who were defined as the actors who were "terrorizing" the innocent settlers. It is the so-called "unprovoked" attacks by "savages" on the civilized "white settlers" that functions as an incitement to the expansion and consolidation of Empire.

A second analytic principle concerns the practices put into play in power struggles. In the political arena, symbolic action is understood by the actors and spectators to be a more or less calculated strategy for dealing with a social situation. As regards *political* power struggles involving organized contending parties, symbolic action is a calculated means to achieve strategic objectives in the teeth of organized resistance by an opponent. Victimage ritual, in this sense, is a rhetorical weapon employed to achieve a political goal. The agents of the U.S. power elite are self-aware and knowledgeable strategic actors who deploy victimage ritual as a calculated means to exercise political power. If a smoothly functioning and stable Empire is the objective, it can only be accomplished by a two-pronged rhetorical strategy. On the one hand, victimage ritual must function to constitute the "enemies of empire" and to inspire and support military action and warfare to create and extend the dominion of Empire. On the other hand, victimage ritual must also function to limit "public opinion" and silence anti-war discourses by attacking dissenters as "traitors."

The vilification of Colonel Moammar el-Qaddafi as a state-sponsor of terrorism exemplifies the cycle of Empire → Resistance → Victimage Ritual (see "Timeline: Col. Moammar el-Qaddafi," *New York Times* 2011). The dominant discourse: Qaddafi assumes power after leading a successful revolution against the Libyan colonial regime of King Idris I in 1969, forcing the withdrawal of British and American forces from Libya. The U.S. shoots down two Libyan fighter jets in 1981. Intelligence sources report Libyan involvement in efforts to overthrow Sudan's government and assistance to rebels in Chad in rout of government forces in 1983. U.S. officials link Libya to two December 1985 terrorist attacks at airports in Rome and Vienna. The U.S. bombs Tripoli and Benghazi in April of 1986. Qaddafi's agents are blamed for two terrorist attacks in 1988: an April West Berlin nightclub bombing and the December 22 bombing of Pan Am Flight 103 over Lockerbie, Scotland. American warplanes shoot down two Libyan fighters in January 1989. And, so on. The denouement: Qaddafi is executed by Libyan "revolutionaries" with massive support from American and NATO forces, October 2011. His bloody body is displayed for public viewing.

No questions are raised about the deployments of U.S. and NATO military forces in the region. Their presence is taken for granted. Qaddafi's ritual victimage was a way to cover-up an act of political violence. These underlying power relations are the cultural unconscious of Empire. As an example of this dynamic, consider the 1988 bombing of Pan Am Flight 103 over Lockerbie, Scotland (Ruthven 2009). The Libyans are assumed to be the responsible party. There is a discourse that traces the cause of the Lockerbie attack to U.S. violence. The shooting down of the *civilian* airliner over Lockerbie was "retaliation" for the July 1988 U.S. downing of an Iranian civilian airliner over the Persian Gulf (all 290 people aboard civilian Flight 655 were killed). The Iranian government denounced the act as a "barbaric massacre" and threatened "bloody" retaliation (Ruthven 2009, Ibrahim 1988). This possibility is not pursued. It threatens to expose the political unconscious of Empire. It might raise questions about why an American warship that killed 290 civilians was deployed in the Persian Gulf in the first place. It also might lead to an understanding that the global deployment of U.S. military forces is a constant provocation to resistance and "terrorism," which, in turn, can warrant a further expansion of Empire.

A third and final point concerns the tactical use of discourse in power struggles. Politicians must speak to multiple and, at times, conflicting constituencies, as well as take account of their opponent's shifting tactics in order to gain a plurality of support and achieve their political goals. Leaders must deploy multiple discourses to appeal to different and conflicting constituencies, opening them up to the charge of hypocrisy or cynical opportunism. Moreover, a second contingency arises once a campaign is launched. Discourses are mobile and polyvalent, allowing for a turning-of-the-tables to take place. Words can be selected and recombined in novel strategies. The discourse of terrorism is particularly mobile and polyvalent. As we shall see, once the U.S. invaded Iraq and provoked an insurgency, the Bush regime countered this insurgence by denouncing it as a terrorist campaign organized by Al Qaeda.

Diagram 3.2 below presents a schematic analysis of the two principle ways victimage ritual functions in support of Empire. In the domestic political context, it functions to differentiate loyal patriots from unpatriotic traitors. A good example of this kind of tactic, a legacy of the Viet-Nam war era, is the silencing of dissent by means of the vilification of anti-war dissenters as unpatriotic and treasonous. They were accused of aiding and abetting the enemy because they undermined public morale and did not support the troops. In foreign context or the situation of Empire an effective victimage discourse divides the field of power relations into enemies and friends. The specific cast of characters, the actors cast into the roles of friends and enemies corresponds to shifts in the field of geostrategic power relations. The vilification of Al Qaeda, Osama bin Laden and their "Taliban allies" as "terrorists" was central to the invasion and occupation of Afghanistan. Once the

Political Context		
Discourse	**Domestic**	**Foreign**
War	**patriots vs. traitors**	**allies vs. enemies**
Liberal	**security, freedom**	**security, freedom**

Diagram 3.2   Victimage Rhetoric in Domestic and Foreign Contexts

Bush regime decided to invade and occupy Iraq, the tyrant and alleged "sponsor of terrorists," Saddam Hussein, emerged as the chief villain.

The cycle of Empire →Resistance →Victimage Ritual produces a shifting cast of melodramatic characters. The specific villains change as the specific moves made in the power game change: the agents and agencies of Empire make a geostrategic move—in this case the U.S. Each move in the power game provokes resistance and a more or less organized form of insurgency emerges, agents and agencies of resistance, who are categorized as enemies and / or terrorists and terrorist organizations. The agents of Empire respond to resistance with counter-***terrorism***.

Chapter 4

War on Terrorism

The compulsive repetition of the cycle of Empire → Resistance → Victimage Ritual constituted by the world war against terrorists is the "cyclical night" of contemporary political fright. In turn, these violent episodes provoke new emergencies, new cycles, and more violence. These cycles are determined by the strategic objectives of those parties who make up the contemporary U.S. power elite and, and, who, in their capacity as self-aware and knowledgeable global actors, advance the cause of Empire.[1]

The Israeli-Palestinian struggle exemplifies the cycle at a regional scale. Israel is constituted in resistance to the British Empire in the wake of the Second World War (*c.* 1948). The "British Foreign Office" categorizes the Zionist campaign as "terrorist." After the successful establishment of an Israeli state, the settlement and occupation of Palestinian lands recapitulates the pattern. Israeli dominance provokes organized resistance. This movement was categorized as terrorist. A victimage ritual against "terrorists" is the pretext for an intensification of settlements in Palestinian territory, surveillance of the Palestinian population, more military assaults, drone attacks, and targeted assassinations. Empire, "Cold-war," and "War on Terrorism," reiterate these patterns at multi-regional scales in the Middle East, Central Asia, and South Asia.

This chapter presents the results of an analysis of this vicious cycle of power and subjection by means of victimage ritual in the war on terrorism. The discourse analysis highlights two subjectifying practices that are central to understanding of the war on terrorism. The first practice involves the use of two *systems of differentiation* to narrate the field of power relations: patriots versus traitors and friends versus enemies. The second practice involves amplifying and elaborated these differentiations through the use of two melodramatic devices: the vilification of opponents (foreign and domestic) and the glorification of the leaders and troops as heroes. The aims of the analysis are threefold: to measure the extent, intensity and dynamics of the victimage ritual targeting the "terrorist" villains, to show how the actors cast into the role of villains have changed in tandem with the shifting theater of power relations, and to demonstrate how political actors glorify the hero

---

1   White (1989, 1993, 1995) found the repression / resistance pattern in the Northern Ireland case. The pattern of conflict is fractal, involving the same cycle operating at different scales, with shifting casts of characters. See Goldstone and Useem's (1999) discussion. The micro-dynamics of the "prison revolt" replicates the macro-dynamics of a full scale "political revolution." The multiplier effect of simultaneous micro-revolts can cause a critical mass that constitutes a full-scale revolution or war.

to sustain violent power struggles. It begins by setting the scene of these power struggles and victimage rituals through a brief geostrategic history of relevant U.S. activities in the Middle East and Central Asia.

Empire

The war on terrorism constitutes a global theater in which the leading agents of Empire can stage speeches, hold press conferences, grandstand and gloat, while they vilify threats to Empire and identify themselves with heroes struggling against villainous powers. By these means the leaders of the "free-world" [particularly the agents representing the U.S. power elite, for example, the President of the U.S. as the self-appointed leader of the "free-world"] assert their political authority and dominance. The 9/11 attack on the American homeland was a symbolic act. Even though it was impossible to say so in public without being attacked as unpatriotic traitors and not so veiled threats of violence, the attacks were certainly understood by many this way as a melodramatic symbol of resistance to a U.S. led Empire. This is why the question, "Why do they hate us?" was so irritating to some. Instead, the question was ruled out of order. The perpetrators were categorized as "terrorists" who represented an ultimate threat to the very foundation of modernity. The "extremists" and their ideas were the origin of the acts. Any discussion of the historical background of these acts was denounced as a violation of the norms of appropriate public discourse. By this means the historical background of Empire was disassociated from the memory of the event. The decision to respond with military force could be portrayed as an ultimate battle for the survival of the American way of life and the free world. This is why the U.S. Department of Defense (DOD), ever mindful of the role of public opinion and its influence on public morale, could call the military campaigns in Afghanistan and Iraq, without any evident irony, "Operation Enduring Freedom" and "Operation Iraqi Freedom."

The Bush and Obama regimes have reiterated the denial of Empire in numerous speeches on the war on terror.[2] It is about "our way of life" or the "free-world," or the "civilized" or "modern" world. The Bush regime emphasized the similarity between past struggles against fascism (World War II) and communism (the Cold-

---

2   Again, the use of Bush's and Obama's names are simply short-hand devices for designating specific historical regimes that work to advance the interests of the U.S. power elite (Domhoff 2010). These agents play leadership roles in advancing the cause of Empire (Hardt and Negri 2000). There is no implication that these two individuals who uttered these statements or delivered these speeches are the individual origin of the ritual practices and discourses analyzed in this analysis. There is ample evidence that these statements were socially produced, vetted and modified by speech writers and numerous relevant players in the regime. They are best understood as part and parcel of a specific regime's strategy of "psychological warfare" (Simpson 1994).

War)—"totalitarian empires," and the fight against Al Qaeda. On the occasion of the September 2006 memorial to 9/11, the Whitehouse had Bush deliver speeches articulating its preferred understanding of the issue:

> So this week I've given a series of speeches about the nature of our enemy, the stakes of the struggle, and the progress we have made during the past five years. On Tuesday in Washington, I described in the terrorists own words what they believe, what they hope to accomplish, and how they intend to accomplish it. We know what the terrorists intend, because they have told us. ***They hope to establish a totalitarian Islamic empire across the Middle East, which they call a Caliphate, where all would be ruled according to their hateful ideology*** ... [emphasis added: bold = glorifier / bold + italic = vilifier] ("Fifth Anniversary of September 11 Attacks," Weekly Whitehouse Speech, September 9 2006)

The clear implication is that the Bush regime, as agents of the U.S. power elite, did not seek Empire in prosecuting the war on terrorism. They wanted "to protect and to defend" the weak and liberate the oppressed from the brutality of those villainous powers who seek to create and/or maintain "totalitarian" empires. Denying the "desire for power" by attributing it to "tyrants" and "terrorists" is the standard pretext of Empire as it expands its scope to new territories and populations. The rhetoric of the Bush regime can be reduced to the following gloss: we do not desire Empire; we make wars to liberate the oppressed.

The denial of Empire is reiterated in President Obama's Weekly speeches as well, particularly those delivered in celebration of the annual Fourth of July holidays (July 3, 2009, 2010). The American Revolutionary war is invoked as evidence of the benign character of U.S. intentions, tactfully avoiding any reference to the British, our current ally in advancing the cause of Empire. The denial is explicit (some complained that it was, in fact, too apologetic) in Obama's December 2011 speech to the troops at Ft. Bragg, North Carolina, on the occasion of the so-called end of the U.S. Iraq war:

> ...Unlike the old empires, **we don't make these sacrifices for territory or for resources. We do it because it's right...There can be no fuller expression of America's support for self-determination than our leaving Iraq to its people. That says something about who we are**...[emphasis added: bold = glorifier / bold + italic = vilifier]

> The war in Iraq will soon belong to history. **Your service belongs to the ages. Never forget that you are part of an unbroken line of heroes spanning two centuries — from the colonists who overthrew an empire, to your grandparents and parents who faced down fascism and communism, to you—men and women who fought for the same principles in Fallujah and Kandahar, and delivered justice to those who attacked us on 9/11** ("Remarks by the President and First Lady on the End of the War in Iraq," December 14, 2011).

These "denials" seem morally obtuse and deceptive in the extreme when placed in the context of U.S. geo-political and military activities (hence, the insistent need to rhetorically deny reality). The geostrategic history of U.S. in the Middle East and Central Asia since World War II specifically contradict these persistent denials. The sequence of victimage rituals orchestrated by Empire that have unfolded in that region correspond exactly in stimulus / response pattern to the history of U.S. geopolitical moves in the Middle East and Central Asia. Moreover, these geopolitical moves and dramatic events have increased in frequency and intensity since World War II. They have assumed different forms, nuclear crises, nuclear threats directed against the Soviets during the Cold-war, covert CIA operations to destabilize and overthrow unfriendly regimes or install friendly regimes (Iran 1953, Afghanistan 1986, Iraq 1958), as well as overt military interventions and armed conflicts in the region (Afghanistan, Iraq, Afghanistan again).

Among the important power moves leading the U.S. down the road to the global war on terrorism was the creation of a U.S. / Saudi alliance in 1945. President Franklin D. Roosevelt had a meeting with King Abdul Aziz of Saudi Arabia to initiate an alliance based on oil for security (Unger 2004: 289). A second move was the covert CIA operation in 1953 that overthrew the Iranian government and installed the Shah of Iran in power. Steven Kinzer (2006: 111–128) argues that this action was doubly significant. It established the "cold-war" pattern of U.S. led Empire (in a post "Imperial Era") by means of a CIA "covert operation," publically orchestrated as a victimage ritual against communists who desire world domination—"Despotism and Godless Terrorism." The alliance with Israel is the third.

These power moves are directly reflected in the pattern of U.S. arms exports recipients from 1950–2010 (see SIPRI 2011). Table 4.1 (opposite) divides the "trend indicator values" before and after the Iranian revolution of 1979. Empire's Cold-War with the Soviet Union determined the top-ten distribution, 1950–1979. Five NATO allies dominate the list: Germany, Italy, Canada, UK, and France. Two Asian allies are on the list: Japan and Taiwan. Two Middle East countries are included. Iran ranks second and Israel sixth on the top-ten list.

After the 1979 Iranian Revolution toppled the Shah's regime and the revolutionaries occupied the U.S. embassy in Teheran, holding American hostages for months, the U.S. abandoned Iran and strengthened its security alliance with Saudi Arabia. The shift from Asia to the Middle East as the locus of Empire is evident in the top-ten list for 1980–2010. U.S. allies in the Middle East include Saudi Arabia, Egypt, Israel, and Turkey. Saudi Arabia and Egypt are new to the top-ten list, ranking third and fourth, respectively. This geostrategic shift is also registered in the value distribution of U.S. arms exports to the various recipients evident in Table 4.1. Iran is ranked second on the top-ten list of U.S. arms exports from 1950–1979 ($26.6b), its largest U.S. arms exports after the 1973 Arab Oil Embargo (to be exact, 1974–1978). After the revolution, U.S. arms exports to Iran decreased dramatically ($106 m, 1980–2010). Saudi Arabia displaces Iran as top recipient of U.S. arms exports in the post-revolutionary context ($23.4b, 1980–2010). At the same time, the U.S. provided logistical support to Iraq in its war

Table 4.1   Top-Ten U.S. Arms Exports Recipients Before/After the 1979 Iranian Revolution (standardized to 1990 U.S. dollars)

Rank	1950–1979	1980–2010
1	Germany ($36.4b)	Japan ($37.4b)
2	Iran ($26.7b)	South Korea ($27.6b)
3	Japan ($20.1b)	Saudi Arabia ($23.4b)
4	Italy ($16.3b)	Egypt ($21.6)
5	Canada ($15.0b)	Israel ($19.6b)
6	Israel ($14.7b)	Taiwan ($19.5b)
7	UK ($13.3b)	Turkey ($17.4b)
8	Turkey ($12.9b)	UK ($17.4b)
9	Taiwan ($12.3b)	Greece ($11.9b)
10	France ($11.3b)	Australia ($11.1b)

Source: Data derived from Stockholm International Peace Research Institute, *SIPRI* Trend Indicator Values (standardized to 1990 U.S. dollars), http://armstrade.sipri.org/armstrade/page/toplist.php

against Iran, 1980–1988. Most of this change in the rank structure of U.S. arms exports is due to large increases in U.S. arms exports from 1983–1988).

The change in geostrategic focus from Asia to the Middle East was a direct effect of the Iranian Revolution. Later, the U.S. would mobilize the Saudi military infrastructure to counter the 1990 Iraqi invasion of Kuwait. After the 1990–1991 Iraq war Saudi Arabia again enjoyed a second large increase in U.S. arms exports (1993, 1996–1999). The deployment of American troops to Saudi Arabia would become one of the most important motives Osama bin Laden, speaking on behalf of Al Qaeda, would cite for declaring a war against the U.S.

Table 4.2   U.S. Armed Conflicts by Region Before / After the 1979 Iranian Revolution

	Europe	Middle East	Asia	Americas	Total
1950–1979	0 (.0)	0 (.0)	6 (85.7%)	2 (40.0%)	8 (44.4%)
1980–2010	1 (100%)	5 (100%)	1 (14.3%)	3 (60.0%)	10 (55.6%)
Total	1 (100%)	5 (100%)	7 (100%)	5 (100%)	18 (100%)

Source: Data derived from Uppsala University Conflict Data Program / International Peace Research Institute, Oslo: Armed Conflict Dataset, www.ucdp.uu.se/database (for details and overview, see Harbom and Wallensteen 2009)

Table 4.2 presents further evidence of the consequences of the shifting geostrategic aims of Empire in the Middle East. The U.S. was involved in six armed conflicts in Asia in the years from 1950–1979. The Korean and Vietnamese wars were protracted and intense. In that time period, the U.S. was not involved in any comparable armed conflict in the Middle East. Since 1979 the number of armed conflicts in the Middle East has increased 100 percent, accounting for five of the ten U.S. armed conflicts.

The following is a brief chronology of moves made by the U.S. in its leadership role in Empire (data derived from Grossman, 2011). It describes the increasing number of U.S. overt and covert armed interventions in the Middle East and Adjacent Regions, including Africa and Central Asia:

- 1940s = 1 (Iran 1945–1946)
- 1950s = 4 (Iran 1953, Egypt 1956, Lebanon 1958, Iraq 1958)
- 1960s = 0
- 1970s = 2 (Oman 1970; Middle East 1973, response to Arab Oil embargo)
- 1980s = 7 (Iran 1980, Libya 1981, Lebanon 1982–84, Iran 1984, Afghanistan 1985, Libya 1986, Iran 1987–1988, Libya 1989)
- 1990s = 7 (Liberia 1990, Saudi Arabia 1990–1991, Iraq 1990, Kuwait 1991, Somalia 1992–1994, Liberia 1997, Iraq 1998, Afghanistan 1998)
- 2000s = 6 (Afghanistan 2001, Yemen 2001, Liberia 2003, Iraq 2003,

Somalia 2006, Syria 2008, Yemen 2009)
- 2010–2012 = 2 (Libya 2010, Yemen 2011, Somalia 2011)

"Terrorism" as Violent Resistance to Empire

As the data presented in Chapter 2 showed, the use of the discourse of 'terrorism' by U.S. Presidents to justify political actions to advance the cause of Empire has increased in frequency since World War II. It escalated dramatically in response to the Iranian Revolution. In fact it is invoked in over eighty percent of all Presidential *State of the Union Messages* after 1980 (see Chart 2.1). There were important precedents to the use of this rhetoric in response to resistance. It was deployed against the Viet Cong during the American-Vietnamese war (*State of the Union Messages*, Kennedy 1962, Johnson 1965–1967). The Carter regime went literally ballistic in response to the Iranian revolution (see *State of the Union Message*, 1980), linking "terrorism" to Iran, while at the same time, applauding the fierce resistance of the Afghan people to Soviet "military aggression" in Afghanistan (i.e., from a Soviet standpoint, "terrorism").

> At this time in Iran, *50 Americans are still held captive, innocent victims of terrorism and anarchy. Also at this moment, massive Soviet troops are attempting to subjugate the fiercely independent and deeply religious people of Afghanistan.* [emphasis added: bold = glorifier / bold + italic = vilifier] These two acts--one of international terrorism and one of military aggression--present a serious challenge to the United States of America and indeed to all the nations of the world. Together, we will meet these threats to peace (President Jimmy Carter, *State of the Union Message*, 1980).

As many commentators have observed, Osama bin Laden's leadership role in Al Qaeda emerges from the U.S. sponsored "terrorist" struggle against the Soviet occupation of Afghanistan. As Mann (2003: 169) observed, in spite of the religious rhetoric and violent means, Bin Laden was evidently a "rational man." "There is a simple *reason* why he attacked the US: American imperialism [and] as long as America seeks to control the Middle East, he and people like him will be its enemy." It was the U.S. "occupation" of Saudi Arabia and Iraq that provoked Osama bin Laden's declaration of *Jihad* against America. He clearly articulates his criticism in his statement, "Expel the Polytheists from the Arabian Peninsula":

> *So the people of Islam realized that they were the fundamental target of the hostility of the Judeo-Crusader alliance.* [emphasis added: bold = glorifier / bold + italic = vilifier] *All the false propaganda about the supposed rights of Islam was abandoned in the face of the attacks and massacres committed against Muslims everywhere, the latest and most serious of which—the greatest disaster to befall the Muslims since the death of the Prophet Muhammad—is*

the occupation of Saudi Arabia, which is the cornerstone of the Islamic world, place of revelation, source of the Prophetic mission, and home of the Noble Ka'ba where Muslims direct their prayers. Despite this, it was occupied by the armies of the Christians, the Americans, and their allies. (Bin Laden, 2005: 25).

The following is a partial list of direct attacks by Al Qaeda against U.S. targets in response to the occupation of Saudi Arabia (derived from White 2002: 294):

- 2–26–93: New York City: First World Trade Center bombing
- 11–13–95: Riyadh, Saudi Arabia: Car bombing of U.S. military personnel
- 6–25–96: Dhahran, Saudi Arabia: Truck bombing of U.S. Air Force base
- 8–7–98: Dar es Salaam, Tanzania and Nairobi, Kenya, U.S. embassy bombings
- 12–4–99: Port Angeles, Washington, foiled bombing plot targeting Los Angeles, California
- 10–12–00: Aden, Yemen, bombing of USS Cole
- 9–11–01: New York City, airliner attacks World Trade Center Towers, Washington, D.C., Pentagon, and, foiled airliner attack, Shanksville, Pennsylvania

The Bush regime declared a world war against terrorism within days of the 9/11 attacks. As described in Chapter 3 there are two ways that victimage ritual functions in the genesis and dynamics of wars (see Diagram 3.1). In domestic contexts they can be used to differentiate loyal patriots from traitors who threaten public morale. In foreign contexts victimage rituals can be used to differentiate allies and enemies and the willingness to engage in political violence. The friends vs. enemies system of discourse has been the focus of much research in the genesis and functioning of wars. And, no doubt, the campaign of ritual victimage against Islamic "terrorists" certainly is the linchpin of the war on terrorism. As we shall see later in this chapter, the rhetorical campaign against "terrorists" was protracted and nightmarish in its intensity.

Patriots vs. Traitors

Once the war had been officially declared by the Bush regime a victimage ritual was launched against internal "enemies"—the dynamism of "patriots" denouncing villainous "traitors." After the official discourse articulated by war proponents inside and outside the Bush regime, was locked into place, any public figure who questioned the assumptions behind this discourse or, more radically, articulated a counter-discourse of the meaning of 9/11 and the appropriate response and the subsequent war, were denounced and vilified by supporters within and outside the Bush administration, punished, and threatened with violence if they did not shut up. This campaign was particularly vicious in its attacks on any public figure who dared to contest the central foundations of war proponent's discourse: refusing to call the villains terrorists, contextualizing the perpetrators' motives and characteristics, or discussing the background of power relations involved.

Creating and sustaining public support for the war is a political problem. In part, this problem can be solved by orchestrating periodic campaigns of ritual victimage against public figures who dissent. The implication is that they are internal enemies and traitors. The official, as well as the self-appointed "guardians of the social order," must engage in "moral entrepreneurship" by staging highly publicized "witch hunts" to establish the norms and limits of patriotic and unpatriotic public discourse (see Becker's [1963] account of this phenomenon in political campaigns against deviants and criminals). They actively hunt down disloyal and treasonous "deviants" to "tar and feather." By this means they build their authority as virtuous patriots who stand tall and proud in support of the commander-in-chief and the troops. This practice functions to differentiate loyal patriots from the treasonous "dissenters" who aid and abet the "enemy." Anti-war activists can mount campaigns and elaborate a counter-war discourse that incites direct resistance to the war, one that effectively questions the necessity and legitimacy of the war (Blain 1989, 1994). One counter to this domestic threat is to categorize dissent in the context of war as treasonous. Actors, particularly those with access to the public stage in a society founded on the liberal principle of "freedom of speech," may interject threatening questions or challenging counter-discourses into the arena of public discourse.

The right to assemble and petition the government is enshrined in Article 1 of the *Bill of Rights of the U.S. Constitution*. "Congress shall make no law respecting an establishment of religion, or prohibiting the free exercise thereof; or abridging the freedom of speech, or of the press; or the right of the people peaceably to assemble, and to petition the government for a redress of grievances." In the past this right has been constrained by the emergency constituted by a formal declaration of war by the Congress. In the age of Empire, this problem has been complicated by the leadership role played by the U.S. in "policing" world security threats. The presence of nuclear weapons has augmented a more or less permanent "state of exception" and the development of a national-security state cloaked in secrecy (Wills 2010, Danner 2011b). In the absence of a formal declaration of war in the context of continuous military deployments around the world, the U.S. government cannot legally control public speech. This task is frequently delegated to the public and private agencies for socializing public opinion, particularly the education institutions and the news media.

Noam Chomsky (2011), who speaks with great personal knowledge of this phenomenon, has described the dynamics of this process in precise detail. In a statement Chomsky published in a Swedish publication on the U.S. response to the 9/11 attacks, he asked the question why it is morally acceptable for the U.S. and its allies to use "terrorism" in pursuit of their political goals. He argues that our moral reaction to 9/11 should have met "the most elementary moral standards: specifically, if an action is right for us, it is right for others; and if wrong for others, it is wrong for us." And why, Chomsky asks, does it irritate and provoke such intense moral indignation when dissenters point this out? He cites a few uncontroversial cases of the use of "terrorism": "forty years have passed since President Kennedy ordered that 'the terrors of the earth' must be visited upon Cuba until their leadership is eliminated…Twenty years have passed since President Reagan launched a terrorist war against Nicaragua…leading to condemnation of the U.S. for international terrorism by the World Court and the UN Security Council (in a resolution the U.S. vetoed)… those who accept elementary moral standards have some work to do to show that the U.S. and Britain were justified in bombing Afghans in order to compel them to turn over people who the U.S. suspected of criminal atrocities…Similar questions arise with regard to the 'Bush doctrine' of 'preemptive strikes' against suspected threats" (Chomsky 2011: 150–152).

Chomsky's statement goes on to explain why it is so difficult to discuss this issue. He invokes the principle of good versus evil (also, as I have argued here, the key structuring device in the melodramatic rhetoric of victimage ritual, a political perversion of a religious form of thought), and, therefore, makes manifest the political unconscious of contemporary Empire:

> There is, of course, an easy counter to such simple arguments: **WE are good**, and ***THEY are evil***. [emphasis added: bold = glorifier / bold + italic = vilifier] That useful principle trumps virtually any argument. Analysis of commentary and much of scholarship reveals that its roots commonly lie in that crucial principle, which is not argued but asserted. Occasionally, but rarely, some irritating creatures attempt to confront the core principle with the record of recent and contemporary history. We learn more about prevailing cultural norms by observing the reaction, and the interesting array of barriers erected to deter any lapse into this heresy. (Chomsky 2011)

A more precise hypothesis can be tested by examining a series of examples of public figures attacked as unpatriotic and treasonous for breaching the norms of the official Bush regime "war on terrorism" discourse. These figures challenged the underlying assumptions behind the rhetoric of the war on terror and violated the normative discourse that propelled public and military support for the war. An analysis of the most highly publicized cases makes manifest the cultural code of war as an instrument of Empire (Smith 1991). This "code of conduct" is composed of a system of moral norms that direct more or less consciously the discourse, what speakers/writers can publically write/say that correspond exactly to the melodramatic and maximalist features of the rhetoric of victimage ritual: 1) thou *shalt* not doubt (or minimize) the absolute villainy of the enemy, 2) thou *shalt* not question (or minimize) the absolute innocence and virtue of the victims used to vilify the enemy, 3) thou *shalt* not doubt (or minimize) the absolute heroism of the hero, 4) insiders [especially prominent American citizens or public figures] must not attack the "commander-in-chief" in times of war, particularly in statements to publics outside of the nation, and 5) thou *shalt* not doubt (minimize) that there is one absolutely truth about these assumptions.

The immediate effect of the "shock and awe" of the 9/11 attack was a kind of stunned silence and self-imposed censorship of many, including the most outspoken "shock-jocks" and political comics (McKinley 2001). This silence gave the Bush regime the opening to declare a global war on terror and a new, more aggressive doctrine of military interventionism. When voices were raised against the rush to war, they were silenced. The targets of the victimage ritual included one major news agency, several public intellectuals, religious leaders, academics, political pundits, comics and entertainers. In total, thirty-four cases were examined. The most frequent cases involved celebrities, especially musicians (36%), and academics, particularly university professors (32%). These rhetorical assaults started after the 9/11 attacks and have continued through to the fall 2011, and the Ten Year 9/11 Memorial event.

The *first* norm of war discourse is the maximalist principle of absolute villainy. The "evil" or "pathology" that motivates the enemies who perpetrated the 9/11 action cannot be doubted. Their motives must originate in their evil character, pathological desire for power, and fanatical devotion to the cause. There can be no "sympathy for the devil" or respect for the opponent as a "warrior." The most striking incidence of this norm violation involved the German composer Karlheinz Stockhausen who called the 9/11 attacks "the greatest work of art that is possible in the whole cosmos" and stated that 'You have people who are so concentrated on one performance [presumably Bin Laden and Mohammed Atta], and then 5,000 people are dispatched into eternity, in a single moment." The composer goes on to say, "I couldn't do that. In comparison with that, we're nothing as composers" (quotes from Tommasini 2001).

The editors at the Reuters news agency had a well-established policy of "objective neutrality" on terrorists. It had a rule that its journalists NOT describe actors as "terrorists." This policy violates the maximalist norm of the absolute villainy of the enemy. The editor categorized the use of "terrorist" as not "neutral" or "objective," and too "emotional." As a matter of policy, journalists were instructed by an editor to remain neutral and not take sides in the conflict. The editor was attacked for invoking the principle of "relativism" embodied in the statement that "One man's terrorist is another man's freedom fighter" (see "Reuters explanation," 2001; also "Media spin," 2001).

Susan Sontag, a prominent public intellectual and novelist, was denounced for questioning the assumptions being made about the power relations involved in the attack and the villainy of the attackers. She made statements in the *New Yorker Magazine* (9/19/2001) criticizing the "self-righteous drivel and outright deceptions" broadcast on the airways, and challenging the statement that the country had witnessed a "cowardly" assault on "civilization" ("Media Spin Revolves Around the Word 'Terrorist'," Bohlen 2001). Rather, Sontag argued, it had been an attack on "the world's self-proclaimed superpower, undertaken as a consequence of American alliances and actions." Sontag was the subject of a widely circulated attack by the syndicated columnist, Charles Krauthammer, arguably the most influential neoconservative political pundit in America:

> What Sontag is implying but does not have the courage to say, is that because of these 'alliances and actions,' such as the bombing of Iraq, we had it coming... This is no time for obfuscation. Or for agonized relativism. Or, obscenely, for blaming America first. (The habit dies hard.) This is a time for clarity. At a time like this, those who search for shades of evil, for root causes, for extenuations are, to borrow from Lance Morrow, "too philosophical for decent company" (Krauthammer 2001).

Conservative religious leaders such as Jerry Falwell and Pat Robertson were publically chastised for diluting the absolute "responsibility" and villainy of the 9/11 terrorists. Falwell was attacked for stating on his 700 Club TV program "God gave the U.S. 'What we deserve' " (Harris 2001). He argued (and was supported by Robertson) that various "liberal" groups, including "feminists," "civil liberties groups," and "homosexuals" were partially responsible for the attacks. The attacks were a form of divine retribution.

Tony Bennett (famous American singer and World War II veteran) was subjected to a victimage ritual on the occasion of the Tenth anniversary of the 9/11. He was doing an interview with Howard Stern, a well-known American "Shock Jock" and talk-show host. Stern asked Bennett what his views were about the 9/11 attacks. He was castigated for making the following statement, "they flew the plane in, but we caused it. Because we were bombing them and they told us to stop." "But who are the terrorists? Are we the terrorists or are they the terrorists? Two wrongs don't make a right." He observed that we had been trying to kill Bin Laden prior to 9/11, providing some additional context to the attack. In spite of the 10 years of debate and discussion on the war on terrorism, the response was instantaneous and fierce. Bennett, like many of his predecessors, was forced to seriously qualify his statement and issue a public apology (quotes from Itzkoff 2011).

A *second* norm requires that speakers/writers never utter anything that violates the sacrosanct status of the victims as "innocent" victims. The victims must be innocent and pure of any taint of guilt to function as an effective vilifier. If they can be indicted as complicit with Empire, then their use as devices to vilify opponents loses some of its moral force. Attacking the absolute innocence of the victim would undermine the maximalist principle of the absolute villainy of the enemy.

One highly publicized case of a challenge to the "innocence" of the victim involved Professor Ward Churchill, a "Native American" as well as a Professor and Chair of the Ethnic Studies Department at the University of Colorado, Boulder. Churchill was dismissed from his academic position at the university in 2007 for "academic misconduct" as a result of problems with his scholarly writings on the persecution of "American Indians." Churchill was attacked for publishing an article in 2001, titled "Some People Push Back: On the Justice of Roosting Chickens." In this article Churchill had challenged the assumption at the basis of the declaration of the war on terrorism, by asserting that the victims of the 9/11 attacks "were not innocent victims." He went further by referring to the victims at the World Trade Center and Pentagon as "little Eichmanns" (quotes from Frosch 2009). Churchill knowingly violates the fundamental norm of a war discourse: the innocence of the victims employed to vilify the villains. If the victims are guilty of complicity in "American Conquest and Carnage," then the validity of the innocent victims employed to establish the legitimacy of the pro-war discourse is undermined. As Churchill added, "If you make a practice of killing other people's babies for personal gain, they will eventually give you a taste of the same thing" (Frosch 2009).

The *third* norm in the pro-war code of conduct is that the heroism of the warriors fighting the villain should not be questioned. Their "bravery" and "courage" cannot be challenged. This norm was manifested in the response to Susan Sontag's statements in the *New Yorker Magazine*. As an example of the lack of precise understanding in the discourse surrounding the 9/11 attacks, Sontag asserted...

> ***And if the word 'cowardly' is to be used, it might be more aptly applied to those who kill from beyond the range of retaliation, high in the sky,*** than to **those willing to die themselves in order to kill others**. [emphasis added: bold = glorifier / bold + italic = vilifier] In the matter of courage (a morally neutral virtue): whatever may be said of the perpetrators of Tuesday's slaughter, they were not cowards (Bohlen, 2001).

Her statement did not ignite a firestorm like that produced by similar statements made by Bill Maher, a political comic and talk-show host of "Politically Incorrect," a late night talk-show. Maher was in a discussion about the attacks with a "conservative" commentator, Dinesh D'Souza. D'Souza was involved in a public quarrel with the Bush Whitehouse about the President's characterization of the attacks [and attackers] as "cowardly" and made the following statement to Maher, which violates the maximalist norm of not questioning the absolute villainy of the enemy:

> Look at what they did. You have a whole bunch of guys who were willing to give their life; none of them backed out. All of them slammed themselves into pieces of concrete. **These are warriors**. [emphasis added: bold = glorifier / bold + italic = vilifier] (Bohlen 2001)

Maher retorted to D'Souza along the same lines as Sontag had:

> We have been the cowards, lobbing cruise missiles from 2,000 miles way. ***That's cowardly***. **Staying in the airplane when it hits the building, say what you want about it, it's not cowardly.** [emphasis added: bold = glorifier / bold + italic = vilifier] (Bohlen 2001)

Maher's retort (as did Sontag's) contained an explicit attack on the absolute courage and bravery of the American military. As a consequence of pressures by advertisers and others including ABC affiliates and the Whitehouse Press secretary, Maher's popular show, "Politically Incorrect," was canceled by the American Broadcasting Company. This would set the pattern of absolute adherence to the normative prescription that everyone (including peace activists) should fall into line and always preface any statement about that the war with an explicit declaration that they "support the troops."

A *fourth* norm concerns what can be publically stated about the President in his role as "commander-in-chief" in times of war. The leader's authority cannot be doubted. This norm was clearly manifested in the so-called "conservative" and "patriotic" response to the "Dixie Chicks," a country-western oriented band (John 2003). The episode occurred at a London concert, March 10, 2003, on the eve of the Iraq war. Natalie Maines told the audience, "Just so you know, we're ashamed the president of the United States is from Texas" (quotes from John 2003). Maines' action created an opportunity for moral entrepreneurship, provoking a well-orchestrated victimage ritual by so-called pro-war, patriotic, and loyal "conservatives" against the band. The fact that the statement was made "outside" the U.S. to an "outsider" audience (although, the British were "friends" and "allies" in the prosecution of the wars in Iraq and Afghanistan) compounds the moral outrage. It was a sign to the "world" that not all Americans were on board with the war—which, some argued at the time, encourages the enemy to prosecute the war, which undermines national unity and morale in support of the war, and reveals the existence of "insider" divisions the 'enemy' might exploit. The speaker/writer who violates this norm is vilified as, at the very least, "disloyal" and "unpatriotic," and at the very worse, as a "traitor" who is aiding and abetting the enemy.

The Dixie Chicks were subjected to a highly publicized victimage ritual including radio boycotts, CD burnings, and explicit "death threats." Questioning the patriotism of Hollywood "liberals" has a history that goes back to Jane Fonda's anti-Viet Nam war activism. Over the years, the hostility to "liberals" in the entertainment industry has inspired the creation of websites with titles like, Boycott-Hollywood.us and Famousidiot.com. Maines, like many others, issued an apology for uttering something that challenges the dominant discourse on the meaning of the "war on terrorism." At the time, many journalists added to the fire by covering the story as a "cautionary tale," a warning that "celebrities" should not use their access to the "public stage" and "influence" to criticize the war in general and the "commander-in-chief" in particular.

A *fifth* and final norm manifested in these controversies is the absolute sovereignty of a politics of truth. One final episode can be employed to sum up the larger philosophical and social scientific problem of the rhetoric of victimage ritual and the politics of truth in times of war. Edward Rothstein provoked a controversy by launching a frontal attack in a *New York Times* article on the idea of relativism espoused by postmodernists and some social scientists. One of the major targets in that attack was Professor Stanley Fish, a well-known exponent of postmodernism in academic circles. Rothstein's initial salvo was published in the *New York Times*, September 22, 2001, where he posed the question of the truth about the significance of the 9/11 attacks as a political and a philosophical problem for postmodernists such as Fish. Postmodernists like Fish were attempting to undermine the moral fiber of the American people in a time of political crisis. Fish responded to this criticism by attacking Rothstein and his ilk in a paper presented to an academic conference held at the University of Illinois the following summer, 2002. Fish charged that Rothstein did not know what he was talking about with regard to postmodernism and its sociological understanding of the history of various "truths."

Rothstein, in turn, responded with a second article published in the *New York Times* (July 13, 2002) titled in full-tilt irony, "Connections; Moral Relativity is a Hot Topic: True. Absolutely." In this article he attacked "Professors of literature, history, and sociology" like Fish for advocating the postmodern view that there are no absolute and universal standards for judging what is true or not, including the discourse of the war on terrorism. The issue as Rothstein posed it, was the discourse of "postcolonialism, which treats Western Imperialism as the Original Sin of modern history." This discourse was viewed as threatening the Rothstein truth that this discourse does not work with enemies of the type targeted in the war on terrorism, "Avatars of absolutism—terrorist Islamic fundamentalists— [who] are challenging the liberal democratic societies of the West, objecting to their power, their values, their differing creeds, their modern (and postmodern) perspectives" (quotes from Rothstein 2002).

Friends vs. Enemies

The successful staging of a victimage ritual like the war on terrorism requires a second discourse that clearly differentiates enemies from allies as well as patriots from traitors. The Clinton regime initiated the campaign against Osama bin Laden and his terrorist network. Clinton made reference to "terrorism" in all eight *State of the Union Message* (1993–2000), including one explicit reference to the threat posed by "Osama bin Laden's network of terror" (1999). The public discourse categorizing Bin Laden as a terrorist predates the 9/11 attack. Chart 4.1 (below) graphs the number of *New York Times* articles containing Osama bin Laden's name by year. The regime's campaign to kill Bin Laden first appears in print in September 1998, one month after the August cruise missile attacks. Over ninety percent of these articles link Bin Laden to international terrorism.

Al Qaeda's September 11, 2001 attacks symbolize the politics of resistance to a liberal form of Empire (World Trade Center, Whitehouse, Pentagon). In retaliation the Bush regime launched a reign of rhetorical terror to complement the Clinton military campaign against Al Qaeda. The data presented in Chart 4.2 (below) indicates that the number of references to terror in Weekly Whitehouse speeches fluctuated wildly each month/year period after 9/11. The number of

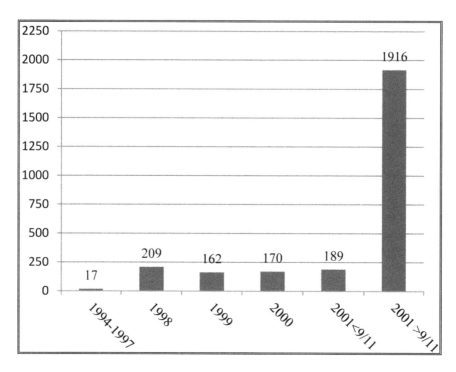

Chart 4.1   Number of *New York Times* Articles referencing Osama bin Laden, Before / After 9/11

Source: Data derived from *New York Times* archive, Times Topic, Osama bin Laden

terror speeches and references to terror per unit time are treated as indices of the dramatic intensity of the on-going victimage rituals. The logic goes this way. The higher the frequency of speeches and use of vilifying terms deployed in a time period then the more intense the victimage ritual and the rhetorically generated social need to scapegoat the enemy. As argued in great detail in previous chapters, the "terrorist" category is a vilifier. By turning up the frequency of terror speeches and "terrorist" categorizations, politicians can increase the sense of emergency and alarm, increase the anger and vengeful desires directed toward the category vilified, and incite violent attacks to destroy their enemies (e.g., Al Qaeda, Taliban, Saddam Hussein, etc.).

To test these propositions 557 Weekly Whitehouse Speeches were analyzed with a text-processing program to track and monitor the number of terror speeches delivered and word frequencies as the war unfolded. These speeches are brief, topically focused, and regular statements of a Presidential Administration's current issue agenda. They are ideal for detecting shifts in discursive tactics and strategic priorities over time. A speech is released each Saturday in an attempt to influence

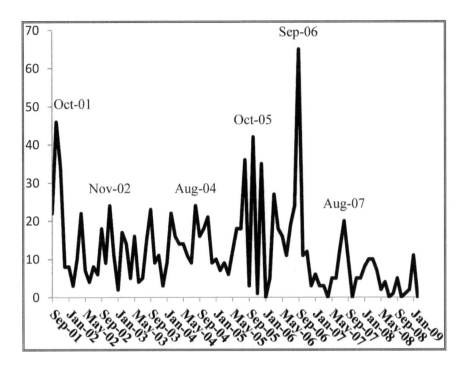

Chart 4.2 **Frequency of Terror Terms by Month / Year period in the Bush Regime's Weekly Whitehouse Speeches, 2001–2009**

Sum of terror terms in speeches in each month/year period.

Source: Data derived from http://whitehouse.gov.

the following week's news cycle. The speeches included in this analysis date from the start of the Bush regime (January 2001) through the third year of the Obama regime and the tenth-year anniversary of the 9/11 attacks (September 2011).[3]

Two statistics are treated as indicators of the intensity of victimage ritual, the frequency of speeches in a particular time period and the number of references to terrorism per speech. The more frequent the terror speeches or references to terror per speech in a specific time period, then the greater the intensity of victimage

---

3 Each Weekly Whitehouse speech was downloaded from http://Whitehouse.gov into a Word file. WordCruncher 6.0 (2004), a text indexing and rapid retrieval program, was employed to process and analyze the texts. WordCruncher computes descriptive statistics for every unique term in the text file. Each speech was placed in chronological order, and coded for title, date, and political context. Once indexed, the analyst can retrieve text containing specific terms or combinations of terms employing Boolean logics (e.g., "terror AND security", or "terror OR freedom"; or [terror AND (security AND freedom]).

ritual. The results show that the Bush regime (2001–2009) engaged in frequent and intensive rhetorical attacks on "terrorists." After the 9/11 attacks, fifty-six percent of the 417 weekly speeches contained at least one reference to terror. This is in striking contrast to the one speech the Bush regime deployed on terrorism in the thirty-three Weekly Speeches before 9/11 and the nine terror speeches delivered by the Obama regime in three years. These results are consistent with the rhetorical pattern in annual *State of the Union Messages*, 2002–2011. Terrorism is discussed in every *Message* after 2002. The intensity of the concern is indexed by the frequency of terror terms in each Message. After 2001, the average frequency of references to terror by the Bush regime was twenty-four times per speech. Again, in striking contrast, the Obama regime's speeches on average made only two references to terrorism per speech.

If the number of terror speeches and references to terror per unit time are treated as indicators of the dramatic intensity of the on-going rhetorical war, then what caused that variation? One of the central tenets of a genealogical analysis of discourse is that rhetoric is a tactical component of a strategy. Changes in rhetorical tactics are responses to actor's changing calculations of political opportunities. The 9/11 attacks presented the Bush regime with a range of domestic and global geo-political opportunities. The 9/11 attacks provided the U.S. power elite with a new mission statement for Empire that would function to fill in the discursive black-hole created by the historic end to the Cold-War against communism. A global war against terrorism provided a new rationale for Empire. The Bush regime responded to 9/11 with a sustained and unrelenting campaign of rhetorical terrorism. As the war on terrorism gathered momentum, the political context and structure of opportunities also shifted. These shifts were determined by geopolitics, particularly the shift of focus from the European to Near East and South Asian theaters, and the post-9/11 decisions to invade Afghanistan and Iraq, and domestically by the cycle of U.S. electoral politics.

Twelve political contexts were differentiated (see Table 4.3). The intensity scores for the first months of the Bush presidency, prior to the 9/11 attacks, is extremely low (1/33 or 3% of speeches made reference to terrorists, at an average rate of .03/speech). Terrorism is mentioned once in one speech in thirty-three Weekly Speeches before the 9/11 attacks. This speech is devoted to "National Security" and argues for a ballistic missile defense system to defend the U.S. against "high tech terrorists" ("National Security," February 10, 2001; also mentioned almost verbatim in the 2001 *State of the Union Message*). The context after the 9/11 attacks is defined as the "Afghan War / Homeland Security." Sixty-six percent of the Weekly Speeches during this time reference terror at least once. The percentages in context are highest during the Afghan war (66%), Iraq war debate (67%), Iraq invasion (63%), 2004 Presidential Election (64%), and 2006 Congressional election (62%) On average, each of these speeches makes more than three references to terror. In the last years of the Bush regime, after the 2006 congressional elections produced an anti-Iraq war democrat controlled congress and a "new" U.S. counterinsurgency campaign was implemented in

Table 4.3   Indicators of Victimage Ritual Intensity, 2001–2011

Context (Number Speeches)	Intensity		Correlation of Terms		
	Percent Speeches[#]	Average Terms[##]	Terror / Security	Terror / Freedom	Security / Freedom
Bush Regime Pre- 9/11/2001 (33)	3	0	.28	-.11	-.24
Afghan War 9/11/2001–2002 (53)	66	3	.30*	.08	-.05
Iraq Debate 2002–2003 (27)	63	3	.67**	.15	.10
Iraq War 2003 (21)	67	2	.42	.57**	.52*
Iraqi Insurgency 2003–2004 (21)	48	3	.65**	.67**	.70**
U.S. Election 2004 (42)	64	4	.68**	.40**	.60**
Regime Change 2004–2006 (66)	53	3	.14	.59**	.06
U.S. Election 2006 (39)	62	5	.45**	.58**	.40*
Anti-War Congress 2006–2007 (33)	52	1	.47**	.23	.17
Iraq Surge 2007–2009 (82)	43	1	.72**	.03	.11
Obama Regime 2009 (48)	6	0	.30*	.05	-.09
Afghan Surge 2010–2011 (88)	7	0	26*	.09	.14

*Perc*ent speeches in context with at least one reference to terror

*Mea*n and standard deviation (S.D.) based on number of references to terror per speech

* *Biva*riate correlation coefficients, Spearman's rho (two-tailed), * p < .05, ** p < .01

Source: Data derived from www.Whitehouse.org

response to the critique of the Iraq war (2007–2009), both intensity scores dropped dramatically.

Another indicator of the intensity of the victimage ritual is the strength of the correlation of key liberal and terror terms. The coefficients of correlation between terror, security, and freedom invoked in the war of words are reported in Table 4.3. The coefficients range from -1 through 0 to +1. Zero indicates no association. The increase and decrease in these coefficients index the degree of concern regarding the terrorist threat to a "liberal" form of security and / or freedom. The asterisks flag the likelihood that the association is not due to chance. The higher the positive correlation coefficient, the stronger the terrorist threat to security and freedom. The fluctuations in these correlations can be compared across contexts.

The highest coefficients for the terror / security correlations occur in the contexts of the 2003 Iraq war debate, 2004 Iraqi insurgency against the U.S. occupation (.65), and the 2004 Presidential election (.67). The correlations involving freedom are strongest after the invasion of Iraq and ensuing insurgency against occupation. The contexts within which the terror / security / freedom terms are highly correlated are indicated in gray shade. The use of all three terms in individual speeches escalates during the Iraq war. Saddam's tyranny or the terrorist insurgency against the U.S. occupation threatens freedom. The precise function of the war against terrorism is directly implicated. The insurgency threatens the security and freedom of the Iraqi people as well as Empire.

There is a structural pattern to the discourses of the war on terror. This pattern is evident in the pattern of correlation coefficients during the years of the Bush regime. The terror / security link dominates the discourse from 9/11 through the Iraq war debate from September of 2002 until the U.S. invasion of Iraq in March of 2003. Once the decision to go to war had been made and the U.S. and allies invaded Iraq the terror / security couplet is linked to regime change, the democratization of Iraq, and the project to make the Iraqi people "free." Table 4.3 marks this shift. The correlations are strong and positive. After the Iraq insurgency throws a wrench into the machinery of extending Empire to Iraq and the 2006 election resulted in an explicitly anti-Iraq war congress, the Bush regime dropped the liberation discourse.

The rhetoric in the initial phase of the war focused primarily on a rather abstract category of "terrorists" as a singular threat to U.S. national and "homeland" security. The following excerpt invokes the memory of 9/11 and links it directly to the threat terrorism poses to the "Homeland":

> **Next week, our nation will pause to honor and remember the lives lost on September the 11th.** [emphasis added: bold = glorifier / bold + italic = vilifier] We must also remember a central lesson of the tragedy: our homeland is vulnerable to attack, and we must do everything in our power to protect it.
>
> We protect our country by relentlessly pursuing terrorists across the Earth; assessing and anticipating our vulnerabilities, and acting quickly to address

those vulnerabilities and prevent attacks. America needs a single department of government dedicated to the task of protecting our people....

One essential tool this new department needs is the flexibility to respond to terrorist threats that can arise or change overnight. The Department of Homeland Security must be able to move people and resources quickly, without being forced to comply with a thick book of bureaucratic rules ("Afghan War," September 7, 2002).

There is no reference to the need to engage in preemptive strikes or democratization in dealing with "regimes" that support terrorists. It is all about the "security" of the American people. The urgent need to suspend a "thick book of bureaucratic rules" that frustrates "flexibility" would play a prominent role in the Bush and Obama regime's violations of international laws and domestic constitutional freedoms (Cole 2004, 2009).

The discourse of "terrorism" as threat to "security" continued to dominate Bush regime discourse in the lead up to the Iraq war. The first week of the Iraq war in March of 2003 the discourse makes an explicit link between the war against terrorism and the "campaign against the regime of Saddam Hussein" and liberation of the Iraqi people:

American and coalition forces have begun a concerted campaign against the regime of Saddam Hussein. In this war, our coalition is broad, more than 40 countries from across the globe. Our cause is just, the security of the nations we serve and the peace of the world. And **our mission is clear, to disarm Iraq of weapons of mass destruction, to end Saddam Hussein's support for terrorism, and to free the Iraqi people** [emphasis added: bold = glorifier / bold + italic = vilifier] ("Iraq War," March 22, 2003)

By the fall of 2003 the strategic goal of "Operation Iraqi Freedom" was rearticulated as "regime change":

We have a strategy in Iraq and a mission. **We will fight and defeat the terrorists there, so we don't have to face them in America. And we will help transform Iraq into an example of progress and democracy and freedom that can inspire change and hope throughout the Middle East.** [emphasis added: bold = glorifier / bold + italic = vilifier] ("911 and the War on Terrorism," September 13, 2003)

Shifting Cast of Villains

The cycle of Empire →Resistance →Victimage Ritual produces a shifting cast of melodramatic characters. The actors cast into the role of villains change as the specific moves made in the power game change and as the agents and agencies of Empire make a geostrategic move—in this case, the U.S power elite playing its leading role in Empire. Each move in the power game incites resistance and a more or less organized form of insurgency emerges. The agents and agencies of resistance, in turn, are categorized as enemies and / or terrorists and terrorist organizations. The agents of Empire respond to resistance with counterinsurgency or counterterrorism.

Two war-zones (Afghanistan and Iraq) are differentiated in Tables 4.4 and 4.5 to differentiate the geopolitical contexts and corresponding subjects of victimage ritual. The distribution of vilifiers (Table 4.4) and glorifiers (Table 4.5) follow the cyclical pattern. The leaders of Empire vilify the enemy to move the public and the troops to launch a war → Empire intervenes in a new geopolitical space → Empire glorifies the heroes implementing the policy of liberation and sacralizes the sacrifice of life to sustain the struggle to realize a victory. As observed above, the discourse of the enemy shifted as the political and geostrategic context of the war changed. The analysis that follows describes the system of vilifiers and glorifiers at each stage of this game: Afghanistan (2001–2002), Iraq (2003–2008), and full-circle, back to Afghanistan (2009–2011).

The Bush regime responded to the spectacular 9/11 attacks by declaring a global war against terrorism (Department of Defense [DOD] acronym = GWOT) and issue an ultimatum to the Taliban regime ruling Afghanistan—turn over Bin Laden and the other terrorists right now or else. The threat was made on September 20, 2011; the U.S. and British forces launched an invasion on October 7, 2001. The DOD called it "Operation Enduring Freedom."

> In recent days, many members of **our military** have left their homes and families and begun moving into a place for missions to come. Thousands of Reservists have been called to active duty. Soldiers, sailors, airmen, Marines and Coast Guardsmen are being deployed to points around the globe, **ready to answer when their country calls**. Our military families have accepted many hardships, and our nation is grateful for **their willing service** [emphasis added: bold = glorifier / bold + italic = vilifier].

> The men and women of **the Armed Forces are united in their dedication to freedom and they will make us proud in the struggle against *terrorism.***

> International cooperation is gaining momentum. .Canada and Japan…countries, from Russia to Indonesia…**America is grateful** to the nations that have cut off diplomatic ties with the ***Taliban regime in Afghanistan, which is sheltering terrorists***.

> **The United States respects the people of Afghanistan and we are their largest provider of humanitarian aid.** But we condemn the Taliban, and welcome the

Table 4.4 **Correlation of Vilifiers in "Weekly Whitehouse" Speeches, 9/11/2001 – 9/11/2011**

Context (Number Speeches)	War zone	Enemy#	Terror	Extreme	Killer	Tyrant	WMD
				Vilifiers			
Afghan War 9/11/2001–2002 (53)	Afgh.	Al, Ta	.34*	.31*	.08	-	-
	Iraq	-	-	-	-	-	-
Iraq Debate 2002–2003 (27)	Afgh.	-	.56**	-	.26	.24	.04
	Iraq	Sd	.52**	-	.27	.86**	.93**
Iraq War 2003 (21)	Afgh.	-	.61**	-	.47*	.14	.05
	Iraq	Sd	.47	-	.49*	.75**	.65**
Iraqi Insurgency 2003–2004 (21)	Afgh.	Al, Ta	.66**	-	.61**	-.25	.51*
	Iraq	Sd	.77**	-	.41	.60**	.26
U.S. Election 2004 (42)	Afgh.	Ob	.41**	-	.13	.07	.37*
	Iraq	Sd, Za	.42**	-	.61**	.47**	.19
Regime Change 2004–2006 (66)	Afgh.	Ta, Ob	.40	-.08	.23	.48**	.003
	Iraq	Za, Sd	.63**	.23	.54**	.49**	.11
U.S. Election 2006 (39)	Afgh.	Ta	.37*	.16	.19	.19	-.02
	Iraq	Za, Al	.66**	.24	.54**	.50**	.10
Antiwar Congress 2006–2007 (33)	Afgh.	-	.27	.20	.09	-	-.08
	Iraq	Al	.50**	.73**	.32	-	-.15
Iraq Surge 2007–2009 (82)	Afgh.	Ta	.29**	.28**	.31**	.15	.15
	Iraq	Al, Sd	.50**	.66**	.56**	.18	.08
Obama Regime 2009 (48)	Afgh.	Al	.25	-.06	-.06	-.04	.16
	Iraq	-	-.07	-.05	-.05	-.04	-.09
Afghan Surge 2010–2011 (88)	Afgh.	Al	.43**	-.04	-.10	-.06	.32**
	Iraq	-	.35**	.31**	.07	.05	-.06

*Abbr*eviations: Al Qaeda (Al); Taliban (Ta); Osama bin Laden (Ob); Saddam (Sd); Abu Musab al-Zarqawi (Za)

* *Biva*riate correlation coefficients; Spearman's rho (two-tailed): * p < .05, ** p < .01

Source: Data derived from www.Whitehouse.org

support of other nations in isolating that regime. ("Progress Made in War on Terror," Weekly Whitehouse Speech, September 29, 2001)

These early speeches set the system of differentiation that structures the ritual rhetoric of the war:

- Enemies = "Taliban," "nations that sponsor terrorists;" "oppress their women," "terrorize their citizens," "prefer to attack the helpless" [but NOT the "Arab world," but NOT "Islam," but NOT "people or citizens in nations that sponsor terrorists"];
- Heroes = "our military," "men and women of the Armed Forces," "humanitarian," "dedicated to freedom";
- Allies = "the civilized world," "nations that stand with us against the terrorists

U.S. forces (with the U.K. and coalition forces) launched the Afghanistan War with military attacks against the Taliban regime on October 7th, 2001. Notably, Weekly Whitehouse speeches that fall did not invoke Osama bin Laden or Al Qaeda by name (in fact, Bin Laden's name does not show up in any of these speeches until February of 2004). The speeches on the war that fall focused exclusively on "terrorists" and the "Taliban." The Bush regime had the sublime spectacle of the 9/11 attacks at their backs. In the aftershock of this unprecedented spectacle, they could focus on other objectives than capturing or killing Osama bin Laden. The October 6 speech reiterates the September 20 ultimatum to the Taliban regime—"time is running out." As all of these speeches imply, the Taliban are directly associated with the guilt of the 9/11 "terrorists." This speech works hard to precisely differentiate the villains [terrorists] from the heroes [the Americans and their allies]. The paradigmatic contrasts are indicated in brackets:

> THE PRESIDENT: Good morning. Today I want to update Americans on our global campaign against terror. The United States is presenting a clear choice to every nation: **Stand with the civilized world,** *or stand with the terrorists* [emphasis added: bold = glorifier / bold + italic = vilifier]. And for those nations that stand with the terrorists, there will be a heavy price.
>
> *America is determined to oppose the state sponsors of terror*. Yet we are equally determined to respect and help the men and women those regimes oppress. [paradigm contrast] **Our enemy is not the Arab world**. Many friendly Arab governments are themselves, the targets of extremist terror. **Our enemy is not Islam**, a good and peace-loving faith that brings direction and comfort to over one billion people, including millions of Americans. And **our enemy is not the people of any nation**, even when their leaders harbor terrorists. *Our enemy is the terrorists themselves, and the regimes that shelter and sustain them*.

Afghanistan is a case in point. *Its Taliban regime has made that nation into a sanctuary and training ground for international terrorists—terrorists who have killed innocent citizens of many nations, including our own. The Taliban promotes terror abroad, and practices terror against its people, oppressing women and persecuting all who dissent.*

The Taliban has been given the opportunity to surrender all the terrorists in Afghanistan and to close down their camps and operations. Full warning has been given, and time is running out. ("Humanitarian Aid to Afghanistan," Weekly Whitehouse Speech, October 6, 2001)

This speech employs a series of paradigmatic contrasts (i.e., binary oppositions) to precisely define the objectives of Empire in the emerging conflict—the terrorists are NOT the same or synonymous with "the Arab world," or "Islam...a good and peace-loving religion," or the "people" who happen to be in regimes that harbor or sponsor "terrorists" (differentiating allies from enemies). The "Taliban" and the "terrorists" are the true enemies. They kill the innocent, including their own people. They "oppress women" and persecute "dissenters."

The signifiers of villainy and glory are driven home with the rhetorical force of violence in an October 13, 2001 speech:

This week, we opened some important new fronts in the war on terror. We're taking the war to the enemy and we are strengthening our defenses here at home...

On Sunday, American and British forces launched strikes at terrorist camps and Taliban military targets in Afghanistan. **Our men and women in uniform are performing as they always do, with skill and courage** [emphasis added: bold = glorifier / bold + italic = vilifier]. And they have achieved the goals of the first phase of our campaign...

[paradigmatic contrast]...***Our enemy prefers to attack the helpless.*** He hides from our soldiers. But we're making a determined effort to take away his hiding places. The best defense against terrorism is a strong offensive against terrorists. That work continues.

At the same time, we are taking further action to strengthen our protections against terrorism here at home ("New Fronts in War," Weekly Whitehouse Speech, October 13, 2001).

On November 17, the week before the quintessentially American "Thanksgiving" holiday, Laura Bush steps in for President Bush to deliver the Weekly Whitehouse Speech, adding a "woman's" perspective on the significance of the Afghan war. The speech inaugurates "a world-wide effort to focus on the brutality against women and children by the Al-Qaida terrorist network and the regime it supports in Afghanistan, the Taliban." A feminist rhetoric of women's liberation is enlisted in the service of Empire. The triumphal tone of imperial arrogance rings through loud and clear, "That regime is now in retreat across much of the country," she states, "and the people of Afghanistan—especially women—are rejoicing (Laura Bush, "Brutality against women and children," November 17, 2001). The terrorists and the Taliban are brutal villains who persecute women and children. The Taliban persecuted "girls" by forbidding them from going to school. The Americans are heroes triumphing over brutal villains, liberating the powerless and innocent women and children of Afghanistan from "degradation" at the hands of patriarchal tyrants.

The discourse of national "liberation" from an oppressive and brutal "Taliban regime" is reiterated in future speeches, setting the pattern of discourse that would be reiterated in the prosecution of the Iraq war. A March 2002 speech is typical:

> In one week boys and girls in Afghanistan will start a new school year. For many girls this will be the first time in their young lives that they will have set foot in a classroom. ***Under the Taliban regime, educating women was a criminal act.*** Under the new government of a liberated Afghanistan, educating all children is a national priority ("Children of Afghanistan," March 16, 2002).

A December 2002 speech glorifies the accomplishments of the war on terror to that date, the creation of a new "Department of Homeland Security" and the liberation of Afghanistan, and looks forward to a new front in the global war:

> In 2002, the war on terror that began with **the liberation of Afghanistan** [emphasis added: bold = glorifier / bold + italic = vilifier] continued on many fronts. **Working with our allies** around the world, **we** captured top Al Qaeda leaders, destroyed terror training camps and froze millions of dollars in terrorist asset.
>
> In the New Year, **we will prosecute the war on terror with patience and focus and determination**. With the help of a broad coalition, **we** will make certain that ***terrorists and their supporters*** are not safe in any cave or corner of the world.
>
> The war on terror also requires us to confront the danger of catastrophic violence posed by ***Iraq and its weapons of mass destruction***. The United Nations Security Council has unanimously affirmed that ***Saddam Hussein is a danger to his neighbors and to the peace of the world***. The burden now is on ***Iraq's dictator*** to disclose and destroy his arsenal of weapons. **If he refuses, then for the sake of peace, the United States will lead a coalition to disarm the Iraqi regime and free the Iraqi people** ("Proposals for a New Year," December 28, 2002).

Agitation by the Bush regime for going to war against Iraq, the second war-zone, starts in the fall of 2002. The cast of characters must change to meet the changed circumstances of a new theater of warfare.

Afghan War → Iraq War

The change in context from Iraq war to Iraqi insurgency produced a new cast of characters:

- Enemies = Saddam Hussein, a homicidal dictator, a tyrant, who desires to have and use weapons of mass destruction (Saddam is not a "terrorist" per se, but a "sponsor of terrorists"; Abu Musab a-Zarqawi, leader of Al Qaeda in Iraq)
- Heroes = U.S. military, the troops;
- Allies = Britain, "coalition of the willing"; after invasion, cooperative Iraqis (but conspicuously and in striking contrast to Afghanistan, not France, not the U.N., not NATO),

In striking contrast to the Afghan war, the target of the victimage ritual mounted to goad the American public into a war against Iraq is personified by a single man, Saddam Hussein. He symbolized the rationale for the war. He is a tyrant who violates the universal principles of security and freedom, who "terrorizes" his own people; who "wants" and "desires" to exercise tyrannical power by terrorizing the U.S. and the world with WMD. The Bush regime delivers four Weekly speeches in September and November of 2002 specifically focused on the threat posed by Saddam Hussein and the Iraqi regime.

The first speech in September 2003 sets the pattern by personifying the threat in terms of Saddam Hussein's desires as a tyrant and a homicidal dictator:

> Saddam Hussein's regime *continues to support terrorist groups and to oppress its civilian population* [emphasis added: bold = glorifier / bold + italic = vilifier]. It refuses to account for missing Gulf War personnel, or to end illicit trade outside the U.N"'s oil-for-food program. And although the regime agreed in 1991 to destroy and stop developing all weapons of mass destruction and long-range missiles, *it has broken every aspect of this fundamental pledge.*

> Today this regime likely maintains stockpiles of chemical and biological agents, and is improving and expanding facilities capable of producing chemical and biological weapons. *Today Saddam Hussein has the scientists and infrastructure for a nuclear weapons program, and has illicitly sought to purchase the equipment needed to enrich uranium for a nuclear weapon. Should his regime acquire fissile material, it would be able to build a nuclear weapon within a year.*

The former head of the U.N. team investigating Iraq's weapons of mass destruction program, Richard Butler, reached this conclusion after years of experience: ***"The fundamental problem with Iraq remains the nature of the regime itself. Saddam Hussein is a homicidal dictator who is addicted to weapons of mass destruction."*** ("Saddam Hussein," Weekly Whitehouse Speech, September 14, 2002)

In a second speech that September, titled "Iraqi Threat," the focus is very specifically on Saddam's villainous character. It is rhetorically directed toward producing a U.S. Congressional resolution in support of "unilateral" military action against Iraq (duly passed, shortly thereafter). To maximize its rhetorical effect, the threat was described as ultimate and imminent:

We know that the Iraqi regime is led by [Saddam] ***a dangerous and brutal man***. We know he is ***actively seeking the destructive technologies to match his hatred*** [emphasis added: bold = glorifier / bold + italic = vilifier]. And we know that **he must be stopped**. The dangers we face will only worsen from month to month and year to year. To ignore these threats is to encourage them—and when they have fully materialized, it may be too late to protect ourselves and our allies. ***By then, the Iraqi dictator will have had the means to terrorize and dominate the region***, and each passing day could be the one on which the Iraqi regime gives anthrax or VX nerve gas or someday a nuclear weapon to a terrorist group ("Iraqi Threat," Weekly Whitehouse Speech, September 28, 2002).

After much debate about Iraq's nuclear weapons program and a failed political campaign to garner a U.N. resolution in favor of a military campaign to invade and overthrow Saddam's regime (featuring Hans Blix, the U.N. nuclear weapons inspector, in the role of spoiler), the Bush regime launched a "unilateral" and "preemptive war" against Saddam's regime in March of 2003. Subsequently, the occupation of Iraq by Empire provokes a fierce and determined cycle of victimage ritual. The correlation of vilifiers reported in Table 4.4 associates Saddam and his Sunni supporters with the "terrorism" of the Iraqi insurgency that emerged against the U.S. occupation in the fall of 2003 (Rho .77, p ≤ .01).

The following Weekly Speech made in response to the August 2003 attack on the U.N. headquarters in Baghdad, exemplifies the rhetorical use of vilifiers and glorifiers in this global victimage ritual: the use of innocent victims to vilify opponents as "terrorists" who resist the good (civilization; the free world; liberal regime of security and freedom), and, working in point-counterpoint tandem, the use of heroic terms to glorify the "freedom-fighters" struggling against the terrorists. It manifests, by means of a point-counterpoint sequencing of paradigmatic contrasts, the melodramatic structure of victimage ritual as a mode of power and subjection. The majority of people are good and humanitarian (i.e., the Americans, United Nations, allies, freedom-loving, self-sacrificing, determined and resolved in the struggle against evil) are placed in paradigmatic opposition to the "violent few" who are willing to murder and kill the innocent.

THE PRESIDENT: Good morning. Earlier this week, *terrorists struck the United Nations headquarters in Baghdad.* [paradigmatic contrast] **The U.N. personnel and Iraqi citizens killed in the bombings were engaged in a purely humanitarian mission** [emphasis added: bold = glorifier / bold + italic = vilifier]. Men and women in the building were working on reconstruction, medical care for Iraqis, and the distribution of food. **Among the dead was Sergio Vieira de Mello, the U.N. representative for Iraq—a good man serving an important cause.**

These two bombings reveal, once again, the nature of the terrorists, and why they must be defeated. In their malicious view of the world, no one is innocent. **Relief workers and infants alike are targeted for murder.** Terrorism may use religion as a disguise, but terrorism violates every religion and every standard of decency and morality.

The terrorists have declared war on every free nation and all our citizens. ***Their goals*** are clear. ***They want more governments to resemble the oppressive Taliban*** that once ruled Afghanistan. ***Terrorists commit atrocities because they want the civilized world to flinch and retreat so they can impose their totalitarian vision.*** There will be no flinching in this war on terror, and there will be no retreat.

In most of Iraq, there is steady movement toward reconstruction and a stable, self-governing society. ***This progress makes the remaining terrorists even more desperate and willing to lash out against symbols of order and hope, like coalition forces and U.N. personnel.*** **The world will not be intimidated.** *A violent few will not determine the future of Iraq, and there will be no return to the days of Saddam Hussein's torture chambers and mass graves.*

[paradigmatic contrast] **Working with Iraqis, coalition forces are on the offensive against these killers.** Aided by increasing flow of intelligence from ordinary Iraqis, we are stepping up raids, seizing enemy weapons, and capturing enemy leaders. **The United States, the United Nations, and the civilized world will continue to stand with the people of Iraq as they reclaim their nation and their future.**

This speech is exemplary for a second reason. It clearly shows how the cast of characters changed as the geopolitical context of Empire changed. The U.S. military move into Iraq provoked resistance. The speech references Afghanistan (e.g., the Taliban) and other fronts in the world war, reasserting the global scale of the war, but the focus is on the new theater of combat and the new villains beyond the Taliban and Saddam, the Iraqi and foreign "terrorists and remnants of that regime" resisting the inevitable advance of freedom.

> ***From Afghanistan to Iraq, to the Philippines and elsewhere, we are waging a campaign against the terrorists and their allies*** wherever they gather, wherever they plan, and wherever they act. [emphasis added: bold = glorifier / bold + italic = vilifier] This campaign requires sacrifice, determination and resolve, and we will see it through. Iraq is an essential front in this war. ***Now we're fighting terrorists and remnants of that regime who have everything to lose from the advance of freedom in the heart of the Middle East.***

> ***We're determined, as well, not to let murderers decide the future of the Middle East. A Palestinian state will never be built on a foundation of violence.*** **The hopes of that state and the security of Israel both depend on an unrelenting campaign against terror waged by all parties in the region.** *In the Middle East, true peace has deadly enemies.* **Yet America will be a consistent friend of every leader who works for peace by actively opposing violence.**

> All nations of the world face a challenge and a choice. In continued acts of murder and destruction, ***terrorists are testing our will, hoping we will weaken and withdraw.*** Yet across the world, **they are finding that our will cannot be shaken. Whatever the hardships, we will persevere. We will continue this war on terror until all the killers are brought to justice. And we will prevail** ("War on Terrorism, Weekly Whitehouse Speech, August 23, 2003).

This speech also illustrates the emergent—some might argue tragic— logic of Empire and the power struggles it provokes. All resistance to liberal Empire is equated to terrorism. Once Empire makes its move into a new geo-political space and the battle has been joined, there is no turning back, no surrender, no retreat. The war must be won by all necessary means. Why? If the agents and agencies of Empire show signs of "weakness" and "withdraw" or "retreat," then the opponents of "freedom" will be emboldened to engage in further resistance. It does not matter that the war may have not been justified in the first place. The "terrorists" in the world are watching. A new motive for the war emerges from the war. This emergent feature is also observable, as we shall see, in the glorification of the war heroes who have died in the war. Their sacrifice shall not be in vain. It is in their name that the war must be won.

As the Iraqi insurgency emerged in the fall of 2003 and the U.S. presidential election in November of 2004 approached, a new personification of the "enemy" emerged. The capture of Saddam Hussein (December 14, 2003) did not end the resistance. An effective victimage ritual, in true melodramatic fashion, must have a personifier of the negative. Abu Musab al-Zarqawi (leader of Al Qaeda in Iraq) is added to the cast of villains and moved into the center of the stage as chief antagonist threatening Empire:

Saddam Hussein doubted our resolve to enforce our word. Now he sits in a prison cell while his country moves toward a democratic future. **Today in Iraq, our coalition faces** *deadly attacks from a remnant of Saddam's supporters, joined by foreign terrorists.* [emphasis added: bold = glorifier / bold + italic = vilifier] *Recently we intercepted a letter sent by a senior Al Qaeda associate named Zarqawi, to one of Osama bin Laden's top lieutenants. The letter describes a terrorist strategy, to tear Iraq apart with ethnic violence, to undermine Iraqi security forces, to demoralize our coalition and to prevent the rise of a sovereign, democratic government. This terrorist outlines his efforts to recruit and train suicide bombers, and boasts of 25 attacks on innocent Iraqis and coalition personnel. And he urges Al Qaeda members to join him in waging war on our coalition and on the people of Iraq.*

Zarqawi and men like him have made Iraq the central front in our war on terror. The terrorists know that the emergence of a free Iraq will be a major blow against a worldwide terrorist movement. In this, they are correct ("War on Terrorism," Weekly Whitehouse Speech, February, 21, 2004).

Notice how the discourse subtly equates "free Iraq" with the achievement of goals "in our war on terror." Implicit in this assertion is the logologic of *our* "security" insures *their* "freedom."

Iraqi Insurgency → U.S. Elections

The next major change in political context was the approaching presidential and congressional elections of 2004 and 2006. In March of 2003, going to war against Saddam's regime was very popular. At the time more than seventy percent of Americans thought going to war was the right decision. By November 2004, the percent believing it was the right decision had declined to forty-eight percent (Pew Research 2011: 153–154, "Detailed Tables"). Significantly, the Presidential election of 2004 would pit John Kerry, the anti-Viet Nam war activist and "liberal" Massachusetts Senator, against the incumbent "war" president and "conservative," George Bush. The intensity levels of rhetorical terror observed during the election cycles of 2004 and 2006 return to the levels observed during the very intense Afghan and Iraq wars (60% + of Weekly speeches) The Bush regime deployed the victimage ritual against terrorism to run the gauntlet of electoral politics. The election, they argued, represented a fateful choice, two candidates with two different views of the terrorist threat:

...Since September the 11th, 2001, I have led a relentless campaign against the terrorists. We have strengthened homeland security. We removed terror regimes in Afghanistan and Iraq. We are on the offensive around the world,

because the best way to prevent future attacks is to go after the enemy.
[emphasis added: bold = glorifier / bold + italic = vilifier]

[paradigmatic contrast] *My opponent has a different view. Senator Kerry says September the 11th didn't change him much, and his policies make that clear. He says the war on terror is "primarily an intelligence and law enforcement operation." He has proposed what he calls a "global test" that would give foreign governments a veto over American security decisions. And when our troops in Afghanistan and Iraq needed funding for body armor and bullets, Senator Kerry voted against it.*

The direction of the war on terror is at stake in the election of 2004. And when you go to the polls on Tuesday, remember this: [paradigmatic contrast] **I will do whatever it takes to defend America and prevail in the war on terror, and I will always support the men and women who do the fighting** ("2004 Election," Weekly Whitehouse Speech, October 30, 2004).

The Bush regime won this election by a narrow margin. The single most important reason given by voters for casting a vote against the incumbent was opposition to the Iraq war. According to exit poll data, ninety-four percent of respondents who strongly disagreed with the decision to go to war against Iraq, voted against Bush, and 74% of those who somewhat disagreed voted against him (forty-six percent of the total respondents, CNN Election Results 2004). The Weapons of Mass Destruction fiasco (that the case against Saddam's secret nuclear weapons program, had been fabricated) on top of a growing sense that the war itself was provoking more "terrorism," had forced the Bush regime into a defensive posture. Thomas Powers (2004, 2010, Jervis and Powers 2010) has detailed how the Bush regime pressured intelligence analysts at the CIA to provide the "smoking cloud" that provided the specter of a nuclear "mushroom cloud" to justify going to war against Saddam's regime. The following speech given in response to a *National Defense Estimate* issued in July 2006 by the CIA captures the sense of urgency:

> *...Some in Washington have selectively quoted from this document to make the case that by fighting the terrorists in Iraq, we are making our people less secure here at home. This argument buys into the enemy's propaganda that the terrorists attack us because we are provoking them...*[emphasis added: bold = glorifier / bold + italic = vilifier] The terrorists are at war against us because they hate everything America stands for, and because they know we stand in the way of their ambitions to take over the Middle East. We are fighting to stop them from taking over Iraq and turning that country into a safe haven that would be even more valuable than the one they lost in Afghanistan.

> Iraq is not the reason the terrorists are at war against us. Our troops were not in Iraq when terrorists first attacked the World Trade Center in 1993, or when

terrorists blew up our embassies in Kenya and Tanzania, or when they bombed the USS Cole, or when they killed nearly 3,000 people on September the 11th, 2001. *Five years after the 9/11 attacks, some people in Washington still do not understand the nature of the enemy.* The only way to protect our citizens at home is to go on the offense against the enemy across the world ("National Intelligence Estimate," Weekly Whitehouse Speech, September 30, 2006).

This speech deploys a familiar tactic. Vilify the "internal enemies" by suggesting they oppose America's special mission to defend Empire's "freedom." Indict them for "not understanding the nature of the enemy" and being "obtuse" and "blaming America first." The Bush regime had lost control of the message justifying the Iraq war. The Democrats ran against the discourse linking the Iraq war to the war on terrorism. As a result, the Bush regime and its allies inside the Republican Party lost control of U.S. Congress in November of 2006.

Anti-War Congress → Iraq Surge

A new military strategy emerged from the Bush regime's 2006 political defeat. While one might have expected a withdrawal of the military from Iraq, the Bush regime doubled-down by implementing a "surge" (i.e., short for counterinsurgency) strategy to defeat the "terrorists" (Al Qaeda) and "extremists" (Sunni Arabs, "remnants of the Saddam regime") involved in the insurgency against the U.S. led occupation. The "surge" was led by a new commander, General David Petraeus, and a new Ambassador to Iraq, Ryan Crocker. The new "surge" strategy is detailed in a June 2007 Weekly Speech:

> … It recognizes that our top priority must be to help the Iraqi government and its security forces protect their population—especially in Baghdad. And its goal is to help the Iraqis make progress toward reconciliation and build a free nation that respects the rights of its people, upholds the rule of law and is an ally in the war on terror.

> So America has sent reinforcements to help the Iraqis secure their population, go after *the terrorists, insurgents and militias that are inciting sectarian violence.* [emphasis added: bold = glorifier / bold + italic = vilifier], and get the capital under control. The last of these reinforcements arrived in Iraq earlier this month, and the full surge has begun. One of our top commanders in Iraq, General Ray Odierno, put it this way, "We are beyond a surge of forces. We're now into a surge of operations." ("Independence Day," Weekly Whitehouse Speech, June 3, 2007)

Fifteen months later the Whitehouse announced that a progress report to the Congress made by General Petraeus and Ambassador Crocker on the situation in Iraq reported that the "surge" had begun to show positive results:

> Since the surge began, American and Iraqi forces have made significant progress. While there's more to be done, sectarian violence, civilian deaths, and military deaths are down. Improvements in security have helped clear the way for political and economic progress. The Iraqi government has passed a budget and three major "benchmark" laws. And many economic indicators are now pointed in the right direction (Weekly Whitehouse Speech, "Iraq," March 12, 2008).

By the last months of the Bush regime's tenure following the election of Barack Obama to the presidency, the Weekly Whitehouse Speeches were touting the "surge" as an historic success story. The following excerpt is from a speech on "Iraq, Defense" that announced a new "Strategic Framework Agreement" with Iraq, including a planned withdrawal of military forces:

> ..Only a few years ago, such an agreement was unimaginable. ***Chaos and violence were consuming Iraq. Terrorists were seizing new ground and using violence to divide the Iraqi people along sectarian lines. And the nation was nearing the point of political collapse and civil war.*** [emphasis added: bold = glorifier / bold + italic = vilifier]

> **Today, violence is down dramatically. Our forces have struck powerful blows against Al Qaeda. The Iraqi military is growing in capability, taking the lead in the fight against the extremists, and working across sectarian lines** ("Defense, Iraq," Weekly Whitehouse Speech, December 6, 2008).

The regime's final reference to the "surge" comes in a Weekly speech delivered in January 2010 reporting the content of a "farewell" speech Bush had delivered "to the men and women of "America's" Armed Forces in a ceremony at Fort Myer, Virginia. The theme of the speech is the "valor" of those "brave Americans" who had served the President in his capacity as "Commander-and-Chief":

> **We saw their valor in battle-tested warriors who signed up for a second, or third, or fourth tour—and made the troop surge in Iraq that I announced two years ago today one of the great successes in American military history.** [emphasis added: bold = glorifier / bold + italic = vilifier]

> **America's Armed Forces have liberated more than 50 million people around the world—and made our Nation safer. They have taken the fight to the terrorists abroad so that we have not had to face them here at home. And the world has seen something that almost no one thought possible: More than seven years after September the 11th, there has not been another terrorist attack on American soil** ("Defense," Weekly Whitehouse Speech, January 20, 2009).

The "surge" was a response to the stalemate in Iraq and the election of an "anti-Iraq war" Congress controlled by the Democratic Party. The Democrats had never seriously questioned the legitimacy of the Afghan war. They complained that the Bush regime had made a historic "strategic" blunder by diverting its attention from Al Qaeda and the Taliban, and not finishing the job in Afghanistan. To wit: Osama bin Laden was still alive and the Taliban had mounted an effective insurgency against the new regime in Kabul and the foreign occupiers while the Bush regime had mounted its unwarranted war (based on the false Weapons of Mass Destruction claim) against Iraq. As we shall see, once the Obama regime took office it would ultimately organize a "strategic" withdrawal of the U.S. military from Iraq and double-down on the war in Afghanistan, mimicking the Bush regime tactic of mounting a "surge" against the Taliban and Al Qaeda.

Obama Regime → Afghan Surge

President Barack Obama defeated Senator John McCain in the presidential election, November 2008. Once in command of the Whitehouse, the Obama regime implemented a change in strategy and rhetorical tactics. In part, these changes were direct implications of the anti-Iraq war critique advanced by the Democratic Party against the Bush regime and the Republican Party. The Obama regime would carry out the agreement to withdraw military forces from Iraq by the fall of 2012. In the meantime, they would refocus attention on finishing "the job" in Afghanistan.

The change in rhetorical tactics involved minimizing the tactics of vilification and, as we shall see in the analysis of glorifiers, maximizing the glorification of the troops. The quantitative data directly reflect this change. The Obama regime turned down the frequency of terrorism speeches to a barely audible level. As Table 4.3 reports, the Bush Whitehouse only issued one speech on terrorism before the 9/11 attacks (3% of the total). In the seven years following the 9/11 attacks the Bush regime devoted fifty percent of all its Weekly Whitehouse Speeches to terrorism. Since taking control of the Whitehouse, the Obama regime has delivered only nine Weekly speeches on terrorism, about 7 percent of the total. Only two of those speeches mention the word more than once. This represents a radical reduction in the intensity of the victimage ritual rhetoric against terrorism. The changes in discourse recycle the original "Afghan" cast of characters supplemented by new ones in Pakistan:

- Enemies = Osama bin Laden, Al Qaeda, extremists, Taliban in Iraq and Pakistan
- Heroes = "troops," "dedicated to freedom";
- Allies = NATO, Afghan regime, President Hamid Karzai, President of Afghanistan, Pakistan government and military (ambivalently)

In effect these changes represented a decision on the part of the regime to recycle an earlier covert, counterinsurgency strategy. General David Petraeus would direct the campaign. The fight would be against Al Qaeda and its supporters. The regime has augmented a vicious "predator war" against "terrorists" and "militants" in Pakistan (Mayer 2009). One study reports the following distribution of drone strikes in Pakistan: 2004–2007 = 9, 2008 = 33, 2009 = 53, and 2010 = 118. ("Year of the Drone," New America Foundation, 2011; also *Rise of the Drones I and II* 2011) At the same time, while the Obama regime toned down the victimage rhetoric they moved to redeploy military assets from the Iraq war and mount a new "surge" in the Afghan war.

After the Obama regime pondered the policy behind the wars in Iraq and Afghanistan for a year, the January 2, 2010 Weekly speech articulates the rationale behind the regime's decision. It sets the context of the speech with a brief account of the details of a Christmas Day (December 25, 2009) attempt by "Al Qaeda in the Persian Gulf" to blow up an airliner on its way to Detroit. The speech goes on to recall the day Obama took the oath of office as President and reasserts his "solemn responsibility ...to protect the safety and security of the American people":

> **On that day I also made it very clear-our nation is at war against a far-reaching network of violence and hatred ...**
>
> It's why I refocused the fight-bringing to a responsible end the war in Iraq, which had nothing to do with the 9/11 attacks, and dramatically increasing our resources in the region where Al Qaeda is actually based, in Afghanistan and Pakistan.
>
> It's why I've set a clear and achievable mission—to disrupt, dismantle and defeat Al Qaeda and its extremist allies and prevent their return to either country.
>
> And it's why we've forged new partnerships, as in Yemen, and put unrelenting pressure on **these extremists wherever they plot and train-from East Africa to Southeast Asia, from Europe to the Persian Gulf** ("The Fight against Al Qaeda," Weekly Whitehouse Speech, January 21, 2010).

This speech reaffirms the U.S. commitment to fight a world war against the "extremists" behind the terrorism. The object is President Obama's personal desire to defend the "safety and security" of the American people. The speech makes no mention of Empire or the interests behind the presence of the U.S. in these far-flung places. The link to Empire is revealed in the speech's characterization of the terrorist scapegoat and enemy as "a far-reaching network of violence and hatred." While the specific focus has shifted from Iraq to Afghanistan, the scope of the war includes the "extremists wherever they plot and train from East Africa to Southeast Asia and Europe to the Persian Gulf."

Glorifying Human Sacrifice

As the war on terrorism proceeded, the shift in the discourse of victimage ritual from an emphasis on vilifying opponents to glorifying the war fighters as heroes was striking. The glorification of human sacrifice is central to how ritual victimage functions in warfare. This is not a new idea. Ritual human sacrifice—the crucifixion of Jesus and the torture of criminals are paradigm examples, is a powerful mode of subjection (see Nietzsche 1967: 60–62, also Blain 1976, Foucault 1977: 3–72). As such it is a key to how religious and political memorials function in society. This complex is also central to how memorials can function as victimage rhetoric in the war on terrorism. There are two types of discourse and victims: the heroic martyrs who have sacrificed their lives fighting for the cause, and the leader / scapegoat, who personify the enemy. Once the military battles were joined in Afghanistan and Iraq, and the casualties mounted, the number of speeches glorifying heroic martyrdom also increased. It then becomes possible for the agents of Empire to use these heroic martyrs to inspire the public and the troops to honor their sacrifice and fight on to victory.

The frequency of references to sacrifice in the Weekly Whitehouse "Memorial Day" speeches reveal the pattern. The speeches average 1 to 2 references in the four speeches delivered 2001–2004. The number of references increases to five references per speech 2005–2008. This pattern is also reflected in the distribution of correlations in Table 4.5 (below). The Bush regime glorifies the troops as liberators from the beginning of the Afghan war. This association is invoked repeatedly in the Bush Weekly speeches that memorialize the troops and their sacrifice. It disappears with the Bush regime. The association between the troops and bravery (including their great "valor") begins during the Iraq war debate, particularly in those speeches referencing the Afghan war. This association continued to dominate speeches about the troops right through the first two years of the Obama regime; it was particularly intense in the first months of the Obama regime. The sacrificial motive first emerges as a major theme during the Iraq war debate and mainly in references to the troops and the Afghan war. It really emerges as a persistent theme during the 2004 election. The heroic martyrs of the Afghan and Iraq wars were regularly invoked in the annual memorials. Once public opinion shifted toward opposing the wars, the glorification of the troops as brave and heroic martyrs to the cause has become a primary focus of speeches devoted to the war. The motivation to fight is sustained by the tragic logic that those heroic martyrs who have given their lives will have died in vain if we do not continue to fight.

The discourse of heroic martyrdom adds rhetorical force to the drama of ritual victimage. Each new generation of warriors is goaded into killing and dying for the national cause by symbolically identifying their current actions with the actions of the patriot dead. Marx (1852) once observed that in the face of a crisis, the "tradition of all the dead generations weights like a nightmare on the brain of the living." And precisely at such times, rather than choosing the revolutionary possibilities, people "anxiously conjure up the spirits of the past to their service

Table 4.5   Correlation of Glorifiers in Weekly Whitehouse Speeches, 9/11/2001 – 9/11/2011

Context (Number Speech)		War zone	Troops	Hero	Brave	Liberator	Sacrifice
		Glorifiers					
Afghan War	Afgh.	.50**	.22	.22	.32*	.10
9/11/2001–2002 (53)	Iraq	-	-	-	-	-
Iraq Debate	Afgh.	.07	-	-.12	.47*	-.08
2002–2003 (27)	Iraq	.40*	-	-.25	.09	-.18
Iraq War	Afgh.	.50*	-.10	.47*	.27	.46*
2003 (21)	Iraq	.69**	-.22	.19	.73**	.21
Iraqi Insurgency	Afgh.	.25	-	.55*	.35	.34
2003–2004 (21)	Iraq	.44*	-	.33	.44*	.26
U.S. Election	Afgh.	.03	-	.30	.05	-.03
2004 (42)	Iraq	.42**	-	.45**	.40**	.46**
Regime Change	Afgh.	.34**	.09	.54**	.42**	.53**
2004–2006 (66)	Iraq	.42**	-.03	.38**	.25*	.51**
U.S. Election	Afgh.	.10	-.14	.52**	-.03	.23
2006 (39)	Iraq	.20	.06	.51**	.45**	.64**
Antiwar Congress	Afgh.	.20	.40*	.37*	-	.66**
2006–2007 (33)	Iraq	.73**	.12	.27	-	.35*
Iraq Surge	Afgh.	.52**	.21	.32**	.35**	.33**
2007–2009 (82)	Iraq	.72**	.17	.51**	.36**	.57**
Obama Regime	Afgh.	.71**	.46**	.74**	-	.38**
2009 (48)	Iraq	.85**	.55**	.64**	-	.47**
Afghan Surge	Afgh.	.51**	.22	.27**	-	.25
2010–2011 (88)	Iraq	.36**	.34**	.25*	-	.26

* Bivariate correlation coefficients; Spearman's rho (two-tailed): * $p < .05$, ** $p < .01$

Source: Data derived from www.Whitehouse.org

and borrow from them names, battle cries and costumes in order to present the new scene of world history in this time-honored disguise and this borrowed language" (1963: 15). In spite of all the rhetoric about how the 9/11 attacks had changed everything, Marx's observation also applies to the current political crisis and "new scene of world history."

Americans celebrate the sacrifices of the patriot-dead several times a year in national holidays (including Memorial Day, Armed Forces Day, Flag Day, Veterans Day), but most emphatically as part of Memorial Day celebrations held in the month of May. Durkheim (1951: 217–40) was the first sociologist to explicitly note the cultural force of memorial rites that celebrate the "altruistic suicide" by soldiers who have "given their life" fighting for their nation. The sacrifices of the World War Two generation loom largest in the American imagination (Warner 1959). Blain (1974, 1976) extended these ideas to the politics of death in the context of the Viet Nam War and U.S. military interventions. The traditions of the "patriot dead" continue to weigh like a nightmare on the brain of the living. These signifiers are most likely to be used by politicians to add dignity, honor, and glory to the heroic sacrifices of the present generation. The following excerpt from a pre-9/11 Memorial Day speech illustrates this type of discourse. In the absence of an ongoing military conflict, it summons the public at large to fulfill its patriotic "duty" by honoring the "cost" in human lives that has been paid for their "free lives":

> …Memorial Day, when we pause to reflect **on the cost of the free lives we live today.** [emphasis added: bold = glorifier / bold + italic = vilifier]…**With their sacrifice comes a duty that will go on through the generations to honor them in our thoughts, in our words and in our lives.**
>
> **Every Memorial Day we try to grasp the extent of this loss and the meaning of this sacrifice. But it always has seemed more than words can convey. In the end, all we can do is be thankful; all we can do is remember and always appreciate the price that was paid for our own lives and our own freedom** ("Memorial Day," Weekly Whitehouse Speech, May 26, 2001).

This symbolic practice is infused with new power by the war on terror and the "blood spilled" by a new generation of heroic martyrs. The Bush regime glorified their courage and sacrifices in fighting the Afghan and Iraq wars by linking their sacrifices to the generation that fought World War II:

> …Monday is Memorial Day and all across America this weekend, people are **remembering those who fought for freedom and who gave their lives in service to their country.** [emphasis added: bold = glorifier / bold + italic = vilifier]

The World War II Memorial will stand forever as a tribute to the generation that fought that war, and **to the more than 400,000 Americans who gave their lives**. Because of their sacrifice, tyrants fell; fascism and Nazism were vanquished; and freedom prevailed.

Today, freedom faces new enemies, and a new generation of Americans has stepped forward to defeat them. Since the hour this nation was attacked on September the 11th, 2001, we have seen the character of the men and women who wear our country's uniform. In places like Kabul and Kandahar, Mosul and Baghdad, we have seen **their decency and brave spirit**. And because of **their fierce courage**, America is safer. And two terror regimes are gone forever, and more than 50 million souls now live in freedom ("Memorial Day," Weekly Whitehouse Speech, May 29, 2004).

As the years of war have passed by this discourse played an increasingly more central role in the campaign to support and sustain the war on terrorism. In ritual fashion, the same words are repeated verbatim in every Memorial Day speech, 2004–2008:

On Memorial Day, we also pay tribute to Americans from every generation who have given their lives for our freedom. [emphasis added: bold = glorifier / bold + italic = vilifier] From Valley Forge to Vietnam, from Kuwait to Kandahar, from Berlin to Baghdad, **brave men and women have given up their own futures so that others might have a future of freedom. Because of their sacrifice, millions here and around the world enjoy the blessings of liberty.** And wherever these patriots rest, we offer them the respect and gratitude of our Nation ("Memorial Day," Weekly Whitehouse Speech, May 26, 2007).

The Obama regime intensified this rhetorical practice. It was elected to end the wars and bring the troops home, to leave Iraq and finish the job in Afghanistan. To accomplish these objectives, the Obama regime had to shift political and public attention from the "terrorists" and the "tyrants" to the heroism and sacrifice of the troops. This maneuver allowed the regime to ward off domestic opposition to ending the Iraq war, withdrawing our troops, and the criticism that it represented an unpatriotic and cowardly retreat from our duty to protect and defend that country. At the same time, the rhetoric of patriotic pride—"the finest fighting force on Earth; that make the United States military the best the world has ever known; and that make all of us proud to be Americans" (Obama, "Tragedy at Fort Hood," Weekly Whitehouse Speech, November 7, 2009)—could be mobilized to sustain political and public support to surge the war in Afghanistan and "finish the job":

Our calling on Memorial Day is different [than Veterans Day]. On this day, **we honor not just those who've worn this country's uniform, but the men and women who've died in its service; who've laid down their lives in defense**

of their fellow citizens; who've given their last full measure of devotion to protect the United States of America.... [emphasis added: bold = glorifier / bold + italic = vilifier]

There are any number of **reasons America emerged from its humble beginnings as a cluster of colonies to become the most prosperous, most powerful nation on earth. ...the hard work, the resilience, and the character of our people...the ingenuity and enterprising spirit of our entrepreneurs and innovators....the ideals of opportunity, equality, and freedom...**

But from the very start, there was also **something more. A steadfast commitment to serve, to fight, and if necessary, to die, to preserve America and advance the ideals we cherish.** It's a commitment witnessed at each defining moment along the journey of this country. It's what led a rag-tag militia to face British soldiers at Lexington and Concord. **It's what led young men, in a country divided half slave and half free, to take up arms to save our union. It's what led patriots in each generation to sacrifice their own lives to secure the life of our nation,** from the trenches of World War I to the battles of World War II, from Inchon and Khe Sanh, **from Mosul to Marjah...**

That commitment—**that willingness to lay down their lives so we might inherit the blessings of this nation**—is what we honor today... (Obama, "Honoring the Fallen," Weekly Whitehouse Speech, May 29, 2010).

The U.S. power elite, as the leading agents of contemporary Empire, must summon the warriors to battle by tying their sacrifice to the debt owed to previous generations who have sacrificed their lives for "our" freedom. The "heroic martyrs" function as the reason for the ritual sacrifice of the scapegoated enemy. Finishing the job, or the final moment in the cycle of ritual victimage, would logically entail the ritual executions of the tyrants and terrorists who had functioned as personifiers of the war.

Moment of the Kill

There are two discourses of human sacrifice evident in the Weekly Presidential Speeches. The first discourse glorifies the heroic struggle against the enemy. The warriors in the global struggle against terrorism do not kill the enemy to revenge the innocent victims of 9/11. They fight and die heroically to protect and defend and multiply human life. The warrior's heroic sacrifice is linked to the bio-political motive of fighting and dying so that others might live. Killing the enemy, in this sense, is a biopolitical act. The *second* discourse dramatizes the moment of the kill — the taking of the enemy's life. The ultimate and final dramatic act in a victimage ritual is the destruction of the villainous scapegoat.

The "targeted-killing" of Osama bin Laden on March 2, 2011 is a paradigm case of this phenomenon. The direct link this killing has to the history of American involvement in Empire is coded in the very name given to the mission. "Operation Neptune's Spear" was the name given to the Navy Seals mission to capture or kill Bin Laden in a raid on bin Laden's compound in Abbottabad, Pakistan. "Geronimo" was the code the Seals used to alert their commanders that they had visually identified their target. Geronimo was the Apache war-Chief, a "warrior" well-known for his intelligence and bravery, who fought the last "Indian War" in the 1880s against the Americans and was described as a "terrorist" at the time. And, ultimately, "Geronimo-EKIA" was the coded message to confirm that they had killed Bin Laden. As it turned out, he was unarmed.

The killing of the leaders of the "terrorist" movement or war is a highly charged symbolic act. The leader is perfected in the role of personifier and incarnation of the "villainous power" that must be destroyed. There have been a series of these spectacular moments:

- Saddam Hussein: 'tyrant,' linked to 'terrorism' (Iraq: December 30, 2006);
- Abu Musab al-Zarqawi: Al Qaeda 'terrorist,' alleged link between Al Qaeda and Saddam's regime (Iraq: June 7, 2006);
- Osama bin Laden, Al Qaeda 'terrorist' (Pakistan: May 2, 2011);
- Anwar al-Awlaki, Al Qaeda 'terrorist,' American born Imam (Yemen: September 11, 2011);
- Col. Muammar el-Qaddafi: 'tyrant,' linked to 'terrorism' (Libya: October 20, 2011).

The ritual killing of these high-profile "tyrants" and "terrorists" consummates the rhetorically generated desire to kill that was stirred up through a protracted, politically motivated campaign of subjection by means of victimage ritual.[4]

4　Predictably and controversially, the 2012 campaign to re-elect President Obama used the occasion of the one-year anniversary of the "killing of bin Laden" to launch its campaign against his opponent, Mitt Romney. As stated by Vice President Joe Biden, "Bin Laden is dead and General Motors is alive" (Baker and Shear, "Obama Trumpets Killing of Bin Laden, and Critics Pounce," 2012). Supporters of Obama put out a web-video making invidious comparisons to Romney, implying Romney would not have made the decision to kill Ben Laden. Senator John McCain of Arizona, perennial "Viet Nam war hero" and Romney supporter, countered, "Shame on Barack Obama for diminishing the memory of September 11th and the killing of Osama bin Laden by turning it into a cheap political attack ad."

Chapter 5

Dangers of Security

The Bush regime's reign of victimage ritual and rhetorical terror generated a dense symbolic fog. That fog provided cover for a swarming of new surveillance mechanisms, particularly in the United States. This chapter describes two power effects of the heightened [in]security associated with the war on terrorism.[1] The first effect has been to radically intensify the policing of the American population. The second effect has been in the order of knowledge—the birth of "terrorism" and "the terrorist" as objects of serious scientific research.

As we have seen, the discourse of 'terrorism' functions as a tactical element in a complex strategy of Empire. As such, it operates as a crucial relay between the politics of victimage ritual and an intensified biopolitics of security. The "U.SA Patriot Act" was passed by the congress within weeks of the 9/11 attacks and signed into law by President Bush on October 26, 2001. The following year the Bush regime orchestrated a massive reorganization and consolidation of existing federal "domestic security" programs in a new government agency with cabinet level status in the regime, the Department of Homeland Security. The fact that it could happen so fast is attributable to the political opportunity created by the intense drama surrounded the 9/11 event and the Bush regime decision to declare a world war. These events created an historic opportunity for the Bush regime to implement a preexisting emergency program called "Plans for Continuity of Government" (COG). Scott (2007: 7–9, 214–228) provides a detailed account of the origins of this plan devised by a "cabal" of actors inside the U.S. national security state that included Vice President Dick Cheney.

As this massive reorganization of the federal government was underway, the Central Intelligence Agency created a global network of "Black Sites" and "Detention Centers" for the interrogation and incarceration of "enemy

---

1   The war on terrorism has generated a critical discourse that attempts to measure its economic costs in dollars spent (e.g., Stiglitz 2008, "Commission on Wartime Contracting…" 2008, Belasco 2011, Cox 2011, "The Reckoning…" 2011). From a power elite perspective, these "economic costs" are interpreted as "benefits" that produce a massive Keynesian stimulus in the form of defense and "homeland security" contracts worth trillions of dollars to sustain corporate profits, economic growth, and employment (Domhoff 2010: 38–43; on the origins of this "warfare state" system, see Hooks and McQueen 2010). A critical discourse has also focused on measuring the biopolitical "cost" of the war in human lives (Roberts et al. 2004, "The Reckoning…" 2011, *Iraqi Deaths…* 2012). The "costs" of the war to American civil liberties has also been a constant theme (e.g. Cole 2004, *Enduring Abuse…* ACLU 2006, *A Call to Courage…* ACLU 2011).

combatants." Part and parcel of this development was a recrudescence of torture in the guise of "enhanced interrogation." This move to "the dark side" was justified by the imminence of the 'terrorist' threat and the need to produce "actionable intelligence" to counter the danger. Subsequently, the CIA would also launch a vicious "Predator War" employing "unmanned aerial vehicles" to engage in "targeted killings" of hundreds of 'terrorists' and 'militants' who opposed the U.S. led war to defend and extend Empire.

A second power effect has been in the order of knowledge. The intense victimage ritual targeting "terrorists" documented in the previous chapter, has produced a parallel new subject/object of knowledge. "Terrorism" as a phenomenon has emerged as a sui generic "social fact" and legitimate field of research. The Department of Homeland Security has funded the creation of "Centers of Counterterrorism" at universities. Their practical aim is to provide useful knowledge to the U.S. power elite as managers of Empire.

Liberalism, Security, Surveillance

Michel Foucault's analysis of security systems in modern liberal societies is directly applicable to an understanding of the dangerous social consequences of the war on terrorism. He argued that the historical constitution of liberal societies and the human and social sciences were a response to the emergency of French revolutionary terror. Foucault invented the words biopower and biopolitics to designate a new cluster of practices organized around "the management of life rather than the menace of death" (Foucault 1978: 147). The biography and personal life of each and every individual had become an object and target of political power. He contrasted this mode of power to the practices of Sovereignty and the Law that functions primarily by ritual victimage, public torture and spectacular warfare, and systems of state terror. Biopower, on the other hand, is a strategy that seeks to deter and prevent crime through an intensification of surveillance of populations and individuals. Foucault linked biopower with the rise of liberalism. By liberalism he meant a cluster of practices aimed at governing the everyday activity of "living beings" and "free" subjects (Rose 1999, Rabinow and Rose 2003). Each individual's personal biography had to be tracked, monitored, and regulated. This new approach to managing society operated by means of an intensification of police surveillance at the grassroots level of society and individual behavior. He traced the origins of these practices to Christianity and the institutions of the Roman Catholic Church. The modern police, in this sense, constitute a secular political pastorate.

The omnipresent possibilities of detection by surveillance regimes, police on patrol, video cameras, satellites, and drones, realizes Jeremy Bentham's panoptic dream of designing a perfectly efficient mode of social domination. Foucault thought the prison was a paradigm of this kind panoptic mode of power. These systems are designed to deter "deviance" and "criminality" through the more or less continual presence of the police and surveillance technologies in close proximity to the targeted individuals in a population. The very possibility of detection exerts a power effect on the behavior of the governed or enemies of the state. By the peculiar logologic of liberal modes of government and security, more surveillance can mean more freedom and liberty.

Agamben (2005) was among the first to see the biopolitical significance of the war on terrorism. His point of departure was President George Bush's November 13th, 2001 executive order authorizing the use of indefinite detention of "illegal enemy combatants" and "terrorists" in camps such as those built at Guantanamo Bay, Cuba, and Bagram Air Base, Afghanistan. The declaration of a state of emergency—wars or domestic turmoil, creates "a state of exception" that allows the Sovereign to exercise emergency powers outside and above the law—the Bush regime's resort to extraordinary rendition and torture, for example. In the current emergency, a U.S. President's executive order is the law. The concept of a "state of exception" creates a gap in the political and legal theory at the basis of modern liberal democratic societies. In the face of a crisis that threatens the survival of liberty and freedom, it may be necessary to abandon democracy for a certain period of time. This concept had been worked out by Karl Schmitt (1976, 1985), a legal theorist. Later, it would be used to legitimate the Nazi seizure of emergency powers and constitute a totalitarian regime. In the wake of a "terrorist" attack by Communists on the Reichstag in 1934, the Nazis invoked this theory, disbanded the German Parliament and introduced "emergency rule."

On one point Agamben (1998) departs from Foucault's account of modern society. The biopolitical paradigm of social modernity is not the prison, as Foucault had argued, but the exclusionary [as opposed to disciplinary] regime of the concentration camp like the one the Nazis built at Auschwitz. Agamben draws a historical parallel between Auschwitz and the detention center the Bush regime built at Guantanamo Bay. For Foucault, the prison was a disciplinary mechanism like a school. The prison was designed to rehabilitate—a regime aimed at fashioning normal, productive, members of society. Agamben argues that the "state of exception" produced by a declaration of a global war on terrorism and the camps it authorized, is based on a paradigm of government in which the law encompasses living beings by means of the law's own suspension. It is in the profoundest sense an exclusionary rather than disciplinary regime. He draws a striking parallel between the Nazi subjection of Jews in "death" camps and the current treatment of terrorists. Defined as "illegal enemy combatants," they are relegated to a status of "bare life" outside of the frameworks of existing International and U.S. laws, most especially the Geneva Conventions. That is, they were stripped of their liberties and rights under U.S. or international laws. The result was a program of torture and indefinite detention was implemented.

Danner (2004, 2009, 2011) has elaborated Agamben's thinking through a detailed account of the logic of torture at Black Sites, the sordid events that took place at Abu Ghraib prison in Iraq, the "extraordinary rendition" of suspected terrorists, and the indefinite detention of prisoners at places like Guantanamo Bay and Bagram. No need to repeat the excruciating details of that history here. The return of torture and military violence clearly represents a return to sovereign modes of power and subjection in the guise of a liberal discourse of 'security."

Empire and Surveillance

There has been a more or less continuous interplay of the practices of surveillance and policing in liberal societies and in their far-flung colonies (Stoler 1995, Parenti 2003, McWhorter 2009). The same power elite that manages Empire, also manages so-called western "liberal societies." Stoler (1995) described this phenomenon in her study of the "education of desire" and the biopolitics of "race" and "sexuality" in the colonial order of things. Her analysis is focused on what this "polyvalent mobility" of discourses and practices can mean (particularly, the relay between the practices of subjection in European societies and their colonies). She uses examples from the development of pedagogical practices designed to discipline the colonized to have racially appropriate, sexual desires. Good examples would be the schools developed by the Americans to civilize "Indian children" and turn them into productive members of American society.

This interplay of Empire and domestic society is also evident in the American colonization of the Philippines at the turn of the 20th century. Alfred McCoy (2009) has made this interplay central to his detailed history of U.S./Philippine relations and the policing of Empire. McCoy argues that many of the "imperial" techniques developed to administer a Philippine population resistant to U.S. occupation after their "liberation" following the Spanish American war (1898), were gradually reintroduced into American society. He describes how the "information revolution" going on at the time of the occupation allowed American imperial administrators to establish an intense system of surveillance to pacify and manage a resistant Philippine population. They were able to improvise special techniques of "cadastral mapping, census taking, geography, photography, and police surveillance, and scientific reconnaissance" (McCoy 2009: 44). The situation in the Philippines, away from the internal politics of a liberal society that rejected such draconian practices, constituted a "protracted social experiment" in the use of police power as an instrument of domination. The Americans, he claims, developed three policing practices that would be reintroduced into American society during the World War I as a part of an emergent surveillance state: the use of informants, the use of civilian auxiliary organizations to collect information on the population, and the organization of counter-intelligence agencies. He describes how these systems of surveillance were put to use against German-Americans during the war, the "Reds" and other subversives after the war, the internment of the Japanese during World War II, and against "communists" in the 1950s. These practices returned to the U.S. with the personnel who had developed them and by the development of new policies, providing a basis for the intensification of surveillance and domination of the homeland.

More recently, the intensification of surveillance has been driven by the compulsive repetition of victimage rituals targeting illegal drugs, drug abusers, and organized crime (Blain 2002). Scott (2003) found direct linkages between CIA involvement in the illegal drug trade, the political-economy of oil, and America's wars in Afghanistan, Columbia, and Indochina. These developments are also reflected in the increased involvement of federal police agencies across international borders. Nadelmann (1993, also Andreas and Nadelmann 2006) describes how this phenomenon was a result of the increased involvement of U.S. federal agencies in spreading the American "drug prohibition" regime and policing at a global level.

The relay between these colonial practices and policing is evident in the ongoing "militarization" of American policing. Kraska's (1997a, 1997b) survey of 548 nonfederal police departments found an historic rise in the number of "police paramilitary units"—SWAT teams, and their level of activity, a development he argued had been made possible by the forging of many direct links between the military, private contractors who sell new technologies, and the military. He concluded that these paramilitary units had become a normal feature of mainstream policing. The menace of drugs, like terrorism, is tactically polyvalent, at once a "domestic problem" as well as a problem for administering Empire in the face of organized and violent resistance financed by revenues from drug trafficking. The illegal drug industry cuts across national boundaries. The "cocaine" cartels in Latin America must move product in the U.S. market, the largest market for illegal recreational drugs in the world, to maximize profits. This can only be accomplished by establishing direct domestic links to "homegrown" drug dealers.

Homeland Security and the Swarming of Surveillance Technologies

These studies are directly relevant to an assessment of the impact of the war on terrorism in liberal societies like the U.S. It is no exaggeration to say that the heightened "terror" of the U.S. population and emergence of "homeland security" has caused a proliferation of new surveillance technologies. The proliferation of these new technologies provides strong support for the epochal changes described by social theorists focusing on the social and political implications of the new information age (Poster 1984; Melluci 1996; Castells, 1996, 1997).

One index of the revolutionary impact of the computerization of new information systems on the intensification of police surveillance in American has been the enormous growth in the number of new federal government programs and agencies associated with "Homeland Security." Looking only at organizations at the top secret level in counterterrorism and intelligence, Priest and Arkin (2011) found the following:

> ...twenty-one new organizations created in just the last three months of 2001, among them the Office of Homeland Security and the FBI's Foreign Terrorist

Tracking Task Force. In 2002, thirty-four more organizations were created. Some tracked weapons of mass destruction, others joined the cyberwar and collected threat tips. Still others coordinated counterterrorism among different agencies, attempting to tame the growing information load. Those were followed the next year by thirty-nine new organizations, from the formidable Department of Homeland Security to Deep Red, a small naval intelligence cell working on the most difficult terrorism problems. In 2004, yet another thirty organizations were created or redirected toward the terrorism mission. That was followed by thirty-four more the next year and twenty-seven more the year after that; twenty-four or more each were added in 2007, 2008, and 2009. (2011: 86–87).

After a two year investigation they estimated that the sheer number of organizations affected included thousands of government agencies and private companies located at over seventeen thousand locations across the U.S. In total, the authors claim that there were over 3,900 organizations involved with programs related to counterterrorism, homeland security, and intelligence. They honed this number down to 263 new organizations and radically refashioned programs.

Two new types of programs and agencies illustrate the themes discussed here. The first type was inspired by the controversial dream of creating a total information awareness system (see Priest and Arkin's 2011: 104–127, "One Nation, One Map"). In the post 9/11 world, responsibilities for internal security have shifted from city and state to the federal level, particularly the Department of Defense. The "terrorist" threat constitutes a national emergency and national response. Only the federal government and the military can meet that emergency need. "Through Northern Command," an old program spawned by the Cold-War and Soviet nuclear threat, "no fewer than eighteen generals and admirals—men who once commanded combat troops in Iraq and Afghanistan, or prepared for missions against the Soviet Union and China—have as their sole focus defending the North American continent" (Priest and Arkin 2011: 105). Northern Command, in turn has spawned a number of new programs, including the use of state level National Guard units, to play new roles in domestic surveillance as well as to implement martial law in the event of a national emergency. The mapping of the whole nation fell mainly to the National Geospatial-Intelligence Agency (NGA). Responding to the needs of two new organizations—NorthCom and the Department of Homeland Security on the civilian side—this agency applied to the U.S. the mapping matrix it has used for battles overseas. A new program inside NGA called the "Homeland Security Infrastructure Program," includes hundreds of layers of data (Priest and Arkin 2011: 107–108).

The National Security Agency (NSA) is a second existing program and agency to get transformed by 9/11 by an infusion of multi-billions of dollars of new resources to realize the dream of a total information awareness system. The NSA was established in 1952 as part of the Cold-War. It is located in the state of Maryland and operated by the Department of Defense. The agency's original mission was to protect national security information systems and collect foreign signals intelligence (Bamford 2008, 2012). Like many other programs, NSA has been expanded to meet the new counterterrorism mission. The agency information network includes geostationary satellites, an Aerospace Data Facility (Buckley Air Force Base, Colorado), NSA Georgia (Fort Gordon, Augusta, Georgia), NSA Texas (Lackland Air Force Base, San Antonio). NSA Hawaii (Oahu), domestic listening posts, overseas listening posts, Utah Data Center (Bluffdale, Utah), Multipurpose Research Facility (Oak Ridge, Tennessee), and NSA Headquarters (Fort Meade, Maryland). The Utah Data Center will receive data collected by the satellites, foreign and domestic listening posts, and secret monitoring rooms in telecom corporations throughout the U.S.

A second type of program includes the creation of sixty-nine new state level "fusion centers" to integrate information and coordinate operations at the grassroots, state and local level. The majority of the affected organizations were existing federal, state, or local agencies, and large private corporations that experienced an infusion of new funds to create new counterterrorism programs. The bulk of the private contractors were located in the information technology sector. The Pentagon's Defense Intelligence agency that deals in information from around the world grew from 7500 employees in 2002 to 16,500 in 2010. At the same time, on the domestic surveillance front, the number of FBI Joint Terrorism Task Forces increased from 35 to 106. These joint task forces include members from the military, intelligence, law enforcement, and the private sector. The ultimate dream driving these new programs is the capacity to point to any neighborhood in America and gain instant access to all the relevant digitalized data.

This massive build-up of *domestic* surveillance and intelligence gathering capability has also been associated with the emergence of new discourses, constituting new types of terrorists. By February 2009, the "homegrown terrorist" operating as a "lone wolf" engaging in "terrorism" in the "homeland" emerges as a new threat alongside of "international networks" like Al Qaeda. In a statement made to the congress by Janet Napolitano, the secretary of the Department of Homeland Security, state and local police are in the best position to deal with this problem (Priest and Arkin 2011: 126). As a consequence in some locales portable road signs started appearing that displayed messages like "Report Suspicious Activities" and "Terrorist tips?" The sixty-nine new state level "fusion centers" have rapidly transformed themselves into "analytical hubs for all crimes, from school vandalism to petty drug dealing" (Priest and Arkin 2011: 137). More state and local law enforcement began to investigate a range of politically "suspicious" characters such as anti-war protesters, environmentalists, and animal rights activists.

These episodes were subtly encouraged by the diffusion of an array of new technologies that had been developed for use by elite military units to identify "terrorists" in Iraq and Afghanistan (Priest and Arkin 2011: 130). These technologies were developed to meet the needs of Elite Special Operations Units tasked with killing or capturing terrorists in war-zones. They were marketed to police departments by the same private contractors who had developed them to meet these needs. Corporate advertising emphasized the effective use of these technologies in identifying insurgents and clandestine activities in war zones. Many of these new tools were designed to identify large numbers of people without their knowledge. They include handheld wireless fingerprint scanners, thermal infrared cameras, and devices to record license plate numbers. The needs of Elite Special Operations Units for techniques of rapid analysis in the field that allowed operations in the field to fuse biometric identification, computer records, and cell phone numbers to map the organization structure of insurgent groups. At the same time, the Department of Homeland security and its state and local affiliates moved to use the same technology to collect photos, video images, and personal information about U.S. citizens to detect "homegrown terrorists." All of this information is input to computers linked to the Federal Bureau of Investigation and the Department of Homeland Security. The FBI is currently accumulating a vast repository of computerized information on Americans citizens in a data-base it calls the "Guardian." This repository is accumulating information collected by state and local police as part of the new "Nationwide Suspicious Reporting Initiative." Suspicious activity is defined as "observed behavior reasonably indicative of pre-operational planning related to terrorism or other criminal activity" (quoted in Priest and Arkin 2011: 144).

The use of "Human Terrain Systems" in counterinsurgency warfare directly involves social scientists, particularly and controversially, anthropologists (see Forte 2011). These "systems" involve the use of social science to map the "cultural environment" to facilitate the achievement of military goals in counterinsurgency programs. They have been very extensively employed in Iraq and Afghanistan. This use of this system exemplifies the constant relay of practices and discourse between Empire and domestic society. With financial aid and logistical support from the CIA, the New York Police Department (NYPD) has reintroduced this system into domestic society to monitor "terrorist" activity in the American-Muslim community ("Highlights...," *Associated Press*, 2011). Mapping the demographic and geographic distribution of crimes in cities has been a successful police strategy nationwide. NYPD had an existing "Demographics Unit" that produced maps of the distribution of crimes in the city. The new model was based on a system based on "ethnic identity" deployed by the Israeli's in the West Bank to manage Palestinian "terrorism." The goal of the NYPD program was to "map the city's human terrain."

Psychological Torture

The war on terrorism has exerted multiple power effects in various fields of knowledge. As Foucault demonstrated through the meticulous detail of his multiple genealogies of the human sciences, "...power produces knowledge (and not simply by encouraging it because it serves power or by applying it because it is useful); that power and knowledge directly imply one another, that there is no power relation without the correlative constitution of a field of knowledge, nor any knowledge that does not presupposed and constitute at the same time power relations" (1977: 27).[2] The development of the prison was historically correlated with the birth of new fields of knowledge such as psychology and psychiatry, and criminology and the social sciences. The 9/11 attacks and the subsequent declaration of a world war represent historic moves in a global geopolitical game set into motion by the 9/11 attacks—the latest twist in the genealogy of terrorism. The individual terrorist, the "populations" and "spaces" that produce them, and the incidents of terrorism have emerged as objects of serious social and psychological analysis.

The role of "psychology" in the war on terrorism has been controversial. The participation of psychologists working for the military and CIA have been linked to the "enhanced interrogation" of terrorists employing various techniques of "psychological torture." The aim of these practices was to gain "actionable intelligence." The participation of military psychologists in these practices raised serious questions of professional ethics—particularly, the principles that researchers should do no harm to research subjects (see Mayer 2005, 2008, Soldz 2006, "Resolution adopted by APA..." 2007).

Examined in the light of the history of torture, these "interrogations" as well as the subsequent scandals they provoked can be viewed as a recycling of the pattern of sovereign torture. Foucault (1977: 32–69) described these practices in excruciating detail in his history of the prison and genealogy of the human sciences. Sovereign torture was composed of two interlocking rituals, the first was judicial and secret, and the second political and public. These two rites were tied together by the body of the condemned. Torture played a crucial role in both procedures, first as an instrument of a legally regulated pain—"the poetry of Dante put into laws," to mark the "patient" and produce a confession of the truth of the crime, and second, as part of a public political spectacle carefully choreographed to dramatize the truth of the condemned's crime.

The use of "psychological torture" to interrogate terrorists recapitulates this pattern, albeit in the guise of a "psychological" discourse. These practices are not part of a judicial procedure to obtain a confession of a crime or to punish a criminal. They are "enhanced interrogations" to obtain "actionable intelligence" to prevent and deter future terrorist attacks. The following is a brief extract of an account by Abu Zubaydah, a Palestinian man who was subjected an "enhanced interrogations":

---

2   It should be emphasized that this special sense of power / knowledge relations does not preclude an ethical concern with the politics of truth in the obvious sense that scientific research can be directly perverted to achieve commercial or political goals (e.g., the perversion of "scientific integrity" and the "misuse of science" by scientists, executives, and politicians working on behalf of corporate interests, such as Exxon Mobil in the field of "climate science," Union of Concerned Scientists 2004, Coll 2012: 67–92, Cohen et al. 2012; or the misuse of "science" by actors advancing the cause of tobacco firms in the field of medical research on cancer and heart disease, Kluger 1996).

I woke up, naked, strapped to a bed, in a very white room. The room measured approximately [13 feet by 13 feet]. The room had three solid walls, with the fourth wall consisting of metal bars separating it from a larger room. I am not sure how long I remained in the bed. After some time, I think it was several days, but can't remember exactly, I was transferred to a chair where I was kept, shackled by [the] hands and feet for what I think was the next 2 to 3 weeks. During this time I developed blisters on the underside of my legs due to the constant sitting. I was only allowed to get up from the chair to go [to] the toilet, which consisted of a bucket. Water for cleaning myself was provided in a plastic bottle.

I was given no solid food during the first two or three weeks, while sitting on the chair. I was only given Ensure [a nutrient supplement] and water to drink. At first the Ensure made me vomit, but this became less with time.

The cell and room were air-conditioned and were very cold. Very loud, shouting type music was constantly playing. It kept repeating about every fifteen minutes twenty-four hours a day. Sometimes the music stopped and was replaced by a loud hissing or crackling noise.

The guards were American, but wore masks to conceal their faces. My interrogators did not wear masks. During this first two to three week period I was questioned for about one to two hours each day. American interrogators would come to the room and speak to me through the bars of the cell. During the questioning the music was switched off, but was then put back on again afterwards. I could not sleep at all for the first two to three weeks. If I started to fall asleep one of the guards would come and spray water in my face (quoted in Danner 2009).

Once these activities were publicized through leaks to the mass media, they functioned as political victimage rituals with a complex military / political function. Danner (2009) has also noted the "public" character of these so-called "secret" intelligence procedures:

All classified, compartmentalized, deeply, deeply secret. And yet what is "secret" exactly? In our recent politics, "secret" has become an oddly complex word. From whom was "the secret bombing of Cambodia" secret? Not from the Cambodians, surely. From whom was the existence of these "secret overseas facilities" secret? Not from the terrorists, surely. From Americans, presumably. On the other hand, as early as 2002, anyone interested could read on the front page of one of the country's leading newspapers: "US Decries Abuse but Defends Interrogations: 'Stress and Duress' Tactics Used on Terrorism Suspects Held in Secret Overseas Facilities."

This blending of the "intelligence" and "political" functions of "enhanced interrogations" was captured in President Bush's well-known, public admission after leaving office, "Yeah, we waterboarded Kalid Sheikh Mohammed ...I'd do it again to save lives" (quoted in Froomkin 2010).

What is not so well known is the historical role of psychologists in these activities. McCoy (2006) describes its historical development in great detail. During the Cold-War the CIA and Department of Defense developed a psychological "torture" paradigm that fused two methods, "sensory deprivation" and "self-inflicted pain" (McCoy 2006: 8). The infamous photographic image disseminated on the web of the hooded Iraqi prisoner at Abu Ghraib with his arms extended and wires to hands, exemplifies these two aspects of this procedure. As it turns out, military psychologists played a unique role in the development of these programs and participated directly in the "enhanced interrogations" of terrorists (Mayer 2005).

The road that led to Abu Ghraib starts after World War II, and the convergence of the Cold-War and psychological science. Emerging from World War II, psychology was the most militarized of the social and biological sciences. Some of the psychological research was initially inspired by questions raised by the Stalinist practice of staging "show trials" in which alleged traitors to the Stalinist system would give false confessions (McCoy 2006: 23–32). Many of these individuals had been high-ranking and loyal members of the Stalinist regime. Why had they been so willing to give such convincing false confessions? Many of those involved in the early research thought that one possible answer was that these individuals might have been "brain-washed."

With financial backing from the Central Intelligence Agency (i.e., much of it "laundered" through a variety of federal agencies including the Department of Defense), psychologists were actively enlisted to engage in sponsored research to establish a scientific basis to design training programs for CIA agents and soldiers to resist the "communist interrogation" and "mind control" techniques developed by the Soviet and Chinese communist regimes (depicted in the influential 1962 movie, *The Manchurian Candidate*). Later, it would consider the idea that "psychological torture" might be more effective than "physical torture" in producing good intelligence. Some of these research projects were also designed to test the use of drugs like LSD in intelligence gathering and interrogation (Lee and Shlain 1993). Three lines of research converged to produce the CIA's new psychological paradigm:

> ...At Montreal's McGill University, the discovery, by gifted Canadian psychologist Dr. Donald Q. Hebb, of the devastating impact of sensory deprivation became the conceptual core of the agency's paradigm. Working under direct and indirect CIA contracts, distinguished American behavioral scientists—Albert Biderman, Irving L. Janis, Harold Wolff, and Lawrence Hinkle—advised the agency about the role of self-inflicted pain in Communist interrogation. Finally, a young Yale psychologist, Stanley Milgram, did controversial research under

government grant showing that almost any individual is capable of torture—a critical finding for the agency as it prepared to disseminate its method worldwide. By the project's end in the late 1960s, this torture research had involved three of the "100 most eminent psychologists of the 20th century—Hebb, Milgram, and Janis—as well as several presidents of the American Psychiatric Association and the American Psychological Association (McCoy 2006: 32; Hebb 1949, 1955; Milgram 1964, 1974).

The involvement of leading psychologists, psychiatrists, and neurologists in CIA sponsored research and "intelligence gathering" has been confirmed in research by Moreno (2006) in a book titled, "Mind Wars." Chase (2003) has argued that Theodore Kaczynski's (the Unabomber) involvement in "domestic terrorism," was partly attributable to his participation in a Harvard University experiment. The experiment involved using undergraduate students like Kaczynski "as subjects to examine the role of humiliation in the process of psychic deconstruction."

The military and CIA used the results of this research in subsequent years to fashion its military programs to train American pilots and soldiers to resist interrogation techniques when captured by the "communist" enemies. In the meantime, this psychological knowledge had been extended to training for counterinsurgency campaigns. The curriculum was used to train CIA agents and their foreign allies to use these "interrogation techniques" to conduct counterinsurgency campaigns in Viet Nam, Iran, the Philippines, and Central and Latin America (McCoy 2006: 86–107). They are called SERE programs, which stands for "Survival, Evasion, Resistance, and Escape." The first program was created by the Air Force at the end of the Korean War. After the Viet Nam war it was extended to the Army and Navy. The leading SERE program is at the Army's John F. Kennedy Special Warfare Center and School, Fort Bragg, North Carolina, where the Green Berets train (Mayer 2005). Both types of programs involved some of the following features: Psychological Design (i.e., based on knowledge of psychological techniques), [psychological] Regression (i.e., produced by manipulative techniques), Sensory Deprivation, Isolation, Manipulation, Environment (i.e., the space of questioning), Arrest, Threats and Fear, and Drugs.

This CIA and U.S. military propagated the "psychological paradigm" around the world during the Cold War. There were two phases in this history, the first operated through covert police-training programs in Asia and Latin America and the second through Army teams that advised local counterinsurgency forces, largely in Central America. The spread of this practice to Iran was crucial in provoking the Iranian revolution. In the decades after the coup in 1953 had restored the Shah of Iran to power, the CIA helped to train a secret police force called the Savak to use these interrogation practices. A violent variant of these "interrogation" practices showed up 1972 toward the end of the Viet Nam war. Project Phoenix was a "counter terror" program developed as a joint effort of the Central Intelligence Agency and the Federal Bureau of Investigation. This program was instituted in 1972 toward the end of the Viet Nam war, as the Saigon regime in South Viet Nam lost control of the country-side and the U.S. military faced defeat at the hands of the Viet Cong.

> In Saigon, Phoenix used sophisticated computer information banks to centralize data on the Vietcong infrastructure, identifying key Communist cadres for interrogation or elimination. In the countryside, the program made use of this intelligence through specially trained counterguerrilla teams... attached to the CIA's forty Provincial Interrogation Centers (McCoy 2006: 64).

This practice showed up in the Philippines from 1972 to 1986. It was a key element of the Marcos regime's martial-law rule. A key aspect of all of these episodes has been the public awareness that they were going on. These not so secret "interrogation centers" and "Black Sites" constitute a public "theater" of sovereign terror.

After a hiatus of over a decade following the end of the Cold War—the last known use of the torture manuals was in the early 1990s, and the declaration of a war on terrorism in the fall of 2001, the Bush regime reactivated the use of torture as one of its main weapons in the war with Al Qaeda. They argued that the use of "psychological torture" was justified to gain "actionable intelligence" to deter and prevent horrific acts of "terrorism" like the 9/11 attacks, and win the war. However, when the "tortures" are video-taped and photographed, leaked to the press, and widely disseminated in the media of mass spectacle, they also functioned as part of a campaign of victimage ritual and "psychological warfare." The crucial point is that the ritual pattern that constituted sovereign torture is recapitulated in these episodes. As Foucault argued, these "meticulous rituals of power" functioned as a more or less effective system of state sponsored terror. The use of "enhanced interrogations" by the CIA and military to produce "actionable intelligence" reenacts in a modern rationalized form the judicial and political rites of sovereign power. In this sense, then, one might argue that "enhanced interrogation" of terrorists is a form of sovereign terror. The widespread "leaks" to the mass media of videos documented these activities completes the circuit of sovereign terror. The difference, of course, is that these secret / public rites are staged in far-flung theaters of Empire.

At the time, these sites of sovereign power can constitute a space for biopolitics to function. In the same way that the 19th century prison, according to Foucault (1977: 295–96), assumed an "auxiliary function" as centers of research. The Black sites, interrogation and detention centers spawned by the war on terror can assume a similar auxiliary research function, where psychologists, psychiatrists, and social scientists can collect data and test their theories with financial support from federally sponsored research project. Terrorists incarcerated in these places have been transformed into a ready supply of research subjects. This development has a domestic aspect to it as well. A literal "archipelago" of special units in federal prisons has been created to incarcerate "terrorists" that stretches across the U.S. (Shane 2011).

Jerrold Post, a psychiatrist who has worked with the CIA extensively, repeatedly acknowledges his access to incarcerated 'terrorists' in conducting his research. Post (2002, 2005b, 2007) notes that the materials he collected and reported in his research publications, materials that are designed to reveal the "socio-cultural foundations" of contemporary "terrorism" and "bring the reader into their [terrorist] minds," draws on "semi-structured interviews" with numerous incarcerated terrorists around the world. Post stresses his commitment to this goal in his academically oriented publications. In a 2005 publication in "Joint Force Quarterly," the primary aim of his research is to contribute to "Psychological operations and counter terrorism" (2005a).

The bio-politics of terrorism is on full display in a 2010 *Harvard Review of Psychiatry* article by Ronald Schouten, MD, JD, titled "Terrorism and the Behavioral Sciences." The language of epidemiology structures the discourse and reduces the study of "terrorists" to the search for "risk factors." Epidemiology is the branch of medical science that studies the distribution, causes, and control of diseases in populations. It should also be noted in passing that this article also clearly displays the correlated but vexing issues involved in defining "terrorism" in a way that differentiates it from other forms of political violence and warfare, and the problem of working out the ethical issues provoked by the professional participation of behavioral scientists in fighting the war on terrorism. Typically, diseases unlike behaviors have some kind of operational definition with a clear physical test. Unfortunately, Schouten states, no single definition of terrorism "captures the concept." Nevertheless, all definitions include one or the other of the following elements: use of force or violence, by individuals or groups, directed at civilian populations, intended to instill fear, and a means of coercing individuals or groups to change their political or social positions (Schouten 2010: 369). The problem with this definition is that these same five points also describes political violence in "legitimate" and "just" wars such as World War II or the Viet Nam war.

This confusion may explain why no discussion is presented of the role of psychologists, psychiatrists, and social scientists in supporting the "legitimate" political violence perpetrated by "militaries." As we shall see later in this discussion, there has been some research on the role of the human sciences in the design of military training programs. They have been extraordinarily effective in producing soldiers and pilots who engage in much "legal" political violence. The article does review the existing "Psychological Theories of Terrorism." These theories range from "psychopathology" and "rational choice" to a focus on "group and organization dynamics" and "terrorist networks." In spite of a lack of consensus about which of these theories might be the most valid one, the article states:

> The U.S. government has demonstrated its awareness of the importance of behavioral science and mental health issues in addressing terrorism through its funding of the national Consortium for the Study of Terrorism and Responses to Terrorism (START). Based at the University of Maryland, START is one of the Centers of Excellence academic institutions established by the Department

of Homeland Security to address multiple aspects of the problem of terrorism (Schouten 2010: 374).

After reviewing the problems associated with "Predicting Terrorist Behavior," it concludes that predicting terrorist behavior based on personality or clinical profiles has failed.

Since theories of personality or psychopathology do not work, the article argues that a focus on "Risk Factors for Violence" is a better research strategy. The search for "risk factors for violence" primarily focuses on violent individuals and perpetrators of illegal violence. The best way to proceed is on the assumption that "terrorism" is "a subset of violent behavior and to look to other violence research for insights into the potential for this form of violence." Risk factors for "targeted" as opposed to "random" violence include "(1) individual characteristics of the potential perpetrator(s) that may include trait anger, past history of difficulty handling stress, sense of persecution and being treated unfairly, blaming others for all problems, and mental illness; (2) situational factors, or triggers, such as acute and chronic stressors; and 3) environmental variables, including characteristics of the potential subject of attack, level of security, interactions with the potential perpetrator, the work situation, and the perpetrator's knowledge of the potential victim" The author identifies the following specific factors, although not all them show up in every case: male gender, past history of violence, the presence of mental illness and substance abuse, and psychopathic (antisocial) traits." Applying the analytic framework to the planners and perpetrators of the September 11, 2001 attacks, the article observed the following:

> [They shared] a sense of persecution by the West, a history of violence, and fundamentalist religious, as well as political motivations. Situational factors that may have contributed to the events include the American presence in Saudi Arabia and ongoing conflict in the Middle East. Finally, possible environmental variables includes security gaps in the air travel system" (Schouten 2010: 375).

Again, it should be noted, the author does not review any research on "perpetrators" of "legal" political violence, the use of "force" by the police and the military. The presupposition of the whole review is that "terrorism" is a psychological or social pathology. In this sense, it is best understood in terms of the biopolitics of security and the control and regulation of "deviant" and "criminal" behavior. The idea that the so-called "terrorists" might be "rational-actors"—engaged as soldiers in a war they view as legitimate and just, is never really broached in detail.

Past research on the role of the "psyche" sciences in modern warfare suggests that military discipline and intensive training is effective in producing actors who are ready, willing and able to engage in the terrifying "Shock and Awe" of modern warfare (Blain 1988: 273). In a review of historical research by Stern (1985) on the role German psychologists played in the Nazi military suggests that psychological testing might have had more to do with the efficiency and effectiveness of the

Nazi war machine than did the Nazi regime's ritual victimage of the Jews. Public morale was boosted by vicarious involvement in spectacular public victimage rituals staged by the Nazi party. "Basic training" produced the warriors; the Nazi's political victimage rituals contributed to public support for the war. In other words, we should see two cultural practices involved in political violence—disciplinary technologies and political victimage ritual working in tandem.

Perversion of Social Science

The passage of Homeland Security Act in 2002 has exercised direct effects on "knowledge" in a number of social science fields (Blain 2009b). These effects have been registered in articles appearing in the professional newsletters reflecting the new research opportunities and ethical issues they pose (e.g., "AAA Commission on the Engagement of Anthropology with the US Security and Intelligence Communities" 2007, "The Art and Social Science of War" 2008). New consortiums and institutes of 'Terrorism' have been constituted to produce and disseminate 'knowledge': The National Geospatial Intelligence Agency (2003→), The National Counterterrorism Center (NCTC), the official U.S. agency charged with tracking the incidence of terrorism (2005→) and the National Consortium for the Study of Terrorism and Responses to Terrorism, University of Maryland (START), funded primarily by the Department of Homeland Security. Researchers associated with these institutes operationally define terrorism and code and count incidences of terrorism in ways that are consistent with the interests of a U.S. led Empire.

Some idea of the magnitude of the response of social scientists to the global war on terrorism is reflected in Chart 5.1. The total number of articles coded "Subject Terrorism" produced by a search in late 2011 produced 2300 citations to articles published in refereed journal articles. Eighty-eight percent of these articles were published after the 9/11 attacks and the declaration of a global war, 2002–2010. Two systematic random samples (74: 1990–2008 and 285: 1960–2010) of "terrorism" articles were drawn from the Abstracts (sample 1: 74, 1990–2008 and sample 2: 285, 1960–2010) and each article coded for the presence or absence of a biopolitical orientation, forty percent of the articles could be coded as predominantly biopolitical in character. That is, these researchers accepted the operational definition of "terrorism" as a social fact as defined by the U.S. power elite and from the point of view of Empire. These articles accepted the concepts of "terrorism" and / or "the terrorist" as unproblematic social scientific concepts or "social things" that could be scientifically investigated in the same way that one would study the causes and effects of a disease process. The most frequent causes of "terrorism" were attributed to the "terrorists" pathological political, cultural, ethnic, or religious orientations. Some articles examined the social and psychological effects of the terrorism. Sixty percent of the articles contested these notions in some way or another.

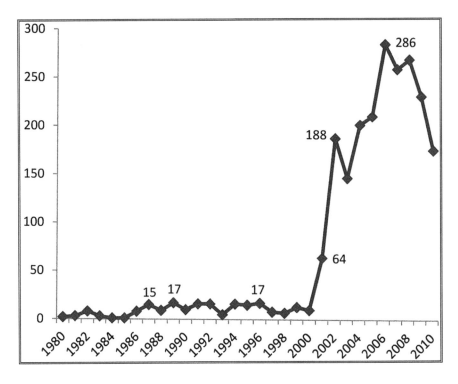

Chart 5.1   Frequency of Peer Reviewed Articles Coded Subject Terrorism by Year in Sociological Abstracts, 1980–2010

Some social scientists were quick to seize the new funding opportunities. On March 30, 2004, the American Sociological Association (ASA) e-mailed its members the following communiqué: "Department of Homeland Security Funding". The purpose of this funding would be to establish two campus-based Centers for Excellence ($7.5 million would go to each center). "One Center will address the 'Psychology of Terrorism' and one will address the "Social Impact of Terrorist Events." A second announcement followed on July 6, 2004: "Department of Homeland Security Announces $12 Million Funding for Social and Behavioral Scientist to Study Terrorism." Proposals were solicited for establishing a university-based Center for Excellence in Behavioral and Social Aspects of Terrorism and Counter-Terrorism. These developments were reported in a front page article appearing in the February 2005 edition of *Footnotes*, the official newsletter of the ASA, "Fighting International Terrorism with Social Science Knowledge" (Ebner 2005). "Social scientists, including numerous sociologists," the article begins, "will unite in defense of national security." A new program associated with the "Center for International Development and Conflict Management," (CIDCM) was to be established at the University of Maryland-College Park. This program was to be dedicated "to reducing terrorism worldwide" (http://www.cidcm.umd.edu/).

The leader of the research team, criminologist Gary LaFree, is quoted as stating: "This may be the social science equivalent of the Manhattan Project." LaFree continues, "Too often, policymakers have had to counter terrorists on the basis of assumptions and guesstimates. Our job will be to give them more solid information to work with" (Ebner 2005: 5; for a critique, see Altheide 2005). The *Footnotes* article does not broach the question of whether or not this kind of "surveillance" and "information gathering" activity is serious social science. It certainly does not deal with ethical questions raised by the rule to "do no harm to research subjects" nor the "Social Responsibility" principle in the American Sociological Association's code of ethics. The transformation of politically useful "information" into scientific "data" is considered unproblematic. As we shall see, the operation definition of "terrorism" continues to be conveniently confused and arbitrary. At least sixty-percent of the social scientists who publish in refereed journal articles on topics relevant to terrorism do not agree with this assumption.

The Center for International Development and Conflict Management (CIDCM) is an interdisciplinary research center that seeks to prevent and transform conflict, to understand conflict and development, and to help societies create sustainable futures. CIDCM "devises effective tools and pathways to constructive change" (Hewitt, Wilkenfeld, and Gurr 2008). For more than 20 years the Center has addressed issues of "security, identity, and distributive justice." The researchers attached to the Center are devoted to the principle that "peace-building and development-with-justice are two sides of the same coin." They might have added that as far as securing large grants from the Department of Homeland Security is concerned, power / knowledge are two sides of the same coin.

The Center's *Peace and Conflict 2008* research report makes many references to terrorism, devoting almost half of the introductory overview of the edited volume to the problem. The implicit perspective of the report is the orientation of the U.S. power elite and the managers of Empire. The analysis emphasizes the concept of a "conflict syndrome" and divides the regions of the world into three types of governmental regimes: democratic, autocratic, and anocratic. "Democratic governance is the norm in the twenty-first century," it asserts, "but in recent years more regimes have edged into anocracy—with an incoherent mix of authoritarian and democratic features (77 democracies and 34 autocratic in 2006; 49 anocratic in 2005)." The anocratic nations are significant because they are more prone to suffer from "conflict syndrome" and be subject "to political instability and armed conflict...to terrorist attacks...to international crises." One might add that anocratic states are also more amenable to invasion. *Peace and Conflict* carefully traces the dangerous propensity for those states (anocratic, unstable, and failing states) to host domestic and international terrorist organizations (Hewitt et al. 2008: 2). A closer reading of the data also reveals a number of glaring exceptions to this pattern (e.g., the conflict in Northern Ireland; also, many terrorist campaigns in the 1970s were located in Europe; the 911 perpetrators were living in Europe and from Saudi Arabia). The idea that these statements might provide a pretext for a U.S. led Empire is not considered.

The introduction concludes with the statement, "Terrorism, especially by Islamists, is an existential threat to security in all world regions" (Hewitt et al. 2008: 3). The careful reader of the rest of the report can only be shocked by the glaring contradiction between these statements and the actual data presented. The evidence presented in a chapter titled, "Ethnopolitical Violence and Terrorism in the Middle East," indicates that most of the 112 ethnic and religious minority groups in the Middle East did not engage in "terrorism" 1980–2004 (Asal, Johnson, and Wilkenfeld 2008: 39–54). And, secondly, the evidence suggests that democratization in the Middle East has generated both conventional politics and terrorism.

Gary LaFree, the criminologist featured in the earlier ASA *Footnotes* article, is the senior coauthor of a chapter titled "Global Terrorism and Failed States" (Lafree, Dugan, and Fahey 2008: 39–54). The strategic character of the power/knowledge relations are strikingly evident in the examples and definitions the authors employ to constitute "terrorism" as an object of knowledge. First of all, Lafree et al. (2008: 39) assert that so-called "modern terrorism" began in the late 1960s. This terrorism is modern because it involves the deliberate use of symbolism and the mass media to attain worldwide attention. The authors cite Bruce Hoffman (1998), scholar on contract to the Rand Corporation, as a source for this convenient idea. The example they describe is the aerial hijacking of an Israeli El Al commercial flight en route from Rome to Tel Aviv in July 1968. The terrorists were three armed Palestinian men belonging to the Popular Front for the Liberation of Palestine. Much discussion follows describing a new Global Terrorism Database (GTD), which is derived from the Pinkerton Global Intelligence Service (PGIS). The data set covers 1970 to the present, which is convenient since the authors restrict their analysis to modern terrorism since the late 1960s.

Lafree et al. (2008) define terrorism in the process of establishing why there are many more cases in the GTD (70,000) than other data-bases maintained by U.S. government agencies like the FBI. Terrorism is defined broadly as "The threatened or actual use of illegal force and violence to attain a political, economic, religious, or social goal through fear, coercion, or intimidation." The U.S. State Department limits its database to "political motivated violence." The operational definition that guides the Global Terrorism Database focuses on the illegality of the political violence. If the political violence is used to obtain one of the listed goals, and it is legal, it is by definition not terrorism. If Empire decides (typically through a resolution of the United Nations' Security Council) to liberate a region from autocratic rule, the political violence involved is by definition legal and not terrorism. In a later publication by Lafree and Ackerman (2009) appearing in the *Annual Review of Law and Social Science*, a more restricted operational definition of terrorism is articulated. Terrorism is "…the threatened or actual use of illegal force directed against civilian targets by nonstate actors in order to attain a political goal through fear, coercion, or intimidation." The next sentence qualifies the object of their analysis by differentiating it from other forms of terrorism: "In particular, we exclude research on state terrorism or genocide, topics that are important and complex enough to warrant their own separate reviews" (2009: 348).

The conceptual problems involved in differentiating terrorism from other forms of violence mount as one examines Chapter 8 of *Peace and Conflict 2008*, "Mass Killing of civilians in Time of War, 1945–2000" by Hugh and Valentino (2008: 79–92). The authors state that 18–25 million civilians have died in wars since 1945. They point out that mass killings of civilians has been a deliberate policy in many wars. They theorize that "intentional killing of civilians during war is often a calculated military strategy designed to defeat powerful guerrilla insurgencies... counterinsurgent forces often choose to target guerrillas' base of support in the population, which can in turn lead to the intentional killing of massive numbers of civilians (2008: 79). Huth and Valentino (2008: 79) define mass killing as "the intentional killing of a massive number of noncombatants ($\geq$ 50,000 over the course of 5 years) during a war." Table 9.1 presented in the report summarizes the actors involved in "Mass Killing in Wars (1945–2000)" by breaking them down into "Civil Wars" (e.g., China-Communists 1946–1949) and "Guerrilla Wars" (e.g., Franco-Algerian of 1945, 1945–1962 and "Korea War 1950–1953. The U.S. does not appear anywhere in this table. Russia is named in "Russia-Chechnya 1994–1996. There is no U.S.-Korea War 1950–1953 or U.S.-Vietnam War 1960–1975. After a careful data analysis of mass killings the authors conclude, "Across all of the statistical models...guerrilla warfare proved to have highly significant and powerful effects on the likelihood of mass killing" (2008: 87). The elision of any reference to U.S. involvement in the intentional mass killings of civilians is a tactical move. By the Lafree et al. definition, many of these mass killings should be coded as cases of terrorism.

The problems with this kind of research strategy are widely recognized in the social science community. The center for "International Studies" at Simon Fraser University devoted a whole issue of *Human Security Research* to the methodological flaws and distortions in these sponsored research projects (*Dying to Lose...*, 2007). The authors of this report identified a number of serious problems with research based on data-bases produced by The Global Terrorism Database and U.S. government agencies: the coding is not reliable, getting accurate counts of injuries and deaths, the decision to only count civilian deaths, and differentiating "terrorism" from "insurgent" or "sectarian" or "criminal" violence. Human Security found the data sets and coding practices were US-centric—influenced by U.S. national security interests that create a "distorted" picture of the global terrorist threat (Charbonneau 2008). Many of the researchers involved in promoting the new institutes exaggerated the level of world terrorism by counting all fatalities after the U.S. invasion of Iraq in 2003. They found, that absent the Iraq war death and injury accounts after the 2003 invasion, there had been no increase international terrorism at the time.

On the other hand, these operational definitions and categorizations coincide perfectly with the biopolitics of terrorism in the context of a U.S. led Empire. This glaring problem was illustrated by the START webpage, June 2010. The page titled, "GTD: Information on Over 80,000 Terrorist Attacks" displayed a map of "Left-Wing Terrorism in Columbia, 1977–1997)." The map was based on research employing GTD by Jason Belcher, a *Department of Homeland Security Scholar*, located at the University of Maryland, and titled, "The Spatial Concentration and Patterns of Left-Wing Terrorism in Colombia (1977–1997)." By January the number of terrorist attacks in the GDT database had increased to 98,000 and it is now possible to get a graduate certificate with a minor in "Think like a terrorist."

Bibliography

"AAA Commission on the Engagement of Anthropology with the US Security and Intelligence Communities." American Anthropological Association. 4 November 2007. <http://www.aaanet.org/_cs_upload/pdf/4092_1.pdf>. Accessed July 15, 2008.

Agamben, Giorgio. *Homer Sacer: Sovereign Power and Bare Life.* Translated by Daniel Heller-Roazen. Palo Alto: Stanford University Press, 1998.

—. *State of Exception.* Chicago: University of Chicago Press, 2005.

Ali, Tariq. *Bush in Babylon: The Recolonization of Iraq.* New York: Verso, 2004.

Allan, Keith, and Kate Burridge. *Euphemism & Dysphemism: Language Used as Shield and Weapon.* New York: Oxford University Press, 1991.

Altheide, David. "Sociology and the Politics of Fear." *Footnotes: Newsletter of the American Sociological Association* 33, no. 8 (November 2005): 10.

American Presidency Project, *Public Papers of the Presidents of the United States (PPPUS).* University of California, Santa Barbara < http://www.presidency. ucsb.edu/ws>. Accessed 5 July 2010.

Anderson, David. *Histories of the Hanged: The Dirty War in Kenya and the End of Empire.* New York: Norton, 2005.

Andreas, Peter, and Ethan Nadelmann. *Policing the Globe: Criminalization and Crime Control in International Relations.* Oxford University Press, 2006.

Archambault, G.H. "Nazis Give French Only Two Choices: All Must Be 'Collaborationist' or 'Terrorist'—No Middle Ground Lies Open." *New York Times*, 2 December 1942, 5.

"The Art and Social Science of War." *Footnotes: Newsletter of the American Sociological Association* 37, no. 6 (July/August 2008): 5.

Asal, Victor, Carter Johnson, and Johathan Wilkenfeld. "Ethnopolitical Violence and Terrorism in the Middle East." In *Peace and Conflict 2008*, edited by J. Joseph Hewitt, Jonathan Wilkenfeld, and Ted Robert Gurr, 55–66. Boulder, CO: Paradigm Publishers, 2008.

Baker, Peter and Michael Shear. Obama Trumpets Killing of bin Laden, and Critics Pounce. *New York Times* 28 April 2012. <http://www.nytimes. com/2012/04/28/us/politics/critics-pounce-on-obamas-trumpeting-of-bin-laden-death.html?emc=tnt&tntemail1=y> . Accessed 8 May 2012.

Bamford, James. *The Shadow Factory: The Ultra-Secret NSA from 9/11 to the Eavesdropping on America.* New York: Doubleday, 2008.

—. "The NSA is Building the Country's Biggest Spy Center (Watch What You Say)." *Wired: Threat Level* 15 March 2012. <http://www.wired.com/2012/3/ff_nsadatacenter/all/1>. Accessed 1 April 2012.

Barrett, Michele. *The Politics of Truth: From Marx to Foucault*. Stanford, California: Stanford University Press, 1991.

Becker, Howard. *Outsiders: Studies in the Sociology of Deviance*. New York: Free Press, 1963.

Belasco, Amy. "The Cost of Iraq, Afghanistan, and Other Global War on Terror Operations Since 9/11." 29 March 2011. *Congressional Research Service*. http://www.fas.org/sgp/crs/natsec/RL33110.pdf . Accessed 27 August 2011.

Bellamy, Francis, *The Pledge of Allegiance*, 1892.

Berlin, Irving. *God Bless America*. 1918, 1935.

Berezin, Mabel. "Politics and Culture: A Less Fissured Terrain." *Annual Review of Sociology* 23 (1997): 361–383.

Berman, Paul. *Terror and Liberalism*. New York: W.W. Norton and Company, 2004.

Bin Laden, Osama. *Messages to the World: The Statements of Osama bin Laden*. Translated by James Howarth. Edited by Bruce Lawrence. New York: Verso, 2005.

—. "Terror for Terror." In *Messages to the World: The Statements of Osama bin Laden*, edited by Bruce Lawrence, 106–129. New York: Verso, 2005 [2001].

Blain, Angeline Kearns. *Tactical Textiles: A Genealogy of the Boise Peace Quilt Project, 1981–1988*. Dubuque, Iowa: Kendall/Hunt Publishing Company, 1994.

Blain, Michael. "Fighting Words: What We Can Learn from Hitler's Hyperbole." *Symbolic Interaction* 11, no. 2 (1988): 257–276.

—. "Group Defamation and the Holocaust." In *Group Defamation and Freedom of Speech: The Relationship Between Language and Violence*, edited by Monroe Freedman and Eric Freedman, 45–68. Westport, Connecticut: Greenwood Press, 1995.

—. "The New U.S. Anti-'Drug War' Movement." In *Anti-Globalization Movements II*, Roland Roth, chair. XV World Congress of Sociology. Brisbane, Australia: International Sociological Association, 7–13 July, 2002.

—. "On the Genealogy of Terrorism." In *Interrogating the War on Terror*, edited by Barbara Staines, 49–66. Newcastle, UK: Cambridge Scholars Press, 2007.

—. *The Politics of Death: A Sociological Analysis of Revolutionary Communication*. www.dissertation.com 2001 [1974].

—. "The Politics of Victimage: Power and Subjection in a US Anti-Gay Campaign." *Critical Discourse Studies* 2, no. 1 (April 2005): 31–50.

—. "Power and Practice in Peace Movement Discourse." In *Research in Social Movements, Conflict and Change. Volume 11*, edited by Louis Kriesberg, 197–218. Greenwich, Connecticut: JAI Press Inc., 1989.

—. "Power, War, and Melodrama in the Discourses of Political Movements." *Theory and Society* 23, no. 6 (1994): 805–838.

—. "The Role of Death in Political Conflict." *The Psychoanalytic Review* 63, no. 2 (Summer 1976): 249–265.

—. *The Sociology of Terrorism: Studies in Power, Subjection, and Victimage Ritual.* Boca Raton, Florida: Universal-Publishers, 2009.

—. "Sovereignty, Biopower, and the Global War on Terrorism." *Discourse and Sociological Practice* 8, no. 2 (2009): 37–58.

Bohlen, Celestine. "Think Tank; In New War on Terrorism, Words Are Weapons, Too." *New York Times* 29 September 2001. <<http://www.nytimes.com/2001/09/29/arts/think-tank-in-new-war-on-terrorism-words-are-weapons-too.html>>. Accessed 15 December 2011.

Borges, Jorge Luis. "The Cyclical Night." In *A Personal Anthology*, edited by Anthony Kerrigan. New York: Grove Press, Inc., 1967.

Borradori, Giovanna. *Philosophy in a Time of Terror: Dialogues with Jurgen Habermas and Jacques Derrida.* Chicago: University of Chicago Press, 2003.

Bowlby, John. "Grief and Mourning in Infancy and Early Childhood." *Psychoanalytic Study of the Child* 15 (1960): 9–52.

—. "Processes of Mourning." *International Journal of Psychoanalysis* 42 (1961): 317–340.

"British in Palestine Ban Use of Word 'Terrorist'." *New York Times*, 4 March 1947, 4.

Bromwich, David. "Euphemism and American Violence." *New York Review of Books (Electronic Edition)* 55, no. 5 (3 April 2008).

Burke, Kenneth. "Dramatism." In *International Encyclopedia of the Social Sciences*, edited by David I. Sills, 445–452. New York: Macmillan & The Free Press, 1968.

—. "Literature as Equipment for Living." In *Sociology of Literature and Drama*, edited by Elizabeth Burns and Tom Burns, 129–138. Baltimore, Maryland: Penquin Books Inc., 1973 [1941].

—. "On Human Behavior Considered Dramatistically." In *Permanence and Change: An Anatomy of Purpose*, 275–295. New York: Bobbs-Merrill Company, 1965 [1954].

—. *Permanence and Change: An Anatomy of Purpose.* 2d rev. ed. Los Altos, California: Hermes Publications, 1954.

—. "The Rhetoric of Hitler's 'Battle'." In *The Philosophy of Literary Form.* 2d ed., 191–220. Baton Rouge: Louisiana State University Press, 1967 [1941].

—. *The Rhetoric of Religion.* Boston: Beacon Press, 1961.

Bush, George W. *Decision Points.* New York: Crown, 2010.

Butler, Judith. *The Psychic Life of Power: Theories in Subjection.* Stanford, California: Standford University Press, 1997.

—. "Violence, Mourning, Politics." *Studies in Gender and Sexuality* 4, no. 1 (2003): 9–37.

A Call to Courage: Reclaiming Our Liberties Ten Years After 9/11. 2011. American Civil Liberties Union. <www.aclu.org>. Accessed 11 September 2011.

Campbell, David. *Politics Without Principle: Sovereignty, Ethics, and the Narratives of the Gulf War.* Boulder, Colorado: Lynne Rienner Publishers, 1993.

Castells, Manuel. *The Power of Identity*. The Information Age: Economy, Society & Culture, vol. II. Malden, Massachusetts: Blackwell Publishers Inc., 1997.

—. *The Rise of the Network Society*. The Information Age: Economy, Society & Culture, vol. I. Malden, Massachusetts: Blackwell Publishers Inc., 1996.

Charbonneau, Louis. "Iraq Figures Distort Terrorism Statistics: Study." *Reuters* 21 May 2008 <http://www.reuters.com/assets/print?aid=USN2139567720080521>.

Chase, A.A. *A Mind for Murder: The Education of the Unabomber and the Origins of Modern Terrorism*. New York: W.W. Norton, 2003.

Chomsky, Noam. *9–11: Was There an Alternative*. New York: Seven Stories Press, 2011.

—. *Hegemony or Survival: America's Quest for Global Dominance*. New York: Metropolitan Books / Henry Holt & Company, 2004.

—. "Objectivity and Liberal Scholarship." In *American Power and the New Mandarins*, 23–158. New York: Pantheon Books, 1969.

"CNN Election Results, American Votes 2004: US / Presidential/ Exit Poll." 11 November 2004. <http://www.cnn.com/ELECTION/2004/pages/results/states/US/P/00/epolls.0.html>. Accessed 26 September 2011.

Cohen, Abner. *Two-Dimensional Man: An Essay on the Anthropology of Power and Symbolism in Complex Society*. Berkeley: University of California Press, 1974.

Cohen, Richard, William Lindzen, Richard Nordhaus, and William Nordhaus. *In the climate casino: an exchange. New York Review of Books* 59, no. 7 26 April 2011 <http://www.nybooks.com/articles/archives/2012/apr/26/climate-casino-exhange/>. Accessed 8 May 2012.

Cohn, Norman. *Europe's Inner Demons: An Inquiry Inspired by the Great Witch-Hunts*. New York: Basic Books, Inc., 1975.

Coll, Steve. *Private Empire: ExxonMobile and American Power*, New York: Penquin Press HC, 2012.

Cole, David. *Enemy Aliens: Double Standards and Constitutional Freedoms in the War on Terror*. New York: The New Press, 2004.

—. "What to Do About the Torturers?" *New York Review of Books* 56, no. 1 (15 January 2009).

Collins, Randall. *Violence: A Micro-Sociological Theory*. Princeton, New Jersey: Princeton University Press, 2008.

—. "C-Escalation and D-Escalation: A Theory of the Time-Dynamics of Conflict." *American Sociological Review* 77, No. 1 (February 2012): 1–20.

Commission on Wartime Contracting in Iraq and Afghanistan. *Transforming Wartime Contracting: Controlling Costs, Reducing Risks*. Created by Congress January 28, 2008. <http://www.wartimecontracting.gov/>. Accessed 30 August 2011.

Conrad, Joseph. *The Secret Agent*. New York: Cambridge University Press, 1990 [1907].

Cox, Amanda. "A 9/11 Tally: 3.3 Trillion." *New York Times*, 11 September 2011, 13.

Cuzzort, Raymond. *Using Social Thought: The Nuclear Issue and Other Concerns.* Mountain View, California: Mayfield Publishing Company, 1989.

Cuzzort, Raymond, and Edith King. "Communication, Art, and Victims." In *20th Century Social Thought*. Third, 327–348. New York: Hold, Rinehart, and Winston, 1980.

Danner, Mark. "How Bush Really Won." *New York Review of Books* 52, no. 1 (January 2005).

—. "The Logic of Torture." *New York Review of Books* 51, no. 11 24 June 2004. <http://www.nybooks.com/articles/17190>. Accessed 10 January 2011.

—. "State of Exception." *New York Review of Books* 58, no. 15 (13 October 2011).

—. *Torture and Truth: America, Abu Ghraib, and the War on Terror.* New York Review of Books, 2004.

—. "US Torture: Voices from the Black Sites." *New York Review of Books* 56, no. 6 (9 April 2009): 69–77.

Dean, Mitchell. *The Constitution of Poverty: Toward a Genealogy of Liberal Governance.* New York: Routledge, 1991.

Der Derian, James. *On Diplomacy: A Genealogy of Western Estrangement.* New York: Basil Blackwell Inc., 1987.

Domhoff, G. William. "Defining the National Interest, 1940–1942: A Critique of Krasner's Theory of American State Autonomy." In *The Power Elite and the State: How Policy is Made in America*, 107–51. New York: Aldine De Gruyter, 1990.

—. *Who Rules America? Challenges to Corporate and Class Dominance, 6th Edition.* New York: McGraw-Hill., 2010.

—. *Who Rules America? Power and Politics, 5th Edition.* New York: McGraw-Hill., 2006.

Donzelot, Jacques. "The Mobilization of Society," translated by Colin Gordon. In *The Foucault Effect: Studies in Governmentality*, edited by Graham Burchell, Colin Gordon, and Peter Miller, 169–180. Chicago: University of Chicago Press, 1991.

—. *The Policing of Families.* Translated by Robert Hurley. New York: Pantheon Books, 1979.

—. "The Promotion of the Social." In *Foucault's New Domains*, edited by Mike Gane and Terry Johnson, 106–138. New York: Routledge, 1993.

Dower, John W. *Cultures of War: Pearl Harbor / Hiroshima / 9–11 / Iraq.* New York: W.W. Norton / The New Press, 2010.

Dreyfus, Hubert, and Paul Rabinow. *Michel Foucault: Beyond Structuralism and Hermeneutics.* Chicago, Illinois: University of Chicago Press, 1982.

Duncan, Hugh D. *Communication and Social Order.* New York: Oxford University Press, 1962.

—. *Symbols in Society.* New York: Oxford University Press, 1968.

Dupuy, Pascal. "La Diffusion Des Stereotypes Revolutionnaries dans la Litterature et le Cinema Anglo-Saxons [The Diffusion of Revolutionary Stereotypes in Anglo-Saxon Literature and Cinema, 1789–1989]." *Annales Historiques de la Revolution Francaise* 305 (1996): 511–528.

Durkheim, Emile. *Suicide: A Study in Sociology*. Translated by J. Spaulding and G. Simpson. New York: The Free Press, 1951 [1897].

Dying to Lose: Explaining the Decline in Global Terrorism. Human Security Brief, 2007. <http://www.humansecuritybrief.info/HSRP_Brief_2007.pdf>. Accessed 25 May 2010.

Ebner, Johanna. "Fighting International Terrorism with Social Science Knowledge." *Footnotes: Newsletter of the American Sociological Association* 33, no. 2 (February 2005): 1, 5.

Edelman, Murray. *Politics as Symbolic Action: Mass Arousal and Quiescence*. Chicago: Markham Publishing Company, 1971.

Edles, Laura. *Symbol and Ritual in the New Spain: The Transition to Democracy After Franco*. New York: Cambridge University Press, 1998.

Elkins, Caroline. *Imperial Reckoning: The Untold Story of Britain's Gulag in Kenya*. Henry Holt, 2005.

Enduring Abuse: Torture and Cruel Treatment by the United States at Home and Abroad. American Civil Liberties Union April 2006 <http://www.aclu.org/safefree/torture/25354pub20060427.html>.

English, Richard. *Terrorism: How to Respond*. New York: Oxford University Press, 2009.

Fanon, Frantz. *The Wretched of the Earth*. New York: Grove Press, Inc., 1963.

Fisher, Margaret. "Contrasting Approaches to Conflict." In *The War System: An Interdisciplinary Approach*, edited by Richard Falk and Samuel Kim, 58–73. Boulder, Colorado: Westview Press, 1980.

Forte, Maximilian. "The Human Terrain System and Anthropology: A Review of Ongoing Public Debates." *American Anthropologist*, March 2011, 1.

Foucault, Michel. *Abnormal: Lectures at the College de France, 1974–75*. Translated by David Macey. New York: Picador, 2003.

—. *Discipline and Punish: The Birth of the Prison*. Translated by Alan Sheridan. New York: Pantheon Books, 1977 [1975].

—. "Governmentality." In *The Essential Foucault: Selections from Essential Works of Foucault, 1954–1984*, edited by Paul Rabinow and Nikolas Rose Rose, 229–245. New York: The New Press, 2003 [1978].

—. *History of Madness*. 1972 [1961]. Translated by Jonathan Murphy and Jean Khalfa. Edited by Jean Khalfa. New York: Routledge, 2006 [1972; 1961].

—. *The History of Sexuality. Volume 1: An Introduction*. Translated by Robert Hurley. New York: Vintage Books, 1978 [1976].

—. *The Order of Things: An Archaeology of the Human Sciences*. New York: Pantheon Books, 1970 [1966].

—. *Society Must Be Defended: Lectures at the College de France, 1975–76*. Translated by David Macey. New York: Picador, 2003.

——. "The Subject and Power," translated by Leslie Sawyer. In *Michel Foucault: Beyond Structuralism and Hermeneutics*, edited by Hubert Dreyfus and Paul Rabinow. First Edition, 208–226. Chicago: University of Chicago Press, 1982.

Freud, Anna. *The Ego and the Mechanisms of Defense*. Translated by Cecil Baines. Revised. New York: International Universities Press, 1966 [1937].

Freud, Sigmund. *Civilization and Its Discontents*. Translated by J. Strachey. New York: W.W. Norton & Company, Inc., 1961 [1928].

——. "Mourning and Melancholia." In *General Psychological Theory: Papers on Metapsychology*, edited by P. Rieff, 164–179. New York: Collier Books, 1963 [1917].

——. *Totem and Taboo*. Translated by J. Strachey. New York: W. W. Norton & Company, Inc., 1950 [1913].

Froomkin, Dan. "Bush's Glib Waterboarding Admission Sparks Outrage." *Huffington Post* 3/June 2010. <http://www.huffingtonpost.com/2010/06/03bushs-glib-waterboarding_n_599893.html?view>. Accessed 03 June 2010.

Frosch, Dan. "Fired Colorado Professor Defends 9/11 Remarks." *New York Times* 23 March 2009. <http://www.nytimes.com/2009/03/24/us/24churchill.html>. Accessed 13 November 2011.

Gamson, William, Bruce Fireman, and Steven Rytina. *Encounters with Unjust Authority*. Homewood, Illinois: Dorsey Press, 1982.

Gareau, Frederick. *State Terrorism and the United States*. Gardena California: Clarity Press, Inc., 2005.

Garland, David. *Peculiar Institution: America's Death Penality in an Age of Abolitiion*. Cambridge, Massachusetts: Harvard University Press, 2010.

George W. Bush, President. "Address Before a Joint Session of the Congress on the United States Response to the Terrorist Attacks of September 11." Washington, D.C., 20 September, 2001.

George, Jim. *Discourses of Global Politics: A Critical (Re)Introduction to International Relations*. Boulder, Colorado: Lynne Rienner Publishers, 1994.

Giddens, Anthony. *The Nation-State and Violence: Vol. 2, a Contemporary Critique of Historical Materialism*. Berkeley, California: University of California Press, 1985.

Go, Julian. "Waves of Empire: US Hegemony and Imperialistic Activity from the Shores of Tripoli to Iraq, 1787–2003." *International Sociology* 22, no. 1 (January 2007): 5–40.

Goebbels, Joseph. *Lie Quote*. <http://thinkexist.com/quotes/joseph_goebbels/>. Accessed 26 July 2011.

Goering, Herman. *War Quote*. <http://thinkexist.com/quotes/hermann_goering/>. Accessed 26 July 2011.

Goffman, *Frame Analysis*. Cambridge: Harvard University Press, 1974.

Goldstone, Jack, and Bert Useem. "Prison Riots as Microrevolutions: An Extension of State-Centered Theories of Revolutions." *American Journal of Sociology* 104, no. 4 (January 1999): 985–1029.

Gordon, Colin. "Governmental Rationality: An Introduction." In *The Foucault Effect: Studies in Governmentality*, edited by Graham Burchell, Colin Gordon, and Peter Miller, 1–52. Chicago: University of Chicago Press, 1991.

—. "Introduction." In *Power*, edited by Paul Rabinow, xi–xli. New York: New Press, The, 2000.

Gray, John. *Al Qaeda and What It Means to Be Modern*. New York: New Press, 2003.

Grossman, Zoltan. "From Wounded Knew to Libya: A Century of U.S. Military Interventions." 2011. <http://academic.evergreen.edu/g/grossmaz/interventions.html>. Accessed 15 August 2011.

Gusfield, Joseph. *The Culture of Public Problems: Drinking-Driving and the Symbolic Order*. Chicago: University of Chicago Press, 1981.

—. *On Symbols and Society*. Chicago: University of Chicago Press, 1989.

Hachey, Thomas, and Ralph Weber, Editors. *Voices of Revolution: Rebels and Rhetoric*. Hinsdale, Illinios: The Dreyden Press, 1972.

Hajjar, Lisa. "Does Torture Work? a Sociolegal Assessment of the Practice in Historical and Global Perspective." *Annual Review of Law and Social Science* 5 (2009): 311–345.

Harbom, Lotta, and Peter Wallensteen. "Armed Conflicts, 1946–2008." *Journal of Peace Research* 46 (2009): 577–587.

Hardt, Michael, and Antonio Negri. *Empire*. Cambridge, Massachusetts: Harvard University Press, 2000.

Harris, John F. "God Gave the U.S. 'What We Deserve,' Falwell Says." *Washington Post* 14 September 2001. <http://www.washingtonpost.com/ac2/wp-dyn/A28620-2001Sep14>. Accessed 15 December 2011.

Hebb, Donald O. "Drives and the C.N.S. (Conceptual Nervous System)." *The Psychological Review* 62, no. 4 (1955): 243–254.

—. *The Organization of Behavior: A Neuropsychological Theory*. New York: Wiley, 1949.

Hewitt, J. Joseph, Jonathan Wilkenfeld, and Ted Robert Gurr, Editors. *Peace and Conflict 2008*. Boulder, CO: Paradigm Publishers, 2008.

"Highlights of AP's Probe Into NYPD Intelligence Operations." *Associated Press* 23 August 2011. <http://www.ap.org/nypd/>. Accessed 15 January 2011.

Hitler, Adolf. *Mein Kampf*. Translated by Ralph Manheim. Boston: Houghton Mifflin, 1971 [1925].

Hoffman, Bruce. *Recent Trends and Future Prospects of Terrorism in the United States*. Santa Monica: Rand, 1998.

Hooks, Gregory, and Brian McQueen. "The Military-Industrial Complex and the Underdeveloped Welfare State." *American Sociological Review* 75, no. 2 (April 2010): 185–204.

Horowitz, Irving Louis. "The Life and Death of Project Camelot." *Transaction* 3 (November-December 1965): 3–7, 44–47.

Hunt, Lynn. *Politics, Culture, and Class in the French Revolution*. Berkeley: University of California Press, 1984.

—. "The World We Have Gained: The Future of the French Revolution." *American Historical Review* 108, no. 1 (2003): xvi–19.

Huth, Paul, and Benjamin Valentino. "Mass Killing of Civilians in Time of War, 1945–2000." In *Peace and Conflict 2008*, edited by J. Joseph Hewitt, Jonathan Wilkenfeld, and Ted Robert Gurr, 79–92. Boulder, CO: Paradigm Publishers, 2008.

Ibrahim, Youssef. "Iran Calls U.S. Action a 'Barbaric Massacre.'." *New York Times* 4 July 1988. <http://www.nytimes.com/1988/07/04/world/iran-calls-us-action-a-barbaric-massacre.html?scp=20&sq=Iranian+airliner&st=nyt>. Accessed 25 October 2011.

Iraqi Deaths from Violence, 2003–2011. Iraq body Count. <http://www.iraqbodycount.org> . Accessed 5 May 2012.

Itzkoff, Dave. "Tony Bennett Apologizes for 9/11 Comments in Radio Interview." *New York Times* 22 September 2011. <http://artsbeat.blogs.nytimes.com/2011/09/21/tony-bennett-apologizes-for-911-comments-in-radio-interview/>. Accessed 22 September 2011.

Ivie, Robert. *Democracy and America's War on Terror*. Tuscaloosa, Alabama: University of Alabama Press, 2005.

—. "Images of Savagery in American Justifications of War." *Communication Monographs* 47 (1980): 279–294.

—. "Literalizing the Metaphor of Soviet Savagery: President Truman's Plain Style." *Southern Speech Communication Journal* 51 (1986): 91–105.

—. "Metaphor and the Rhetorical Invention of Cold War 'Ideologists'." *Communication Monographs* 54 (1987): 165–182.

—. "The Rhetoric of Bush's War on Evil." *KB Journal* 1, no. 1 Fall 2004. http://www.kbjournal.org/fall2004 . Accessed 21 June 2011.

Ivie, Robert, and Oscar Giner. "Hunting the Devil: America's Rhetorical Impulse to War." *Presidential Studies Quarterly* 37, no. 4 (December 2007): 580–598.

Jackman, Mary. "Violence in Social Life." *Annual Review of Sociology* 28 (2002): 387–415.

Jameson, Fredric. *The Political Unconscious: Narrative as a Socially Symbolic Act*. Ithaca, New York: Cornell University Press, 1981.

—. The Symbolic Inference; or, Kenneth Burke and Ideological Analysis." *Critical Inquiy* 4, no. 3 (1978): 507–23.

Jervis, Robert, and Thomas Powers. "The CIA & Iraq- How the White House Got Its Way: An Exchange in Response to 'How They Got Their Bloody Way,' May 27, 1010 Issue." *New York Review of Books* 57, no. 12 (15/July 2010).

Joas, Hans. "The Modernity of War: Modernization Theory and the Problem of Violence." *International Sociology* 14, no. 4 (December 1999): 457–472.

John, Warren St. "The Backlash Grows Against Celebrity Activists." *New York Times* 23 March 2003. <http://www.nytimes.com/2003/03/23/style/the-backlash-grows-against-celebrity-activists.html?emc=eta1>. Accessed 20 December 2011.

Johnson, Chalmers. *The Sorrows of Empire: Militarism, Secrecy, and the End of the Republic*. New York: Metropolitan Books / Henry Hold & Company, 2004.

Jones, Ernest. *On the Nightmare*. New York: Liveright, 1971 [1951].

Kertzer, David. *Ritual, Politics, and Power*. New Haven: Yale University Press, 1988.

Key, Francis Scott. *The Star-Spangled Banner*. 1812. National Anthem, 1932.

Khalidi, Rashid. *Resurrecting Empire: Western Footprints and America's Perilous Path in the Middle East*. Boston, Massachusetts: Beacon Press, 2005.

Kinzer, Stephen. *Overthrow: America's Century of Regime Change from Hawaii to Iraq*. New York: Henry Holt and Company, 2006.

Klapp, Orrin. *Collective Search for Identity*. New York: Hold, Rinehart and Winston, Inc., 1969.

Klein, Melanie. "Mourning and Its Relation to Manic-Depressive States." *International Journal of Psycho-Analysis* 21 (1940): 125–153.

Kluger, Richard, *Ashes to Ashes: America's Hundred-Year War, the Public Health, and the Unabashed Triumph of Philip Morris*. New York: Alfred A. Knopf, Inc., 1996.

Kraska, Peter. "Militarizing American Police: The Rise and Normalization of Paramilitary Units." *Social Problems* 44, no. 1 (1997): 1–18.

—. "The Military as Drug Police: Exercising the Ideology of War." In *Drugs, Crime, and Justice: Contemporary Perspectives*, edited by Larry Gaines and Peter Kraska, 297–320. Prospect Heights, Illinois: Waveland Press, 1997.

Krauthammer, Charles. "Voices of Moral Obtuseness." 21 September 2001. <http://www.jewishworldreview.com/cols/krauthammer092401.asp>. Accessed 15 December 2011.

LaFree, Gary, and Gary Ackerman. "The Empirical Study of Terrorism: Social and Legal Research." *Annual Review of Law and Social Science* 5 (2009): 347–374.

LaFree, Gary, Laura Dugan, and Susan Fahey. "Global Terrorism and Failed States." In *Peace and Conflict 2008*, edited by J. Joseph Hewitt, Jonathan Wilkenfeld, and Ted Robert Gurr, 39–54. Boulder, CO: Paradigm Publishers, 2008.

Lakoff, George. *Whose Freedom? The Battle Over America's Most Important Idea*. New York: Farrar, Straus and Giroux, 2006.

Laqueur, Walter. *No End to War: Terrorism in the 21st Century*. New York: Continuum, 2002.

Lazreg, Marnia. *Torture and the Twilight of Empire: From Algiers to Baghdad*. Princeton, New Jersey: Princeton University Press, 2007.

Lee, Martin, and Bruce Shlain. *Acid Dreams: The Complete Social History of LSD: The CIA, the Sixties, and Beyond*. Grove Press, 1992.

Lewis, Flora. "The New Anti-Terrorism." *New York Review of Books* 46, no. 2 (February 1999).

Longerich, Peter. *Holocaust: The Nazi Persecution and Murder of the Jews*. New York: Oxford University Press, 2010.

Luke, Timothy. "Political Science and the Discourses of Power: Developing a Genealogy of the Political Culture Concept." *History of Political Thought* X, no. 1 (Spring 1989): 125–149.

Mahon, Michael. *Foucault's Nietzschean Genealogy*. Albany, New York: State University of New York Press, 1992.

Mamdani, Mahmood. *Good Muslim, Bad Muslim: America, the Cold War, and the Roots of Terror*. New York: Pantheon Books, 2004.

Mann, Michael. *Incoherent Empire*. New York: VERSO, 2003.

—. *The Sources of Social Power: V. 2. The Rise of Classes and Nation-States, 1760–1914*. New York: Cambridge University Press, 1993.

Marx, Karl. *The 18th Brumaire of Louis Bonaparte*. New York: International Publishers, 1963 [1852].

Mayer, Jane. *The Dark Side: The Inside Story of How the War on Terror Turned Into a War on American Ideals*. New York: Doubleday, 2008.

—. "The Experiment." *New Yorker Magazine*, 11 July 2005.

—. "Obama's Predator War." *New Yorker Magazine*, 26 October 2009.

Mazzetti, Mark, Helen Cooper, and Peter Baker. "Behind the Hunt for bin Laden." *New York Times*, 2 May 2011, A1.

McAdam, Doug, Sidney Tarrow, and Charles Tilly. *Dynamics of Contention*. New York: Cambridge University Press, 2001.

McCormick, Gordon. "Terrorist Decision Making," *Annual Review of Political Science* 6 (2003): 473–507.

McCoy, Alfred W. *Policing America's Empire: The United States, the Philippines, and the Rise of the Surveillance State*. Madison, Wisconsin: University of Wisconsin Press, 2009.

—. *The Question of Torture: CIA Interrogation, From the Cold-War to the War on Terror*. New York: Metropolitan Books, 2006.

McKinley, Jesse. "Comedians Return, Treading Lightly; Excaping Into Work and Feeling a Duty to Keep People Laughing." *New York Times* 26 September 2001. <http://www.nytimes.com/2001/09/26/arts/comedians-return-treading-lightly-into-work-feeling-duty-keep-people.html?scp=3&sq+comics+9%2F11&stnyt&pagewanted=all>. Accessed 22 December 2011.

McWhorter, Ladelle. *Racism and Sexual Oppression in Anglo-America: A Genealogy*. Bloomington: Indiana University Press, 2009.

Melucci, Alberto. *Challenging Codes: Collective Action in the Information Age*. New York: Cambridge University Press, 1996.

Milgram, Stanley. "Group Pressure and Action Against a Person." *Journal of Abnormal and Social Psychology* 9, no. 2 (1964): 137–143.

—. *Obedience to Authority: An Experimental View*. New York: Harper & Row, 1974.

Mills, C. Wright. *The Causes of World War Three*. Armonk, New York: M. E. Sharpe, Inc., 1960.

—. *The Power Elite*. New York: Oxford University Press, 1956.

—. "Situated Actions and Vocabularies of Motive." *American Sociological Review* 5 (1940): 404–413.

Moreno, J. D. *Mind Wars: Brain Research and National Defense*. New York: Dana, 2006.

Mouffe, Chantal. *The Return of the Political*. New York: Verso, 1993.

Nadelmann, Ethan. *Cops Across Borders: The Internationalization of U.S. Criminal Law Enforcement*. University Park: Pennsylvania State University, 1993.

National Commission On Terrorist Attacks Upon the United States. *The 9/11 Commission Report*. Created by the President November 27, 2002. <http://govinfo.library.unt.edu/911/report/911Report.pdf>. Accessed 15 August 2004.

National Counterterrorism Center. *2010 NCTC Report On Terrorism. US Government* <http://www.nctc.gov/witsbanner/docs/2010_report_on_terrorism.pdf>. Accessed 30 March 2011.

National Drug Control Strategy. 2002. The White House Office of National Drug Control Policy: Washington, D.C. < http://www.ondcp.gov>. Accessed 6 July 2002.

National Security Strategy of the United States. September 2002. <www.whitehouse.gov/nsc/nss.html>. Accessed 24 September 2002.

New York Times Historical. . 1860–2006. Editorials. <http://proquest.umi.com>. Accessed 1 June 2006.

Newport, Frank, and Jeff Jones. "Bush Approval Rating Continues to Drop." 26 August 2005. The Gallup Organization <http://gallup.com/pol>.

Niebuhr, Gustav. "After the Attacks: Finding Fault; U.S. 'Secular' Groups Set Tone for Terror Attacks, Falwell Says." *New York Times* 14 September 2001. <http://nytimes.com>. Accessed 27 July 2011.

Nietzsche, Friedrich. *On the Genealogy of Morals & Ecce Homo*. Translated by Walter Kaufmann. New York: Vintage Books, 1967 [1887].

Nisbet, Robert. "The French Revolution and the Rise of Sociology in France." *American Journal of Sociology* 49 (1943): 156–164.

Nygengast, Carole. "Violence, Terror, and the Crisis of the State." *Annual Review of Anthropology* 23 (1994): 109–136.

Obama, Barach, President. "Remarks by the President on Osama bin Laden." East Room, Whitehouse, 2 May, 2011.

Oxford English Dictionary Online. Oxford University Press, 2010.

Ozouf, Mona. *Festivals and the French Revolution, 1789–1799*. Cambridge, Massachusetts: Harvard University Press, 1988.

Pape, Robert. *Dying to Win: The Strategic Logic of Suicide Terrorism*. New York: Random House, 2005.

Parenti, Christian. *The Soft Cage: Surveillance in America from Slavery to the War on Terror*. New York: Basic Books, 2003.

Pew Research. "Beyond Red Vs. Blue: Political Typology." *Center for the People & the Press* 4 May 2011. <www.people-press.org> . Accessed 26 December 2011.

Phillips, Kevin. *American Dynasty: Aristocracy, Fortune, and the Politics of Deceit in the House of Bush*. New York: Viking Press, 2004.

Pontecorvo, Gillo. *Battle of Algiers, The*. The Criterion Collection, 1966 [2004].

Post Jerrold. "Psychological Operations and Counter Terrorism." *Joint Force Quarterly* (2005).

Post, Jerold. *Killing in the Name of God: Osama bin Laden and Radical Islam*. Tech. Rept. No. (Counterproliferation Papers, Future Warfare Series No. 17). Alabama: Air University Maxwell Air Force Base, 2002.

—. *The Mind of the Terrorist: The Psychology of Terrorism from the IRA to al-Qaeda*. New York: Palgrave Macmillan, 2007.

—. "The New Face of Terrorism: Socio-Cultural Foundations of Contemporary Terrorism." *Behavioral Sciences and the Law* 23, no. 4 (July 2005): 451–465.

Poster, Mark. *Foucault, Marxism and History: Mode of Production Versus Mode of Information*. New York: Basil Blackwell Inc./Polity Press, 1984.

Powers, Thomas. "How They Got Their Bloody Way." *New York Review of Books* 57, no. 9 (27/May 2010).

—. *Intelligence Wars; America's Secret History from Hitler to al-Qaeda, Rev. Ed.* New York: New York Review of Books, 2004.

Priest, Dana, and William Arkin. *Top Secret America: The Rise of the New American Security State*. New York: Little, Brown and Company, 2011.

Purdum, Todd S. "Bush Warns of a Wrathful, Shadowy and Inventive War." *New York Times* 17 September 2001: After the attacks: White House. <http://www.nytimes.com/2001/09/17/us/after-attacks-white-house-bush-warns-wrathful-shadowy-inventive-war.html?scp=4&sq=attack+AND+surreal&st=nyt&pagewanted=all>. Accessed 29 September 2011.

Quinby, Lee. *Freedom, Foucault, and the Subject of America*. Boston: Northeastern University Press, 1991.

Rabinow, Paul. *French Modern: Norms and Forms of the Social Environment*. Cambridge, Mass.: Massachusetts Institute of Technology Press, 1989.

—. "Introduction." In *The Foucault Reader*, 3–29. New York: Pantheon, 1984.

Rabinow, Paul, and Nikolas Rose. "Introduction." In *The Essential Foucault: Selections from Essential Works of Foucault, 1954–1984*, edited by Paul Rabinow and Nikolas Rose, vi–xxxv. New York: The New Press, 2003.

"The Reckoning: America and the World a Decade After 9/11." A special report on the decade's costs and consequences, measured in thousands of lives, trillions of dollars and countless challenges to the human spirit. *New York Times*, 11 September 2011, 1–40.

Reich, Wilhelm. *The Mass Psychology of Fascism*. Translated by Vincent Carfagno. New York: Farrar, Straus & Giroux, 1970.

Riefenstahl, Leni. *Triumph of the Will*, 2006 [1935].

Resolution Adopted by APA on August 19: Reaffirmation of the American Psychological Association Position Against Torture and Other Cruel, Inhuman, or Degrading Treatment or Punishment and Its Application to Individuals Defined in the United States Code as "Enemy Combatants." 2007. American

Psychological   Association.   <http://www.apa.org/governance/resolutions/councilres0807.html>. Accessed 15 July 2008.

Reuters Explanation: Policy on not Using the Word Terrorist to Describe Those Who Hijacked Aircraft to Attack the World Trade Center and the U.S. Pentagon, September 11, 2001. 2 October 2001. < http://about.reuters.com/statement3.asp>. Accessed 5 October 2001.

Reynolds, David. *America, Empire of Liberty: A New History of the United States.* New York: Basic Books, 2009.

Rise of the Drones I: Unmanned Systems and the Future of War, Hearings of the Subcommittee on Natural Security and Foreign Affairs Committee on Oversight and Government Reform, House of Representatives, Second Session, One Hundred Eleventh Congress, Serial No.111–118. 23 March 2010. <http://www.gpo.gov/fdsys/pkg/CHRG-111hhrg64921/pdf/CHRG-111hhrg64921.pdf>. Accessed 15 September 2010.

Rise of the Drones II: Examining the Legality of Unmanned Targeting, Hearings Before the Subcommittee on Natural Security and Foreign Affairs Committee on Oversight and Government Reform, House of Representatives, Second Session, One Hundred Eleventh Congress, Serial No.111–120. 28 April 2010.   <http://www.gpo.gov/fdsys/pkg/CHRG-111hhrg64921/pdf/CHRG-111hhrg64921.pdf>. Accessed 15 September 2010.

Roberts, Les, Riyadh Lafta, Richard Garfield, Jamal Khudhairi, Gilbert Burnham. "Mortality Before and After the 2003 Invsion of Iraq: Cluster Sample Survey." *Lancet* 364 (20 November 2004): 1857.

Rogin, Michael. *Ronald Reagan, the Movie and Other Episodes in Political Demonology.* Berkeley, California: University of California, 1987.

Rose, Edward. "The English Record of a Natural Sociology." *American Sociological Review* 25 (April 1960): 193–208.

Rose, Edward, Laurel Richardson, and George Psathas. "The Theoric Construction in the Ethno-Inquiries: Selections from Theory in the World, from Chapter Nine in the Worulde." *Studies in Symbolic Interaction* 16 (1994): 37–62.

Rose, Nikolas. *Powers of Freedom: Reframing Political Thought.* Cambridge: Cambridge University Press, 1999.

Rothstein, Edward. "Connections; Moral Relativity is a Hot Topic? True. Absolutely." *New York Times* 13 July 2002. <http://www.nytimes.com/2002/07/13/arts/connections-moral-relativity-is-a-hot-topic-true-absolutely.html?pagewanted=all&src=pm> . Accessed 15 December 2011.

Ruthven, Malise. "Deception Over Lockerbie?" *New York Review of Books* 56, no. 15 (8 October 2009).

Said, Edward. *Culture and Imperialism.* New York: Alfred A. Knopf, 1993.

—. *Orientalism.* New York: Pantheon Books, 1978.

Saint-Amand, Pierre. *The Laws of Hostility: Politics, Violence, & the Enlightenment.* Minneapolis: University of Minnesota, 1996.

Sanchez-Cuenca, Ignacio, and Luis de la Callez. "Domestic Terrorism: The Hidden Side of Political Violence." *Annual Review of Political Science* 12 (2009): 31–49.

Savage, Charlie. "At White House, Weighing Limits of Terror Fight." *New York Times*, 16 September 2011, National, Frontpage: A1, 6.

Scheper-Hughes, Nancy, and Bourgois Philippe. "Introduction: Making Sense of Violence." In *Violence in War and Peace: An Anthology*, edited by Nancy Scheper-Huges and Philippe Bourgois, 1–32. Oxford, UK: Blackwell Publishing, 2004.

Schmitt, Carl. *The Concept of the Political*. 1927. Translated by George Schwab. New Brunswich, New Jersey, 1976.

—. *Political Theology: Four Chapters on the Concept of Sovereignty*. 1922. Cambridge, Massachusetts: The MIT Press, 1985.

Schouten, Ronald. "Terrorism and the Behavioral Sciences." *Harvard Review of Psychiatry* 18, no. 6 (November 2010): 369–378.

Scott, Peter Dale. *Drugs, Oil, and War: The United States in Afghanistan, Colombia, and Indochina*. Lanham, Maryland: Rowman and Littlefied, 2003.

—. *The Road to 9/11: Wealth, Empire, and the Future of America*. Berkeley, California: University of California Press, 2007.

Segal, Hanna. *Melanie Klein*. New York: The Viking Press, 1979.

Shane, Scott. "Beyond Guantanamo, a Web of Prisons for Terrorist Inmates." *New York Times* 11 December 2011 <http://www.nytimes.com/2011/12/11/us/beyond-guantanamo-bay-a-web-of-federal-prisons.html>. Accessed 11 December 2012.

Simpson, Christopher. *Science of Coercion: Communication Research and Psychological Warfare, 1945–1960*. New York: Oxford University Press, 1994.

Singer, Peter Warren. *Corporate Warriors: The Rise of the Privatized Military Industry*. Othaca, New York: Cornell University Press, 2003.

—. *Wired for War*. New York: Penquin Press, 2009.

Slotkin, Richard. *The Fatal Environment: The Myth of the Frontier in the Age of Industrialization, 1800–1890*. New York: Atheneum, 1985.

—. *Gunfighter Nation: The Myth of the Frontier in Twentieth-Century America*. New York: Atheneum, 1992.

—. *Regeneration Through Violence: The Mythology of the American Frontier, 1600–1860*. Middletown, Connecticut: Wesleyan University Press, 1973.

Smith, Philip. "Codes and Conflict: Towards a Theory of War as Ritual." *Theory and Society* 21 (1991): 103–138.

Smith, Philip, and Alexander Riley. *Cultural Theory: An Introduction*. Malden, MA: Blackwell Publishing, 2009.

Smith, Samuel Francis. "My Country, 'Tis of Thee'." Patriotic song, 1831.

Soldz, Stephen. "Psychologists, Guantanamo and Torture." *Baltimore Chronicle & Sentinel*, 2 August 2006.

Solomon, Norman. "Media Spin Revolves Around the Word 'Terrorist.'." *Common Dreams* 5 October 2001. <Common Dreams, <http://www.commondreams.org/views01/1005-02.htm>>. Accessed 15 November 2011.

Spilerman, Seymour, and Guy Stecklov. "Societal Responses to Terrorist Attacks." *Annual Review of Sociology* 35 (2009): 167–189.

Stern, Fritz. "'Fink Shrinks,' a Review of Die Professionalisierung der Deutschen Psychologie Im Nationalsozialismus." *New York Review of Books* 32, no. 20 (1985): 48–53.

Stiglitz, Joseph. *The Three Trillion Dollar War: The True Cost of the Iraq Conflict*. New York: W.W. Norton, 2008.

Stockholm Institute of Peace Research: Databases. *SIPRI Trend Indicator Values (Standardized to 1990 U.S. Dollars)*. 2011. <http://armstrade.sipri.org/armstrade/page/toplist.php>. Accessed 10 October 2011.

Stoler, Ann Laura. *Race and the Education of Desire: Foucault's History of Sexuality and the Colonial Order of Things*. Durham: Duke University Press, 1995.

Storr, Anthony. *Human Destructiveness*. New York: Basic Books, 1972.

Swidler, Ann. "Culture in Action: Symbols and Strategies." *American Sociological Review* 5 no. 2 (1986): 273–86.

—. "Cultural Power and Social Movements." In *Social Movements and Culture*, edited by Hank Johnston and Bert Klandersmans, 25–40. Minneapolis, Minnesota: University of Minnesota Press, 1995.

Szasz, Thomas. *Ceremonial Chemistry: The Ritual Persecution of Drugs, Addicts, and Pushers*. New York: Anchor Press, 1974.

Tarrow, Sidney. *Power in Movement: Social Movements, Collective Action and Politics, Second Edition*. 2d edn. New York: Cambridge University Press, 1998.

Times Topic: Osama bin Laden. *New York Times*. <http://topics.nytimes.com/top/reference/timestopics/people/b/osama_bin_laden/index.html?scp=1-spot&sq=%20Laden%20Laden%22&st=cse> . Accessed 25 October 2011.

"Timeline: Colonel Moammar el-Qaddafi." *New York Times*. <http://www.nytimes.com/interactive/2011/02/24/world/middleeast/20110224_qaddafi_timeline.html?ref=muammarelqaddafi>. Accessed 25 October 2011.

Tommasini, Anthony. "The Devil Made Him Do It." *New York Times* 30 September 2001. Music. <http://www.nytimes.com/2001/09/30/arts/music-the-devil-made-him-do-it.html.>. Accessed 15 December 2011.

Toolis, Kevin. "Rise of the Terrorist Professors." *New Statesman* 14/June 2004. <http://www.newstatesman.com/print/200406140015> . Accessed 24 May 2010.

Top Secret America: A Washington Post Investigation. October 2011. <http://projects.washingtonpost.com/top-secret-america>. Accessed 15 October 2011.

Turk, Austin. "Sociology of Terrorism." *Annual Review of Sociology* 30, no. 1 (2004): 271–286.

Unger, Craig. *House of Bush, House of Saud: The Secret Relationship Between the World's Two Most Powerful Dynasties*. New York: Scribner, 2004.

Union of Concerned Scientists. "Scientific Integrity in Policymaking: An Investigation into the Bush Administration's Misuse of Science." February 2004 <www.ucsusa.org>.

Uppsala Univerity Conflict Data Program / International Peace Research Institute Oslo Armed Conflict Dataset. 2011. < www.ucdp.uu.se/database>. Accessed 6 October 2011.

Vidal, Gore. *Dreaming War: Blood for Oil and the Cheney-Bush Junta*. New York: Thunder's Mouth Press / Nation Books, 2002.

Wagner-Pacifici, Robin Erica. *The Moro Morality Play: Terrorism as Social Drama*. Chicago: University of Chicago Press, 1986.

Wallerstein, Immanuel, Editor. *Open the Social Sciences: Report of the Gulbenkian Commission on the Restructuring of the Social Sciences*. Stanford, California: Stanford University Press, 1996.

—. "The Three Instances of Hegemony in the History of the Capitalist World-Economy." *International Journal of Comparative Sociology* XXIV, no. 1–2 (January-April 1983): 100–108.

"War Abroad." *New York Times*, 11 September 2011, 6–12.

"War at Home." *New York Times*, 11 September 2011, 13–15.

Warner, W Lloyd. *The Living and the Dead*. New Haven: Yale University Press, 1959.

Weber, Max. "Politics as a Vocation." In *From Max Weber: Essays in Sociology*, edited by H.H. Gerth and C. Wright Mills, 77–128. New York: Oxford University Press, 1946 [1921].

Wess, Robert. *Kenneth Burke: Rhetoric, Subjectivity, Postmodernism*. New York: Cambridge University Press, 1996.

White, Jonathan. *Terrorism: An Introduction*. Belmont, California: Thomson-Wadsworth, 2003.

White, Robert. "From Peaceful Protest to Guerrilla War: Micromobilization of the Provisional Irish Republican Army." *American Journal of Sociology* 94, no. 6 (May 1989): 1277–1302.

—. "On Measuring Political Violence: Northern Ireland, 1969 to 1980." *American Sociological Review* 58, no. 4 (August 1993): 575–585.

White, Robert, and Terry White. "Repression and the Liberal State." *Journal of Conflict Resolution* 39 (1995): 330–352.

Wilgoren, Jodi. "Bin Laden Tape Renews Outrage; a Few Deny It is Authentic." *New York Times* 14 December 2001. <http://nytimes.com>. Accessed 14 December 2001.

Wills, Gary. *Bomb Power: The Modern Presidency and the National Security State*. New York: The Penquin Press, 2010.

Wilson, Joseph. *The Politics of Truth: Inside the Lies That Led to War and Betrayed My Wife's CIA Identity: A Diplomat's Memoir*. New York: Carroll & Graf, 2004.

WordCruncher 6.0. . Provo, Utah: Hamilton-Locke, Inc., 2004.

Year of the Drone. New America Foundation 16 November 2011. <http://counterterrorism.newamerica.net/drones>. Accessed 12 December 2011.

Zygmunt, Joseph. "Movements and Motives: Some Unresolved Issues in the Psychology of Social Movements." In *The Sociology of Dissent*, edited by R. Serge Denisoff, 41–57. New York: Harcourt Brace Jovanovich, Inc., 1972.

Index

References to illustrations are in **bold**